Cdr P.G. 'Jamie' Jameson, who kindly contributed the foreword. Special thanks are due to archivist-historian-author Jinty Rorke for her sage advice on going about this project and to Glenn Pettit, for readily making available his extensive knowledge of World War Two aviation, and to them both for constructive criticism of the manuscript.

Without the encouragement and the innumerable cups of coffee provided by my wife Robin, and her meticulous attention to detail in proof reading, (Mackie, who could never abide mistakes, would, I am sure, have thoroughly approved her professional standards), this biography would never have made it to publication.

Finally, profound thanks to the Mackie family, for their support of this project, and for providing the bulk of the illustrations used therein.

Max Avery
Waihi, New Zealand, 1996

N.B. Christopher Shores notes his gratitude to Paul Sortehaug of Dunedin, New Zealand, who first put him in touch with Evan Mackie during the late 1960s.

Publisher's Note: Many of the pilots mentioned in the text were themselves notable as fighter pilots during either the First or Second World Wars. All such personnel carry footnotes indicating where details of their careers may be found, either in *Above the Trenches* (World War One) or *Aces High* (World War Two), both of which are published by Grub Street. Where biographies or autobiographies have been published by Grub Street in respect of those mentioned, this is also footnoted. Other relevant published material is referred to in a Bibliography.

FOREWORD

by Air Commodore P.G. 'Jamie' Jameson, CB, DSO, DFC & Bar

This is a most interesting and exciting book which has been well researched by the author, Max Avery. It is a true story of a New Zealand country lad of rather humble circumstances who started his working life, during the depression, as the farm hand on a small dairy farm, with no electric power nor machinery apart from an old Model 'T' Ford pick-up truck. Everything had to be done by hand, for which Mackie was paid five shillings a week.

From this job, in January 1941, this same lad joined the RNZAF and started his meteoric rise to 'Stardom'. By the end of the war, he was credited with 21½ enemy aircraft destroyed, and had been decorated with the DSO, DFC & Bar, as well as being appointed a Wing Leader. The fighter Wing Leaders were looked upon as the elite fraternity of fighter pilots and Mackie was certainly one of these.

'Rosie' Mackie was a pilot in 485 (NZ) Spitfire Squadron when I first met him. The squadron was based at King's Cliffe, a satellite of Wittering, in about the middle of 1942. During this period I was the 12 Group Wing Leader based at Wittering and took part in several operations with 485 Squadron, including the big Commando raid on Dieppe, on 19 August 1942. The entry in my logbook concerning the first sortie on the day reads: "Time airborne 1 hour 50 minutes – Led four squadron wing to Dieppe to provide fighter cover for ships and troops." The Wing, on arrival, was attacked immediately by about 100 FW 190s and a few Me 109s. My own section was attacked at least 30 times in as many minutes. Our situation was rather critical owing to the fact that we had to maintain position over, or near the beaches and ships to protect them from air attack. After about ten minutes a further 50 FW 190s were seen coming in from the east to reinforce the first bunch. We were attacked continuously from above and out of the sun. Fortunately the Huns seldom pressed their attacks home to close quarters, often opening fire at 800 yards range. I saw one Spitfire spinning down and the pilot bale out. He was from 611

SPITFIRE LEADER

THE STORY OF WING CDR EVAN 'ROSIE' MACKIE, DSO, DFC & BAR, DFC (US), TOP SCORING RNZAF FIGHTER ACE

MAX C. AVERY WITH CHRISTOPHER SHORES

Published by
Grub Street
The Basement
10 Chivalry Road
London SW11 1HT

This edition first published 1999

British Library Cataloguing in Publication Data
Avery, Max C.
  Spitfire leader
  1. Mackie, Evan, 1917-1986 2. Fighter pilots – New Zealand –
  Biography 3. World War, 1939-1945 – Aerial operations,
  British
  I. Title II. Shores, Christopher, 1937–
  940.5′44′941′092

ISBN 1-902304-26-8

Typeset by Pearl Graphics, Hemel Hempstead

Printed and bound in Great Britain by
Biddles Ltd, Guildford and King's Lynn

10 9 8 7 6 5 4 3 2 1

CONTENTS

ACKNOWLEDGEMENTS

So many people have helped me with the writing of this biography. Amongst those who willingly supplied additional information either from records or their personal knowledge of 'Rosie' Mackie, were Air Cdr H.A. Probert, then Head of the Air Historical Branch, Ministry of Defence (Air) – now retired; Grp Capt W.G. Abel of the Royal Air Force Staff College, Bracknell; the late Grp Capt George Gilroy and his wife Jane, who also proved most accommodating hosts at their home, Auchencairn House; Sqn Ldr C.J. (Chris) Bartle, RAF; C.S. Bamberger; P.J. (Pat) Davoren in Australia; the late L.S.M. 'Chalky' White, always a staunch champion of Mackie; Arthur Rawlinson, that magnificent diarist of 243 Squadron; J.G. Pattison; Sqn Ldr J.M. (Johnny) Checketts, Mackie's fellow New Zealand ace; Dr David Clouston; Sqn Ldr Jim Sheddan; J.R. Duncan; J.E. Miller; the late Sqn Ldr R.L. 'Spud' Spurdle; J.F.P. Yeatman; the late Sqn Ldr M.R.D. (Marty) Hume; the late J.K. (Jim) Porteous; Wg Cdr J.F. 'Stocky' Edwards; historian Trevor Coker; the late Leo Quinn, Mackie's longtime fishing companion; the late Sqn Ldr R.M. Mathieson; Dave Towgood; Owen Eagleson; Mrs C.L. (Cath) Henry; Flt Lt Angelo of the RNZAF Museum; G.H. Jacobi; G.E. 'Bill' Jameson; Jerry Westenra; Hal Thomas, and last, but by no means least, Christopher Shores, who very kindly made all his own writings on Mackie, and all the information in his many publications available to me, as well as researching for me the identities of many of those whom Mackie shot down – little realising that he would eventually be editing and adding to the manuscript!

Further, I am particularly grateful to those who not only contributed information, but took the time to peruse and correct the original manuscript; the late Sqn Ldr Johnnie Houlton; Sqn Ldr Stanley Browne, a welcome stickler for good grammar; Sqn Ldr Harvey Sweetman; Harold C. Payne; Owen Morgan and his son-in-law, Trevor Burnard; Wg Cdr W.E. 'Smokey' Schrader and the late Air

Squadron and was later picked up. I shot one FW 190 down in flames and had several squirts at others. The three squadrons of 12 Group were 485 (NZ), led by Sqn Ldr Reg Grant, 411 (Canadian) led by Sqn Ldr Newton and 610, led by Sqn Ldr 'Johnnie' Johnson. The total score was: three and a half FW 190s and two Me 109s destroyed, one FW 190 probably destroyed, and three FW 190s damaged. We lost five Spitfires and two pilots. I saw one Spitfire dive into the sea on the way back across the Channel. The pilot did not get out.

The pilots of 485 Squadron, of whom Rosie Mackie was one, were superb and one could not have wished for a better team.

Sometimes, when the squadron was stood down for the night, the squadron commander (Reg Grant) would arrange transport for himself and the pilots to go out to one of the local pubs for the evening. During some of these escapades, Rosie Mackie, being of independent disposition, would excuse himself, and later invariably be seen walking across a particular field, from the officers' sleeping quarters, with a blanket tucked underneath his arm. We suspected that the object of these clandestine rendezvous had fewer than three legs, but so far as I know, it was never confirmed!

Later on in 1942 our paths diverged and it was not until September 1944, when I was commanding 122 Wing at Grimbergen, near Brussels, that they re-converged. My three squadrons of Mustangs were replaced by three squadrons of Tempests, 3, 56 and 486 (NZ) Squadrons, from the UK, and these were soon joined by 80 and 274 Tempest Squadrons. I was delighted to welcome Rosie Mackie again and it was not long before he was commanding 80 Squadron. This was when the Wing was based at Volkel in Holland. Rosie was extremely conscientious and loyal, and his quiet, modest disposition in no way detracted from his resourceful determination to win the war – alone if necessary!

Sadly, in mid-April 1945, my Wing Leader, Wg Cdr Brooker, DSO, DFC, was lost in air combat, so it was necessary for me to select a replacement with the required attributes. Rosie's leadership qualities had impressed me so much that it was not a difficult decision to appoint and promote him to this highly prestigious and responsible post.

It was soon after this that the Wing made its last war move, in a 200 mile jump from Hopsten to Fassberg, midway between Hanover and Hamburg. The last fortnight of the the war proved the most intense and concentrated ever experienced by the Wing. On 29 April one of the squadrons destroyed ten enemy aircraft without loss, while the other two squadrons collected 110 road vehicles between them. The next day the Wing accounted for 211 road vehicles. Even this huge total was made to look small during the first three days of May, when over 1,100 vehicles were destroyed or damaged, in addition to 38 enemy aircraft destroyed. On the last of these three days, the Wing gathered in a bag which was surely a record even in this record campaign. 103 sorties were flown by three squadrons. 21 enemy aircraft were destroyed and 14 damaged. Two locomotives were damaged. The road transport score was 96 'flamers' and 395 damaged, for the loss of three pilots. This holocaust mainly took place in the Lübeck-Neumunster area, where two German armies, fleeing desperately from the British advancing from the South and the Russians from the East, converged into one mad, frothing bottleneck of panic, struggling to escape into Denmark.

On 4 May the squadrons were switched to shipping strikes in the Flensburg area. An attack on the seaplane base at Schleswig followed, and this day, with 14 aircraft destroyed afloat or on the ground, proved to be the Wing's final fling, for in the late evening came the news of Germany's collapse.

No other Wing in the 2nd Tactical Air Force could show such an all round record of air and ground success. The "aircraft destroyed" total was beaten by only one Wing, and that by only half an aircraft, but the ground scores were unapproached. An Operational Research section report issued at the beginning of May stated: "nearly 60% of all 2nd TAF's loco attacks were undertaken by pilots of 122 (Tempest) Wing. At this Wing the standard is much above the average."

These tremendous successes, especially in the later stages of the war were due, in no small measure, to Rosie Mackie's great qualities of leadership. His courage and determination and personal example in pressing home attacks, were an inspiration to the other pilots in the Wing.

Authors' note: sadly, 'Jamie' Jameson died in September 1996, before publication of this book took place.

PREFACE

"For many years all lists of the most successful fighter pilots in the RAF failed to mention the name of one New Zealander who had gained for himself a place amongst the select few credited with over 20 air victories in WW II."

So wrote English researcher and historian Christopher Shores in the Spring 1971 issue of *Aero Album*.

"It was not until 1966 that the name of Wing Commander E.D. Mackie, DSO, DFC and Bar finally appeared in its proper place in the list of British Commonwealth top scorers – as New Zealand's equal third-highest scorer, tying with Wing Commander W.V.C. Compton and Flight Lieutenant R.B. Hesselyn with 21½ victories."

Shores was then referring to the 1966 publication of *Aces High*, which he wrote jointly with Clive Williams, and which details Mackie's record together with those other British Commonwealth fighter pilots who claimed five or more enemy aircraft destroyed in the air.

While it is true that many books on air fighting in the Second World War fail to mention Mackie, or total his score at less than 21½, it is equally true that several 1947 newspaper accounts of Mackie's record on his return to New Zealand credit him with 25 enemy aircraft, so he was not unknown. Yet, unlike Wing Commander C.F. Gray, and Wing Commander A.C. Deere, (credited popularly with 27 and 22 victories respectively), Mackie quite failed to retain any of the post-war prominence afforded his fellow New Zealanders.

It is possible that this was because Gray, Deere, Crawford-Compton and Hesselyn all chose permanent careers in the RAF after the war. Mackie on the other hand, chose to return to his previous trade as an electrician. Naturally reticent, he rarely referred to his wartime exploits – and then only while with fellow fighter pilots. He did not join military associations, and rarely attended squadron reunions. Not surprisingly, his exploits were known only to his immediate family and close friends, to the men he flew with, and to a few interested historians.

I first heard about Evan Mackie when we lived at Mount Maunganui, as did the Mackies in the early 1960s, and his son Brian used to hang about my father's service station and go fishing with him. My mother used to recount that Mackie was one of New Zealand's most decorated fighter pilots. His son however, enjoyed fishing with my father, who did not care where the bait was cut up, or how much of a mess the boat got into, as long as the fishing was good.

Evan Mackie, on the other hand, was an absolutely meticulous person. In his boat, the bait was cut up only on the bait board, which was then washed down. There was a place for everything, and everything had to be in its place. Brian, being an average teenager, rebelled against his father's fastidiousness.

One of the few points of similarity between my father and Evan Mackie was that they were both good fishermen. I did not meet Evan Mackie until 1980, when I wrote an article about his wartime exploits for *Home Talk*, a Tauranga newspaper. He had then been retired for two years from his job as Chief Inspector with the Tauranga Electric Power Board, and was taking his harbour fishing quite seriously. Certainly, he was not much interested in me writing about him, and it took some persuading to get him to talk.

The manner of Evan Mackie's fishing says so much about the manner of the man that it is important it be related, and there is no better person to do that than Leo Quinn, his fishing partner for 25 years. Formerly personal assistant to the Chief Engineer of the Tauranga Electric Power Board, Leo Quinn gave this account at his Tauranga home in 1992:

"He would ring up at 8, 9 or 10 o'clock, after hearing the latest weather forecast, say 'five o'clock' or whatever time he wanted to go, and bang down the phone. Just that. No mucking about. I always went to his place and tried to get there five or ten minutes ahead of time. Even so, I would usually be greeted with: 'What kept you?'

"Fishing was his only recreation, as far as I know. He would go out every weekend when there was a low tide early on Saturday or Sunday, from October to June, except at Christmas – there were too many idiots around. He couldn't bear people who couldn't drive a boat properly – or people who used Danforth anchors. Danforths are made for mud, and the bed of the Tauranga harbour is sand.

"He had three or four favourite fishing spots. One was about 150 yards west of the tall marker off Beach Road in Otumoetai, about 20 feet of water, over a mussel bed, which he used on the outgoing tide from mid-tide for a couple of hours. Another was half way across the entrance to the Western Channel in 30 feet of water, which was used from half an hour before low tide to low tide. He used a position in the entrance to the harbour, in a depth of between 110 feet and 119 feet, for about half an hour at dead low tide to catch big snapper. He favoured snapper for eating.

"His spot for catching kingfish was between Panepane Point and No.1 west buoy, in shallow water, on the first hour of the incoming tide – and if we didn't get anything (in that time) we went home. It was not very often that we came home without anything.

"He never spoke much on the boat. He was very quiet. We each had our own separate jobs. When I heard the motor slow I would get the anchor ready and drop it when he said so. I never drove the boat once, or even started the motor. He always fished starboard and I always fished port. The controls were on the starboard side. He fished with three rods, I with one.

"He always caught more fish than me until I changed my tackle to Daiwa – a fawny-coloured supple nylon – and then I caught more fish and he didn't like that. Then he changed to Daiwa tackle and went back to catching more fish than me.

"If we had three fish on, we would keep them in a holding pattern. Evan always did the gaffing for every fish, including mine. I would pass the rod to him and Evan would bring the trace in and gaff the fish while I took the other rods. Whenever we hooked a big fish we would up-anchor and play it for 20 minutes or so if necessary to make sure of not losing it, but we never fought the fish and the tide at the same time.

"I saw him get excited only two or three times, and when he got excited, he got excited. Once was when we caught his 90-pound kingfish. Another time was when he brought an 18-pound conger eel on board. It made a terrible mess of the boat but it also won a $200 prize in the fishing contest. When I caught my biggest snapper, a 26-pounder, he just looked at me and asked: 'Shall we keep it?' He had a very dry sense of humour.

"He would never take any money for petrol. I gave him a cheque once, and said it was for the boat. I found it six months later, pinned to the ceiling in the cabin. His only comment: 'Well, you said it was for the boat!'

"It used to take an hour to clean the boat down with fresh water after fishing – the cockpit as well as the exterior. He was very fussy, very safety-conscious, and had all the gear – lifejackets and flares. We fished in rough water only if there was a contest on. We usually did quite well in contests. At one fishing competition on Bowentown we took four or five prizes – just about scooped the pool.

"I got so used to his fishing pattern that I have never been fishing since he died. I won't go out with anyone else. It would spoil it. We always worked as a team. On the boat he never asked for advice, or for my opinion. But he knew that I was reliable, and I never let him down."

Evan Mackie the fisherman was the same Evan Mackie in just about every sphere of his life. He liked things to be done properly, tidily and neatly. His property reflected this – it would have been a brave blade of grass indeed that was out of place. He preferred situations to revolve around him, rather than he revolve around them.

He wanted very much to be in command of his own orbit at all times.

His service with the Royal New Zealand Air Force reflected that philosophy. Even as a very junior Pilot Officer, Mackie made sure that as far as possible he had taken every precaution to have things the way he wanted them.

His brilliance as a fighter pilot did not rest solely upon his record of enemy aircraft shot down, good though that was. Indeed, fewer than a score of RAF and Commonwealth pilots claimed more. The real brilliance lay in the manner in which he achieved that success, for he did it without ever having any injury inflicted upon himself. Only once was his aircraft hit by bullets from an opposing machine, and that was very early in his war; he was never shot down. Therein lay Mackie's airmanship skills – in his ability to inflict maximum damage while protecting himself; his ability to retain control of what-ever situation he got himself into. Although he tended to decry his marksmanship, it was not that bad. After one successful sortie in which he downed a German aircraft, his armourer checked his guns and found that he had fired only six cannon shells.

At first Evan Mackie was not keen to tell his story. I had been intending to write it for some time, and it was not until I returned from an overseas holiday in late 1985 and found him seriously ill with cancer that I got around to doing anything about it. As I followed him from hospital to nursing home, and back to his own home when he had a brief remission, he gradually became more receptive to the idea and eventually began referring to it as "our project".

I had just completed taping his story when he died in April 1986. I have written it both because I promised him I would, and because he impressed me enormously, to the extent that I believe his character should be recorded.

Evan Mackie was a quiet New Zealander. During the Second World War he saw a job that needed doing, and he did it very well. Having done that, he got on with a constructive life. Our heritage would be the poorer if we did not have the opportunity of knowing what he did, and how he did it.

Additional comment by Christopher Shores: Shortly after my research for the first edition of *Aces High* had drawn to my attention Evan Mackie's outstanding record, I received information from a correspondent of mine in New Zealand, Paul Sortehaug of Dunedin, that he had made contact with Evan. As I was then commencing research for a book about 2nd Tactical Air Force, I requested and received the relevant address, and a long enjoyable correspondence commenced. Evan was extremely generous to the then young researcher, answering all my questions about himself and his experiences, and providing me with a number of photographs from his personal collection which I was able to use in the book when it appeared.

Later I was able to write the article about Evan's air force career for *Aero Album*, which has already been referred to, while subsequently he assisted me again by providing a set of comments – and more photos – which I used in *Fighters over Tunisia*. During the 1970s he and his wife purchased round trip air tickets in order to visit their sons, then resident in South Africa and Canada respectively. The trip included a stop-off in England – the first time the Mackies had returned here since the war ended – and whilst they were in this country, my wife and I had the great pleasure of entertaining them to dinner at our home. At the time I was preparing a history of 80 Squadron, and Evan produced a number of silver squadron crest lapel badges of that squadron which he had had made by a jeweller in 1945. One of these he gave to me, and it remains a treasured possession, and a memento of my friendship with a most outstanding man.

That Evan Mackie was an ace fighter pilot in the popular meaning of the term, there can be no doubt. According to the Shorter Oxford English Dictionary an ace is "an aviator who has brought down three enemy machines, a crack aviator, 1917." By that definition Mackie was an ace seven times over. This is not however the definition that has been widely accepted and has become synonymous with the word in the years since World War I. This later definition identifies an ace as a pilot who has been credited with shooting down at least five enemy aircraft. Indeed, the Concise Oxford Dictionary now identifies ace as "Pilot who has brought down many enemy aircraft."

However, the RAF did not officially acknowledge its best fighter pilots by using the term 'ace', ever. "You seek my advice on the scores of the leading 'aces' and here I must tell you that the RAF does not officially recognise the concept.", Air Commodore Henry

Probert, MBE, MA, then with the British Ministry of Defence's Air Historical Branch advised the author in 1986. "It may help you if I give a little background." he continued.

"Each claim was registered at the time as destroyed, probably destroyed or damaged, and the decisions on whether to confirm these claims were taken almost immediately and normally recorded in the squadron Operational Record Book and the individual's logbook; there was, however, no question of revising these contemporary records in the light of subsequent evidence. While we can be certain that some aircraft claimed as 'damaged' were in fact 'kills', we can be equally sure that a good many claimed as 'kills' were either claimed several times over or not shot down at all. One has only to recall the gross discrepancy between the sum total of 'confirmed kills' in the Battle of Britain and the number of German aircraft that post-war research shows to have been destroyed. Unpalatable as it may be to the pilots concerned, there is no way in which all of them could have shot down all the aircraft each was credited with at the time."

This, of course, is undoubtedly true for all air forces in all wars. It does however neatly let the RAF off the hook of ever having formally endorsed something which later proves open to question.

In spite of the RAF's rejection of aces as such, it is common knowledge that decorations were frequently awarded to fighter pilots according to the number of enemy aircraft they had shot down, and that promotions often followed as a direct result of those scores – which were, of course, a good indication of the individual's ability at their primary task. Such prowess was frequently accompanied by exemplary leadership skills, and the very success brought a degree of immediate respect from other pilots. So the RAF recognised the ace fighter pilot as an ace in all but name – and the wartime public, so starved of good news, seized upon the aerial ace concept first established in World War I, and hailed their aces whenever they had the opportunity to do so. In the early days of the Second World War, before the aces had the opportunity of writing their own realistic accounts, the media sought to persuade their readers that these new heroes flew and died in a flambuoyant aura of glory. For instance, David Masters, in his 1941 publication *So Few, The Immortal Record of the RAF*, wrote:

> "In the messes of Royal Air Force stations all over the British
> Isles may be found modern knights of chivalry whose deeds will
> ring down the ages and become immortal."

Wing Commander Robert Stanford-Tuck, himself credited with 29 aerial victories, put it more in perspective in his foreword to the original 1966 edition of *Aces High*:

> "The term fighter ace always seemed to me to conjure up the mental picture of some gay, abandoned, almost irresponsible young pilot leaping into his aircraft and tearing off into the sky to chalk up victories like knocking off glass bottles in the circus firing range. Nothing could be further from the truth. Any fighter pilot after his first combat is very well aware that air fighting on the scale of the last war was a cold, calculating, cat and mouse type of combat which required great preparation, lightning reactions, first-class teamwork and above all, cool, decisive leadership."

Although it has not been acknowledged previously, Mackie, closely followed by Sqn Ldr R.B. Hesselyn, has the honour of being the top-scoring fighter pilot of the RNZAF. This is because the highest scoring New Zealander, Wg Cdr C.F. Gray, and the other two leading pilots, Wg Cdrs A.C. Deere and W.V. Crawford-Compton, all joined the RAF direct, served only in the RAF, and remained in that service after the end of the war. Mackie and Hesselyn on the other hand, joined the RNZAF, and remained members of that service throughout the war even though they served on operations with units of the RAF.

Per head of population, New Zealanders possibly made a greater contribution to the air war in the Second World conflict than the British or the populations of any other British Commonwealth country. Beyond the RNZAF commitments in the South Pacific (by no means small in their own right), 10,950 New Zealanders served with the RAF, directly or attached, of whom 3,285 died during that service. Among the 1,200 or so most successful fighter pilots of the Commonwealth and its Free European allies, more than 75 were New Zealanders. Their representation amongst the top scorers was disproportionately high, matching closely the totals of the leading British, Canadian, Australian, South African, French and Polish pilots. Here is the life of one of them.

CHAPTER ONE

EARLY LIFE IN WAIHI

Not far south of the Firth of Thames, in the upper half of the North Island of New Zealand, a river has eroded a rocky gorge to divide two ranges of mountains. Over thousands of years, the Ohinemuri has carved out the Karangahake Gorge.

Geographically, the gorge marks the place where the mountains of the Coromandel Peninsula, away to the north, have dwindled to mere foothills. It also marks the place where the mountains of the Kaimai Range begin their sweep to the south, so that they can divide the rich dairylands of the Waikato Plains from the semi-tropical Bay of Plenty.

Within the rock of the gorge and the land east of it there lay other riches – gold. The discovery of gold in the district in 1878 resulted in the creation of the town of Waihi, midway between the gorge and the North Island's east coast. Midway between Waihi and the coast lay a fertile area which would be named Golden Valley by Danish settler Otto Bjerring – not for the metal, but for the flowering gorse introduced by English and Scottish settlers for hedgerows, and which spread and grew there in profusion.

The scene is a two-bail walk-through milking shed on a small farm in Golden Valley. It is a late summer's evening in 1933 and the kerosene lamp has just been lit by the tired 15-year-old farm boy.

Milking is running late, because the bachelor farmer has been in town all afternoon, and the lad has had to get the 26-cow herd in and handmilk most of them himself. It is the flush of the season; the cows' udders are heavy with milk, and the lad's forearms and fingers are aching. The farmer's Ford Model 'T' truck has just rattled up the track, and the farmer sits on a stool to milk one of the last of the herd. He makes a joke which strikes the wrong chord with his work-weary employee.

In a trice the lad is on his feet. He grabs the half-full bucket of milk from under his cow and empties its contents with considerable force and accuracy over his employer's head.

Fred Bjerring, wiping his eyes clear of the warm froth, says: "You can do that as often as you like, until you do it once too often!" and goes on milking.

And Evan Mackie went back to his cow and went on milking too. He knew immediately that he had done a stupid thing. Indeed, it was totally uncharacteristic of him, for he was usually tightly in control of himself. Such outbursts of temperament would rarely be seen in the future.

Fifty-three years on, Evan Mackie talked of his stint on the dairy farm with Fred Bjerring, where he worked seven days a week for five shillings and his keep – and did the cooking: "I know the meaning of work. The cows had to be milked seven days a week. He had 26 cows and they were all milked by hand. There was no power out there, and they didn't have machines then. He was really destitute, you might say, and had only enough to pay his mortgage.

"While he was away – he used to cart his cream into town every day – I worked about the farm after cleaning up the shed. Draining and fencing, you name it, gardening, any old thing at all. Gosh, it was hard to get up early those mornings when it was cold and dark, and if you wanted a cup of tea you had to light the fire first, and when you got down to the shed you had to light the fire there to heat up the water in a couple of kerosene tins ready for washing. And 26 cows take a fair bit of milking in the flush of the season."

Mackie admitted that he must have been in a particularly bad mood the evening he tipped the milk over Fred Bjerring's head. "But I don't think he ever left me to milk them all again!"

Had it not been for the discovery of gold there, Evan Mackie in all likelihood would not have been born in Waihi. It was only the prospect of a job at the Martha goldmine that brought Robert Thomas Bruce Mackie, an Invercargill engine driver, and his family north to the mining town. When Katherine Mackie, nee McIntosh of Taieri Mouth, south of Dunedin, gave birth to Evan Dall Mackie in Nurse Sylvia Burke's Walmsley Road nursing home on 31 October, 1917, the Martha mine was the largest gold producer in New Zealand. About 600 men were employed working three eight-hour shifts every day. The town of Waihi had grown around Martha Hill, and during its 60-year life the mine in the hill produced 8,000,000 ounces of gold.

Underground mining ceased in 1952, but an open-cast mine on the same site began several years ago and today Waihi is as famous for its gold production as it ever was.

Evan was the fourth child in the family, following Doris, Bessie and Allan. Later there was a fifth child, Bruce. Evan explained: "And then we did have a younger brother, who was stricken just after he was born with whooping cough, meningitis, you name it. They couldn't name it in those days, when kids got all sorts of things and died. Some of them lived and they were cripples. I could name four or five similar such cases around Waihi. Anyway, when he was about two or three he couldn't talk and he was crippled. Well, the net result was that he was confined to an institution all his life, and he died when he was 60. More or less a skeleton in the cupboard, but at that time I would say there would be six similar cases."

The Mackie family lived in a house in Cuba Street. Evan described it as "a little old inconvenient house, three bedrooms, outside toilet, outside washhouse, coal stove and candles – a typical miner's cottage." The house is still there, but now the toilet and washhouse are within the living accommodation, and it was wired for electricity soon after 1926, when Waihi was reticulated. Evan recalled:

"We probably had as hard an upbringing as anyone in Waihi. We seemed to do nothing but work. The old man always ensured there was plenty of work for us to do. We used to go collecting bundles of tree sticks from wherever we could get them, carry them home on our backs and cut them up for firewood. We collected pine cones by the sackful and we collected bottles and sold them.

"By hanging around the town tips we finally made up a pushbike for nothing. That was wonderful! If nothing else, it did breed ingenuity and made us resourceful. We were never stuck – we could always make something out of something else."

The Mackie children went first to the Waihi East Primary School which was only a block or so from home. Evan began there at the age of seven. He was a natural scholar. He had the interest and ability to apply himself to his studies and in the Scottish ancestry of his parents there was an in-bred reverence for learning which was a constant support.

Nobody could ever claim that Evan Mackie was given to blowing his own trumpet, so when he commented on his schooldays: "I always used to get top in the class, or that near it didn't matter," it was clearly nothing more than a statement of fact.

Life was not all wood-gathering and schooling, however. "Almost from the day we could walk we were keen on fishing," he said. "We and a few mates used to hike out to the coast. The nearest point would be about five miles from home along country roads. We could perhaps cycle the first three miles and the rest was hiking over the hills. We fished off the rocks at Orokawa, Goat Bay, Boat Bay, Mataura and the like. We occasionally used to get some good, decent-sized snapper – that was the main thing we caught – and it tasted all the better for all the hiking. It was a full day's work to get out there and back."

Another pastime was not quite so popular. "My father, being of

Scottish descent, was rather keen on Scottish and Highland dancing and bagpipes and the like. He played the pipes and he had us four kids taught dancing by the local teacher." Evan and his brother and two sisters danced Highland reels as a team, and flings and sword dances individually. "In those days it was quite a popular sport and we used to travel around to the various sporting fixtures, as far away as Ngaruawahia – cycling, woodchopping, all that sort of thing. We used to do the rounds and we collected a few honours on the way. My sister Doris got about 26 medals and I was the second to last one – I think I got about 14. There were inscribed gold medals, and some silver for second. Sailor's hornpipe and the Highland fling were my forte.

"Typical kids, we all loathed it. We had to be driven to it, and we dropped it as soon as we had an opportunity."

It is an ill wind which blows no good, and later his dancing prowess would help finance him his first motorcycle.

On 2 December 1930 he was granted his Certificate of Proficiency at the Waihi East Primary School. He had recently passed his 13th birthday, and was in Form 2. The next year he began at the Waihi District High School, where John S. MacKenzie, universally known as 'Gummy', was to be his main teacher. Fellow pupils would include Douglas Walker, later Head of New Zealand Forest Products, and Arthur Ellis Kinsella (known at school by his second Christian name), a future Minister of Education. "The High School was about a mile from our home," Evan remembered, "and if we didn't have some sort of bike in operation we would walk. We weren't exactly destitute, but we weren't rich. But you get some good frosts in Waihi, and running around in bare feet it could be mighty cold."

It had been his intention to sit for the Public Service examination, but that year (1931) this was cancelled. "I had no ambition really. I mean, all kids talk about wanting to be an engine driver. But if you got the Public Service examination, that was the key to working in the Public Service, you see, and that was all I had in mind at that time.

"By today's standards we were all very law-abiding at school, probably frightened to do otherwise. They definitely had canes, those teachers!" His favourite subject was mathematics. "I always revelled in that."

By September 1932, on the eve of his 15th birthday, and without even the Public Service examination to work towards, Evan Mackie was keen to leave school and do his bit towards bringing some money into the family. In those days of the big economic depression it was not easy to get work, but the young Mackie had already shown his resourcefulness by getting to know the Danish community out Golden Valley way, to his advantage. "Fred Bjerring, that was the one I took up with, had an old Model 'T' converted into a pick-up truck, and I was a bit mechanically-minded. He had a cream contract, which he used to run each morning.

"We were running two cows at the time – that's how frugal people were – and we used to send away the cream from these cows. I sort of got to know him and the next thing I was on the truck going down to the dairy company, and next thing I'd be out on his farm poking around, and that's how I got my temporary work. I can't even think what he paid me – it might have been a shilling an hour, it might have been less.

"But anyhow, when I persuaded the folk that I should leave school, there seemed to be no other prospect anywhere, and I went out and worked for him."

Leaving the Waihi District School at that time was something which Evan Mackie was later to regret bitterly and hold against his parents – even though he realised it was his own decision. "I should never have been allowed to leave school then. I always blamed my father for that. I could see his point of view up to a point; we were right in the middle of the depression, things were hard and he was bringing up a family of four and I was persuasive. But we all had potential, and for that reason I should never have been allowed to leave – we would have got through the depression somehow. It put a break in my studies which was very hard to recover, and when it came to my own kids I certainly wouldn't have dreamt of letting them leave if they had potential."

In spite of the District High School burning down almost completely during his time there, and being taught in church halls and other temporary accommodation, Evan Mackie continued to perform impressively, as Mr R.G. Andrews, headmaster of Waihi East Primary School, later testified. "Evan Mackie was a pupil at Waihi East School and under my supervision gained his proficiency certificate under a difficult department test. He showed brilliancy in his secondary school work at the DHS, reaching top of his form. At all times I found him thoroughly honest and straightforward. He is a boy of bright and genial disposition with manly bearing and address, courteous and polite."

Douglas Walker of New Zealand Forest Products, 50 years on, remembered the young Mackie as a "good looking, freckled, cheerful fellow, very straightforward and honest, who reflected his good home and parents – popular at school. I followed his RNZAF career with interest and pride."

During the next three years Mackie undertook a variety of jobs, and although most were menial (many with a mechanical flavour), he discharged them with distinction. While doing these tasks he developed the strong physique for which he was later well known in Royal Air Force units – and with it, the high facial colouring which caused him to be nick-named 'Rosie' or 'Rosebud' universally throughout the service.

During the milking season he worked with Fred Bjerring in his bachelor establishment. Evan was also the cook. "We had some rough old meals, believe me, when I was doing the cooking. Stews mostly, and prunes thickened with sago. Not too bad, either. With the appetites we had, or developed, anything went down."

The next season he moved next door, onto the adjoining farm of Kristen Bjerring (usually known as 'Old K'), who was Fred's father. Evan called this a promotion, as his wages went up to ten shillings a week. "At that time I think Fred was doing a bit of courting and he got married just after that."

Kristen Bjerring was a Danish schoolteacher who had followed in the footsteps of his brother Otto to find a new life in New Zealand. He arrived in the Waihi district about 1925 and took up some large tracts of scrub land in the Golden Valley area, which he worked with the help of his large family. To bring in some cash, while they were breaking the country into grasslands for dairying, they established a shelterbelt nursery and sent bundles of Lawsoniana, barberry and other hedging trees and shrubs all over the North Island.

When Evan went to work for 'Old K' one of the girls was living at home and doing the cooking. "I was doing much the same work as before, although they had a bigger herd. Two of the boys were still working there, Karl and Ness, and me, and of course, old Kristen. But he was pretty old by then and he did all the office work as far as the nursery was concerned, and the deliveries. We had to make them up into bundles according to the orders and they had to be delivered to the rail in town. We all worked on the nursery at times, too."

Life was a little easier as far as the dairy herd was concerned, because the milking shed was equipped with a machine powered by a single cylinder stationary engine; however some of the other farm work was more arduous.

"Things were so hard in those days they couldn't afford to concrete their roads and yards as would be done today. They had a lot of rocks around their farm and part of the between-milking duties involved getting out with a 14-pound hammer and smashing up these rocks – no goggles, no protection, nothing. Just get into the paddocks and smash up these rocks into what they called paving stones. Then you would loosen up the earth and get to work and set them into the ground, all against one another. By the time they are trampled down they make a cobbled road, and by Jove, that represents a lot of hard work."

By now the young Mackie was developing a trait for improving himself and his situation which was to become a part of his character. "After a few months with 'Old K', another promotion! I went to work for Chris Christensen, who eventually ended up the Mayor of Waihi, on an adjoining farm. I got 15 bob a week there – a transfer caused by this quest for money." Christen Christensen was also a member of the Danish community in the Golden Valley area. Hard workers, these Danes seized opportunities others passed by – and they obviously saw in Evan Mackie something of their own work ethic. Certainly, in spite of having a bucket of milk tipped over his head, Fred Bjerring had appreciated his farm boy's work output, and never held the incident against him. "This is to testify that Evan Mackie has been in my employ as a farmhand for this past season. I have much pleasure in recommending him to anyone who wants a good worker, willing and capable, and an honest lad. He is a good milker and able to drive horses," he wrote when Evan moved on.

With experience of more primitive facilities, the lad was able to appreciate Christensen's superior establishment. "Machine milking again, and he had slightly less frugal tendencies. He had a beautiful shed for those days, a good machine, and kept everything beautiful."

Christensen was a contractor as well as a dairy farmer, and quite enterprising. He had a sleeve-valve engined Willys-Knight utility which he used in a cream-carting contract, and he rigged up a hay-sweep on the front of the vehicle and used it to gather cut grass for silage. "Usually this was done using two horses towing a boom with a sweep," said Evan. "He just sat there and drove around. He was quite innovative in that way. He made some improvements to the pulsators on the Climax milking machine."

While Evan was working for him, Chris Christensen and his brother Neil operated a sawmill on Otto Bjerring's land – an enterprise which introduced the youngster to a whole new range of mechanical activity.

"The sawmill was about three quarters of the way down the valley leading to Whiritoa and it was run by just Chris and Neil and their farmhands. So after milking we would get onto the back of the old Willys-Knight and go off down to this sawmill.

"The main hauling motor was a Model 'T' (Ford) and I was the engine driver. We used to have thousands of yards of wire rope going from the winch to a block around a tree, to a block tied onto a rock, to another one onto a tree, and eventually we would get to the tree which had fallen. It might have been up the hill, and in that case we would have jacked it down, with the aid of the winch, and eventually got it into a creek bed. And from there on it was hard yakker. We would have a double-purchase around the log itself, back onto an anchor, and eventually it all came down to this Model 'T' which was connected to the winch. You would be surprised at the size of the rimu logs we used to haul along there, anything up to three feet in diameter. We used to have all sorts of fun. We'd follow it up with a timber jack and try and ease it along when she got stuck – all sorts of tricks to help those poor old logs along.

"They would finally arrive at the sawmill, which was driven by the same Model 'T', driving a three foot blade. We milled kauri too. We used to get some darn good timber. There was access for a truck to come in. Beautiful clean timber came out of there."

It was while he was with Chris Christensen that the young Mackie got an urge to own a motorcycle – and it was then that he was able to capitalise on his dancing expertise. "I had a general scratch around of my assets and I came across these 14 medals, which I realised for ten shillings. What a wicked crime! But I wasn't to be deterred!

"I somehow got up to Auckland on the back of someone else's motorbike and went to Robbie's cycle shop in Greys Avenue. Robbie (later Sir Dove-Meyer Robinson, one time Mayor of Auckland) used to have a bike shop there. I always remember going on the back of the bike, right up Greys Avenue, with him driving. Anyway, I bought this bike for £30, a Triumph, 1930 or '32 I just can't remember. Two and three quarter horsepower, inclined cylinder, overhead valve. Oh, it was just what I wanted, just ideal for me.

"We got home mighty late at night, or early in the morning. My wrist was sore for days – you know, metal roads and the suspension was not what it is today. I got this thing into my bedroom – it was a bit rundown – and I pulled it down into every nut and bolt, roller, everything, right down to the last screw. I cleaned it up and over-hauled it and finally took it out and, second kick, away it went. And I was away! It was a damned good bike, actually."

As well as taking money from his medals, and all he had saved, it required the loan of "a few pounds" from his father to finance the Triumph. With the purchase came the knowledge that he would never be able to afford much on a farmhand's wages, and this undoubtedly influenced his next move. He also had the example of his older brother Allan, who was apprenticed as an electrician with the Waihi Gold Mining Company.

"I had seen enough of hard work," he said. "I was getting to the stage where I realised that I would have to get into something in the tradesman line if I was going to get anywhere at all. And to do that I had to be in town where I could attend the School of Mines – something like night classes at college."

Bearing a testimonial from Chris Christensen: "Evan Mackie has for the past 12 months been working for me and I can recommend him to anyone as a trustworthy and conscientious worker", he returned to the family home in September 1934 and began part-time work with a neighbour, Archie Leach. Evan recalled:

"We still had our two cows to milk at home. Archie Leach had about 15 cows, and he was also a trucking contractor up at the mine, loading the trucks all ready for making up into rakes for trains to go down to Waikino. He went down the various shafts and when the empties came in that was his contract – to get them filled and all ready to go to Waikino. So I was part-time working for him on his farm, and I did part-time work up at the mine, helping him to load those trucks, running them under the hoppers to fill them. That was a pretty hair-raising experience."

They had to race four empty trucks down a slight incline, assisted by a big Clydesdale draught horse. "He got up to a gallop with them beside him, and they got enough speed to shoot down a little bit of a dip, and then up and under the hoppers, which were dead-ended. Four of us would be hiding between the supporting legs with sprags with steel on the end. Our job was to sprag the wheels, depending upon the speed these trucks were doing, before they could rebound off the end – but not too soon so that they didn't reach there. And, of course, it's a bit hard to adjust the speed of a Clydesdale running four empty trucks down. Sometimes they came flat out and bounced back. Sometimes we were pushing them, one at a time."

Working in town gave him access to the School of Mines, where he studied mathematics, electricity and technical drawing for two hours each evening. At the time A.H. 'Viv' Morgan, MA, was director of the school, teaching mechanics and mathematics. A.T. 'Archie' Crosher, the mine electrician, took the electrical classes, and mechanical drawing was taught by Tommy Watters, who was employed at the mine as an engineer. "I was having a bit of difficulty with my maths," said Evan. "I got up to the calculus, but that's as far as I got, not that I really needed it for my electrical work. But I did enjoy trigonometry and logarithms."

It was at the School of Mines that he came to know Owen Morgan, son of the director and, like Chris Christensen, a future Mayor of Waihi. The two lads quickly formed a good opinion of each other. "Owen was a very clueful bloke. That's how I got to know him," said Evan, who obviously established an early reputation for not suffering fools gladly. "He was usually in the laboratory or the workshop and he was very keen on photography. That was when I was keen myself. He used to make up all the solutions for developing, and I'd use them. I had a 620 Kodak."

Owen Morgan was actually the laboratory assistant at the school at the time and he remembered that Evan would arrive at about 5.00 p.m., just as he was leaving to go home. "He would study quietly in the library until regular classes started later. Between 4.00 and 5.00 he would have done his home chores, which included milking the house cows, had tea and cycled the mile or so to the school, this effort adding to his already ruddy complexion. At this time he never sought company nor encouraged friendships. He appeared to find total satisfaction in fulfilling his own pursuits."

Even so, a friendship grew. Owen Morgan: "The all-absorbing hobby that Evan enjoyed during these years before the war was photography. As I too had this interest, and as the School of Mining had a well-equipped darkroom, we spent many hours developing, printing and enlarging our masterpieces. One trick shot I have shows Evan giving himself a ride in a wheelbarrow." He remembered Evan as a single-minded and earnest student, yet with a refreshing, slightly off-beat sense of humour. "His only recreational indulgence that I remember was for him to play tennis on the nurses' court at the Waihi Hospital, where his aunt, Miss S.E. McIntosh, was the matron.

"On one occasion, and by now he owned a Morris 8 car which he maintained in an immaculate condition, I with two others went with him on a camping trip around the Rotorua/Taupo area. Looking back, it was basically an educational trip, as after inspecting the thermal areas we studied the Arapuni and Horahora hydro-electric stations in detail before going on to the Huka Falls and Aratiatia Rapids."

Owen Morgan sums up much of the young Mackie's character in the following way: "Everything he did had a purpose and goal. He didn't take unnecessary risks. He was not one of the motorbike boys who created noise and worry for their parents with their dare-devil antics. By their very nature many of these lads were to become heroes during the war, and so it is perhaps surprising that quiet, law-abiding Evan Mackie surpassed them all."

As the friendship between Evan and Owen grew, so did the relationship between Mackie and Owen's father. The young scholar and the scholarly director of the School of Mines established a very good understanding and respect for each other, which resulted in a correspondence between them which lasted through the war years. 'Viv' Morgan had been a radiologist on the hospital ship SS *Maheno* in the First World War. Knowing this, and aware of his interest in the second big conflict, Evan described the campaigns he was engaged in, but never once over-played his own exploits.

"I also exchanged letters with Evan," said Owen Morgan. "but found out little about his achievements until after the war, or by chance when they reached the news."

Soon after he began his studies at the School of Mines, the ever-present urge to better himself came over Mackie again, and in February 1935 he joined Rodney Lockett, a motor mechanic in

Rosemont Road, as a garage assistant. In a sense the work he did at the garage was a practical extension of his evening studies, and he brought with him a testimonial from Archie Leach: "This is to certify that I have known Evan Mackie when going to school and have employed him on farm and work at Waihi Gold Mining Comp. in connection with transport of quartz to Waikino. He is a quick worker and can do a man's work."

By keeping himself within the orbit of men like mine electrician Crosher, through his studies at the school, Evan quickly achieved a short-term objective – in October 1935 he obtained a temporary position with the Martha Gold Mining Coy. (Waihi) Ltd. During the next ten weeks he assisted in the erection of a new electrical winding plant driven by a 907 bhp motor. Even better, at the end of 1935 he passed the junior electrical examination with a mark of 86% – the highest in New Zealand. It was little wonder that 'Viv' Morgan would later write: "He has been an exceptionally brilliant student . . . . ."

The temporary job ended with the completion of the winding gear erection in mid-January, 1936, but he was taken on again temporarily in June that year for two months to make alterations to the mine lighting system. He evidently made a good impression, for immediately on completion of the project he was signed up as an apprentice electrician with the company. His brother Allan had just completed his apprenticeship, and Evan was stepping into his shoes. The apprenticeship was for five years, and his wages started at 15 shillings a week, ending at £2 5s 0d (two pounds, five shillings) a week in his fifth year.

For a young man with ambition in a country beginning to emerge from an economic depression, it was a happy state of affairs indeed. "Oh, great elation, to have landed a job of any description, especially one where you are signed up – set, signed and sealed. This was something. I felt on top of the world. Work was assured for the rest of my life, it seemed to me."

The promise which Mr Morgan had seen in Evan Mackie continued to demonstrate itself. Four months after beginning his apprenticeship he passed his senior electrical examination with 85% – the second highest mark in the Dominion. In 1937 he topped New Zealand with 67% in the practical mathematics examination, and later that year he passed the City and Guilds of London Institute (electrical wireman's) examination in electrical engineering, practical, Grade I (direct and alternating current). He was now working under the direction of Archie Crosher, the mine electrician, and Dick Wynn, his assistant, learning how to maintain a wide variety of electric motors and their associated machinery. While there were a lot of surface installations, like the winding gear at the mine on Martha Hill and the crushing equipment in the batteries at Waikino, generators and compressors, there was also machinery underground, like the 1,200 hp motor driving a huge centrifugal de-watering pump, and the electric lighting system. So a lot of his work was underground too.

The Waihi Gold Mining Company Ltd. (later the Martha Gold Mining Company [Waihi] Ltd.) had its own hydro-electric power generating station at Horahora on the Waikato River. With the introduction of the 40-hour working week by the new Labour government, it was necessary to establish a roster for the manning of what was known as the powerhouse – the point from which the balance of the Horahora generation was distributed after the demand from the Waikino crushing batteries had been established. As the new apprentice became more proficient and was given more responsibility, he took his turn as powerhouse operator. "I think at that time there was an arrangement to take a supply in from the New Zealand Electricity Department to meet any shortfall, and that would have to be strictly adhered to, otherwise it would mean a large expenditure which would have to be explained.

"So it meant running around like a mad thing, up to the last minute of each hour, adjusting the load so that this was neither exceeded, nor was power wasted through not working up to the figure. Load controlling became one of the most enjoyable aspects of my work – seeing how many times I could get it to punch exactly on the figure in the course of a shift. And that happened quite often!"

Soon after he moved back home from the farm he gave up motorcycles, exchanging his Triumph for a bull-nosed Morris Cowley, a 1928 model which had been advertised for sale in Devonport, Auckland. "Dad and I went up in the bus and had a look at the car, not that I knew much about them at the time, except that it went, had all the trimmings, seemed economical enough. Anyhow, I bought the thing and drove it home.

"Not long after that I traded it in on a De Soto two-seater, a sporty-looking thing which was a bit hungry on gas, even though gas was quite cheap at the time. Two shillings a gallon, if I remember right. And one thing that sticks in my mind is pulling into Horace Wrigley's garage one Sunday afternoon. I had a shilling in my pocket and I had the neck to ask him for half a gallon of petrol! He supplied it, and then shook his head and said: 'You know, it doesn't really pay me to come out and serve you. Half a gallon!' But that was the level at which I operated in those days. If I was down to the last shilling or two in my pocket, I put it into petrol or some essential little part for the car. Most of the repairs I did myself, together with friends around town."

Owen Morgan has memories of that too: "At home, in his spare

time, he would repair and re-wind faulty car and motorcycle generators for his friends, myself included, for no charge."

The De Soto was in turn traded in on a more economical 1936
Hillman sedan. Then there was the Morris 8 which Owen remembered
and, in 1938, a new Standard 8, bought from Reg Willis in Waihi's
main street. "That car I put in mothballs during the war, so I had
the use of it when I returned," Mackie recalled.

While it might have seemed unusual for an apprentice to be in a
position of being able to buy a new motorcar, it was simply a matter of
getting one's priorities in order, he said many years later; "Somehow or
another we got by on the smell of an oily rag those days, but not by
depriving ourselves of anything. If we wanted something we were prepared to work for it, and it certainly gave us a great sense of value.
Anything that you worked hard for, you appreciated." Even as an apprentice he went out at weekends to help his Danish friends on their farms.

He continued to shine academically in 1938, passing the wireman's
(written) examination with 88% (one mark below a gold medal) and
obtaining 97% in elementary mathematics – the highest in the country.
He passed the London Institute's Grade II examination at the end
of the same year. The next year his mark in senior mathematics was
third highest in the country, and he achieved a 76% pass in the
wireman's practical examination.

Labour Weekend, 1939, saw him pumping the organ of St. John's
Anglican Church for the wedding of his farm workmate Ness Bjerring
to Doris Pascoe.

By then even isolated New Zealanders were aware of the approaching likelihood of war. Mackie, like many others of his age and
inclination, began to make preparations for the forthcoming conflict.
The Royal New Zealand Air Force had instituted a correspondence
course for prospective aircrew. "For some reason or other I was a
bit slow finding out that several fellows in Waihi had been engaged
in this course for several months. It suddenly struck me, well, what
a wonderful idea. Why aren't I doing it? So without further delay I
borrowed all the past assignments from these other guys in town.
There were three of them; Reggie Upton, Harry Jensen and Mick
'Honk' Miller – he was a mechanic."

A special class had been established by 'Viv' Morgan at the School
of Mines to work through these assignments. Mackie made an
application to join the course register. "By the time that was in hand
I had a heap of previous assignments all sealed up ready to be
despatched. Others came back and in less than no time I was up in
line with these other bods. And it was something I really enjoyed,
because the work was so similar to what I had been doing over the
last few years in connection with my apprenticeship.

"The theory of flight seemed just common sense, and the result was I just flew through and got my joining up papers at the same time and we all went into camp together at Levin."

The odd aspect of this sudden enthusiasm for the RNZAF is that Evan had never had any real interest in flying as such. He had only ever shown the usual interest of a small boy. The first aeroplane he ever saw was the tri-motored monoplane of Sir Charles Kingsford-Smith at Athenree, near Waihi Beach, where he took people for joy rides during barn-storming tours of the Dominion. "I never did go up on any trip. Don't know why, really. I was not particularly interested in flying as such – more interested in the fact that it was an aeroplane. Interested in what made it tick, and interested to see it perform."

Nevertheless, on 27 May 1940, Mackie applied to join the Royal New Zealand Air Force. He was 22 years old and still had a year of his electrical apprenticeship to run. On 16 August 1940 he began the RNZAF educational course No. 3 and completed it on 13 November with a 91% credit and a 'highly commendable' from his examining officer. A few days earlier, on 11 November, he had been advised that his training had been deferred until May 1941, and he had been granted Enlistment Badge No.3189. (The Enlistment Badges were to give those who had volunteered, but had not yet been called up, some evidence of their commitment for King and Country, and to enable them to escape the growing practice of 'white feathering' some able-bodied young men who were trying to escape service with the armed forces. This practice dated from earlier wars, and usually took the form of young women handing white feathers to men thought to be shirking their duty, as a sign of their supposed cowardice).

For some reason not readily evident in the official record, Evan Mackie's entrance into the RNZAF was hurriedly brought forward in the last days of 1940. His apprenticeship contract was formally terminated by mutual consent on 1 January, 1941, while it still had eight months to run. However, Mackie had by then passed all his examinations with flying colours, and under the circumstances was deemed to be a fully-registered electrical wireman.

On 19 January, 1941, he entered the RNZAF. Few Waihi citizens could have guessed that the young man in the pale blue uniform with the white flash of 'aircrew-under-training' in his cap, would next return home as a high-ranking and much-decorated ace fighter pilot, to be honoured with a civic reception.

CHAPTER TWO

TRAINING IN WHENUAPAI AND CANADA

After achieving such excellence in his studies and practical work towards his electrical wireman's ticket, Evan Mackie's progress in the Royal New Zealand Air Force was by contrast rather lacklustre at first.

As always, he was constantly striving to improve himself and his prospects. Above all, he wanted to do it on his own terms. He made this clear in his reasons for joining the RNZAF: "I was still in my apprenticeship, and I could see the way the war was heading. I was going to have to become involved one way or another. I thought to myself, well, it may as well be something I enjoy – and I didn't fancy footslogging. I was more technically-minded, and several of my friends, Mick Miller, Henry Jensen, Reggie Upton and one or two others, had already enlisted as aircrew. I thought, what a jolly good idea. I'll either make it or I won't. I'll have a go."

But before he did so, the canny Mackie ensured that if he was successful, he could be released from his apprenticeship without liability. When he entered the RNZAF he was already registered electrical wiremen No. B3887, even though he was six months short of his qualifying time. In the back of his mind was the determination that, if he did not qualify for aircrew, his second choice would be the electrical section of aircraft maintenance, "where at least I would receive good training which would improve my prospects following the war, if I came out okay."

Evan and several of his Waihi compatriots caught the Taneatua express at Waihi, changed to a south-bound express at Frankton Junction in the middle of the North Island, and steamed on through the night to disembark next morning at Levin, 50 miles north of Wellington, the capital city. Weraroa Camp was just on the outskirts of the small market-garden centre, and there on 19 January 1941, they were kitted out. A six week stint of square-bashing, tempered with a variety of courses, introduced them to the service way of life.

"Plenty of spit and polish," Mackie recalled. "From then on we were in the service and never allowed to forget it. The day began literally before daylight. We were on the parade-ground by six o'clock – and that was after we had washed and shaved, cleaned out our huts, folded our bedding in the approved manner, and cleaned our buttons and everything else on our uniforms."

At Weraroa those on Mackie's initial training course lived in two-man huts which had wooden floors, walls timbered to about four foot, and above that, canvas. Their service clothing included longjohn underwear, and when they went out walking, their greatcoats had to be folded over their arms in conformity with regulations. "Everything was done to a pattern – it was a form of discipline," he recalled. "I don't think it did anyone any harm."

The end of the six-week course saw Mackie, now a Leading Aircraftsman, posted to 4 Elementary Flying Training School at Whenuapai, Auckland. This suited him well, because it was the EFTS closest to his home.

On 3 March 1941, with Pilot Officer Kenneth Russel Clarke at the controls, Evan Mackie left the ground for the first time ever. The aircraft was a De Havilland 82 Tiger Moth, No.789. "I had been below the ground, 2,000 feet or so at the Waihi mine, but never above," he said, recalling being "extremely keyed up and keen. Possibly I was keen to a fault and scared out of my wits that I would miss out through some fault of my own. It was not a good thing, really. One should be more relaxed in these things."

He found that first 20 minutes of air experience "exciting in a way, yet so peaceful. Once you left the ground there you were, just suspended, and everything so peaceful apart from the noise of the engine and the wind."

Just like all the other service personnel on EFTS course, he soon found that there was more to do than admire the scenery and revel in the sensation of being airborne. Under Plt Off Clarke, who would take him right through the course, he buckled down and mastered the basics of practical aviation – and found that flying a DH 82 well did not come easily.

"Of course, the old Tiger Moth was rather a rudimentary aircraft but very suitable for the job, looking back. I wouldn't say it was not hard to fly, and to fly it accurately required all the skills one had. In types like the Tiger Moth, with large control surfaces and under-powered, non-accurate flying was very evident."

Commenting on his instructor, Mackie recalled that Clarke was "a very quiet sort of chap – and as far as I could see there was no deterioration in his health from the time we started until I went solo." Clarke's widow, Mrs Aline Clarke, was later to write: "I know my husband had a very high regard for Evan as a person and always referred to him as 'Mackie Boy' – I don't know why – but imagine they had a good rapport. Ken was very proud of Evan's record."

Mackie soloed with 9 hours 15 minutes of dual instruction in his logbook. "That was roughly average. One or two bright boys went off at eight hours or so. Some took longer and some didn't make it at all." Later on, when he practised aerobatic manoeuvres, he found spinning to be "quite a frightening experience until you learn how to deal with it."

At EFTS the first of only three incidents involving damage to an aircraft for which Mackie alone could be blamed, occurred. (Later there would be a 'deadstick' landing in a Spitfire which ended with the aircraft inverted, and a landing overshoot, also in a Spitfire, both during his early days with his first squadron).

The Whenuapai incident also ended with an inverted aircraft, after a spectacular ground loop. At the time part of the airfield was being re-surfaced, and he was required to land the Tiger Moth on a runway with a cross-wind factor. "Due, no doubt, to my lack of experience, I got into some sort of bounce which perhaps could have been corrected by opening up and going around again. But unfortunately I didn't, and I ended up by veering off the runway and into some ploughed ground, and the aircraft ended up flat on its back.

"And there I was, held with my seatbelt, and my head two or three feet above wet, ploughed ground. And of course, when I pulled the harness-release I landed head-first."

Thanks to the understanding of his instructor and the administration staff, his logbook was not endorsed with the accident, and his training continued. "If they were to turf out everybody who made errors, there would probably be no-one left to continue the war effort," Mackie later commented.

He spent some time on ground instruction in a Link trainer, and learned how to rely entirely on his instruments – "and not the seat of your pants or any other sensation. You've got to glue your eyes on those instruments and believe them. If you don't, you're a dead duck. Because there are times when you could swear that you are flying upside down or turning hard one way or the other, and all the time you are flying straight and level."

The course ended officially with a two-hour cross-country flight to Whangarei and return. "It might not sound very much of an episode now, but in a slow vehicle like the Tiger Moth and with such inexperienced pilots, who at the same time had to keep a flight record of the trip, it was quite an achievement to get there and back. The local folk interested in flying put on afternoon tea for all of us that arrived at Whangarei before we were sent on our way home again."

The next day, 11 April 1941, Mackie and Plt Off Clarke took DH 82 No.683 aloft for 50 minutes of celebratory aerobatics. Then came a ceremonial parade up Auckland's Queen Street, before final leave and embarkation on board the liner *Awatea*, en route to Canada.

Mackie topped No. 11 course at 4 EFTS with an average of 89% for ground studies. With 22 hours 50 minutes of dual instruction and 22 hours 10 minutes of solo flight logged, his proficiency as a pilot was given as "Average" by the Chief Flying Instructor, an assessment confirmed by the school's commanding officer, Squadron Leader John Seabrook. They would have been advised of his progress by Plt Off Clarke, by Flight Lieutenant Firth, who took him for his solo test, by Flt Lt Kenneth Gordon Smith, who took him for his 20-hour and 40-hour tests, and by Plt Off John Desmond Paterson, who supervised his instrument test. Five hours of instruction in the Link trainer also earned him an "Average" assessment.

In the Royal Air Force and the Commonwealth air forces there was provision for flying ability to be graded as Exceptional, Above Average, Average and Below Average. It is perhaps fair to state that "Exceptional" gradings were rare indeed, and that only a relatively small percentage of pilots were ever graded "Above Average".

Mackie's inclination at that stage was towards multi-engined aircraft, and when the course members were given the opportunity of stating their preferences, that was what he opted for: "For no other reason than I thought that perhaps I could handle the responsibility of a multi. I was a bit older than the average candidate at that time – 25, and there were a lot younger than me."

The course had not been without tragedy, and Mackie "thanked my lucky stars" that he was not flying the Tiger Moth which lost a wing during aerobatics. In the resultant crash on 6 March 1941, LAC Frank Robert Traynor lost his life. An investigation, during which all the flying school biplanes were grounded, revealed a faulty flying wire turnbuckle as the cause of the wing failure. But all that was behind him now, and advanced training in Canada beckoned.

"There was great excitement for boarding the *Awatea* in Auckland," Mackie remembered. "For all of us it would have been our first overseas trip on a boat. Mum and Dad had run me up to Auckland in their car. It was fairly late in the afternoon when she came in, and we had to assemble in the drill hall. By the time we were counted and re-counted and sorted out the day went quickly enough." It was 29 April 1941, and the *Awatea* already had on board a contingent of Royal Australian Air Force aircrew in their dark blue uniforms.

"Unfortunately it started to drizzle and rain, and as we sailed out about four or five o'clock, the last we saw of New Zealand was murkiness and clouds," he said.

Mackie had no complaints about the accommodation and revelled in the Pacific crossing. "There were six of us allocated to a cabin – and what a large cabin." In the dining lounge they were seated six to a table, with a steward to each table. "We were treated like kings. Far better than we were used to. I had my first grapefruit on board there, served up as they should be served up, on a silver tray. Sitting up in the big dining lounge, with a great view all around, we felt remote from the war."

Awatea had a smooth crossing, calling only at Fiji and San Francisco, before arriving at Vancouver 17 days later. The ship berthed in the evening and the young servicemen saw little of the city as they entrained immediately for Medicine Hat, travelling via places they had only ever read of before, like Banff and Calgary.

"We woke up next morning well into the Rockies, and for the rest of the day we were all engrossed in watching the scenery. The railways intrigued us no end – their size and the grades."

After two nights and days their train arrived at Medicine Hat, a staging post from where aircrew trainees would be posted to their respective service flying training schools. It was there that Mackie and his companions came up against one of the inconsistencies of service life for the first time – an apparent official predeliction for ignoring expressed preferences. All those in Mackie's draft had expressed a preference for either single-engined or multi-engined aircraft. Their instructors had endorsed their suitability for their choice, and it had been placed on their records. But the Royal Air Force officers in charge of the British Commonwealth Air Training Plan at Medicine Hat had other ideas. They drafted all those who preferred multi-engined machines to single-engined training, and vice versa. What they had not counted on was the colonial reaction to their arbitrary decisions: "We kicked our heels up a bit in what virtually amounted to a strike," said Mackie. "We were duly read the Riot Act and assured that once we learned to fly, once we got our wings, once we got to England, the world was our oyster – we could pick our own type, more or less. Anyhow, quiet prevailed, and we proceeded to our allotted stations. Mine was Moose Jaw, where they were training on Harvards – not that I've ever regretted it, to this day. By the time we had completed our training we were converted and dyed-in-the-wool fighter pilots!"

He was clearly impressed with the new low-wing monoplane trainers with their great radial engines, and he determined to learn everything he could. His new instructor at 32 SFTS was a Canadian, Flying Officer Millar. "Dusty, we used to call him," said Mackie. The Harvard was "quite a swept-up aeroplane", and he was impressed by its size and power, the roominess of the cockpit, and by the sophistications unknown on the Tiger Moth like flaps, wheel brakes and a retractable undercarriage. He was also impressed by the noise it made: "We had to do a certain amount of night flying and these things didn't half make a racket, taking off directly over our barracks. We were in dormitories that held about 60, and they had tin roofs. You can imagine the noise of these things taking off directly overhead. Mind you, we could have slept on a clothesline at that stage, what with the stress of flying, which took place four hours daily, plus our theory studies for the wings exam."

Mackie teamed up with a fellow Kiwi, George Esmond (Bill) Jameson*, who also seemed keen to do well, and they studied together. "He was really capable, that chap," said Mackie. And 50 years on, Jameson recalled a like opinion of Mackie: "Both of us were of a similar bent. Enthusiastic about the job and keen to learn. We had a friendship that we kept up. A very straightforward person." Jameson went on to become a night fighter pilot who claimed 11 enemy aircraft shot down, receiving a DSO and DFC before being manpowered back to New Zealand, where his skills were in even greater demand in agriculture.

"I spent every possible night studying," said Mackie. "I reckoned my chances of coming through depended largely on myself. If I could learn all there was to learn about the game, as taught by others who had flown in combat; if I could pick up all the hints I could on theory and type recognition and become proficient in engine handling, navigation, meteorology and everything connected with flying, I reckoned the better would be my chances of survival.

"It seemed logical to me to do as much as I could for myself. There- fore I spent very little time in the nearby town of Moose Jaw. Most of my time was in studying or flying the Link trainer, which was a great help."

In the cockpit he was equally determined. "A lot of the exercises were solo. We could be told to do a cross-country. Well, you can cut corners, or you can do it properly and teach yourself something. You go up to familiarise yourself with the aircraft and you can just stooge around and have a look at the countryside, or you can put it through all the manoeuvres you can think of, particularly spinning. I know the last time I flew the Harvard I spun it intentionally 11 times."

Mackie admitted that one thing that had him whacked to a certain extent with the Harvard was landing the aircraft. "I was damned if I could guarantee a straight landing run. They were a beggar to veer off to one side or the other after you had touched down. The brakes were too ineffective to hold it once it started to swing. You had to

* (Flt Lt G.E. Jameson, DSO, DFC & Bar; see *Aces High*, page 352.)

anticipate that swing." But he did not always anticipate early enough, and once ground-looped his aircraft three times in succession.

Like others in service flying training schools in flat and featureless central Canada, he had cause to bless the grain industry. "Any town of any note had its own grain elevator, which was like a 20-storied building. Many a pilot owes his safe return to the large lettering on those grain elevators."

Leading Aircraftsman Mackie's progress through the nine-week course at 32 SFTS was fairly standard. He first flew a Harvard on 1 June 1941, and made his first solo flight in one on 11 June, after four hours of dual instruction. His third cross-country Navigational exercise on 30 June involved a two hour flight, his longest to date. A one hour ten minutes flight on 7 July, during which he practised forced landings, gave him more solo than dual hours in his logbook for the first time. On 21 July Squadron Leader W. Cooper, the officer commanding the School's 1 Squadron, certified that LAC Mackie was qualified to spin solo.

On 8 August 1941, with his proficiency as a pilot now assessed "Above Average", and rated as having shown aptitude as a pilot-navigator, Mackie qualified for the coveted flying badge, as the 'wings' were officially known. That same day he was commissioned as a Pilot Officer according to his logbook – although his commission was actually gazetted on 9 August. He had completed 31 hours and 10 minutes dual and 35 hours 25 minutes solo in Harvards, and he topped his course of 68 trainees with an average mark of 91% in the 'wings' examination. His friend Bill Jameson was second.

For both of them, it was the shape of things to come when they began operational flying. Mackie said it was not necessarily those who got the highest marks or who were the best fliers who were commissioned. "No doubt they had their own secret codes by which they selected people. Rather, a large percentage appeared to be commissioned – more than 50 percent. Those who were not commissioned became Sergeant Pilots. It was with great pride, of course, that we sat on our beds and changed our badges of rank, even though we did not have officer uniforms until we got to England."

During the course there had been at least one fatality; most however, had passed the course and won their wings. "It was a very, very sorry one who did miss out. All of them were volunteers and keen to pass, even though a lot of them did fool around and not put their best foot forward."

On one of the rare occasions when Mackie took a break from his studies he was the guest of a nearby resident, a Mrs Flowers, who had a park-like property with facilities for tennis and canoeing, and ran an open home for the airmen during their leisure hours. It was with a touch of homesickness that he learned that Mrs Flowers was related to a Mrs Addy in his hometown of Waihi. "Shows you what a small world it really is."

After the ceremonial 'wings' parade, at which the flying badges were presented, he made a leisurely trip across Canada with a small group of fellow New Zealanders. They had been given open tickets on the railways, and a certain time in which to reach Halifax on the east coast. It was no secret that they were bound for England.

The only hitch occurred when the steam engine hauling their train ran out of water in the middle of nowhere – the fireman having taken it for granted that his predecessor had filled the tender reservoir. "I always remember the figure – it held 18,500 gallons," said Mackie.

Their most noteworthy stop on the long journey was a visit to Niagara Falls, although they found most aspects of Canadian life of interest.

In Halifax they boarded *Dominion Monarch*, and made an unescorted seven day dash across the Atlantic, untroubled by enemy submarines or surface raiders. A destroyer escorted them on their last day as they approached the coast of England. The weather as they moved up the Solent in early September 1941 and berthed at Southampton was reminiscent of their murky departure from Auckland. They saw little of the port city before they were bussed off to Bournemouth.

CHAPTER THREE

TRAINING IN THE UK

When he landed at Southampton, Mackie's future was uncertain. While initially he had an inkling that he might be best suited to multi-engined aircraft, he had tasted the excitement of flying a responsive single-engined fighter trainer – and he liked it. He had shown ability as a pilot/navigator, yet at that stage of the war it was generally believed that fighter pilots needed less navigational ability than did the pilots of other types of aircraft.

His contingent was mustered and kitted-out at nearby Bournemouth, and finally paraded to learn what their fate was to be. Mackie did not particularly mind whether it was fighters or bombers – but after hearing that he was posted to fighters, he really was quite pleased about it. "By this time, having flown the single, I had no misgivings about my posting to Grangemouth for further training on Spitfires at 58 Operational Training Unit."

Grangemouth, situated in Scotland on the Firth of Forth, about midway between Edinburgh and Glasgow, was a fair haul from the Channel coast seaside resort of Bournemouth, and the train journey gave the young New Zealander a good opportunity to assess the organisational ability of the Royal Air Force. He was impressed. "It seemed to be very good everywhere we went. Buses and barracks were there in readiness for our arrival. En route, at certain stations in England, there was a party of women with lunch packs ready to hand out to our particular number."

Most of his journey north was made in daylight and he got a fair look at the country in which he was to spend the next 12 months.

Mackie arrived at Grangemouth in mid-September 1941. Operational Training Units (OTUs) were a fairly new and essential element in the production of service pilots in general, and fighter pilots in particular, and 58 OTU was just getting into its stride. Even so, he was later critical of it, claiming that the standard of training it provided was inadequate.

During much of the First World War the Royal Flying Corps, and later, the fledgling Royal Air Force, suffered severe pilot losses which were made good by replacements straight out of elementary flying schools. Some had never even flown the service machines in which they were then sent out to fight. Patsy Adams-Smith in *The Anzacs* (Thomas Nelson, Australia, 1985) claimed: "The life expectancy of those young pilots was said to be three weeks on 'active service'." But accounts written soon after that conflict by people who were involved, like Elliott White Springs, indicate that many of those inexperienced replacements died on the Western Front after only a few hours, or at best, days. Many never returned from their first patrol.

By the late stages of that first great conflict in the skies, training schools for the pilots of fighting scouts had indeed been set up, where those returning from the Front for a rest from operations were able to pass on the benefits of their experience. The reduction of the RAF to little more than a cadre after the conclusion of hostilities had seen these schools disappear, and not until the outbreak of the new war were they to be reformed.

The introduction of the fast new single-seater monoplane fighters, the Hawker Hurricane and Supermarine Spitfire, posed new problems in training since the difference in performance and the sophistication presented by retractable undercarriages, flaps and enclosed cockpits, proved something of a gulf when compared with the biplanes generally in use for training. Initially the newly-equipped fighter squadrons were able to provide such training for the relatively few new pilots posted to them from the training establishments. Once, however, the duties of wartime were imposed, this facility became a luxury which could no longer be considered available. As new squadrons were formed at an increasing rate and the flow of newly-trained fighter pilots increased correspondingly, the need for specialist advanced training units of this type became vital. Fighter Command had the nucleus available in two Pilot Pools, serving the main Groups, Nos 11 and 12, whilst Bomber Command possessed a number of non-operational training squadrons. From these two basic resources, a huge network of Operational Training Units to meet the needs of all the operational commands of the air force, at home and overseas, was born.

Already however, the Service Flying Training Schools had begun to introduce high powered monoplanes to begin bridging the gap between trainer and operational fighter aircraft, such as the Harvard, on which machine Mackie had already gained experience in Canada. During mid-1938 the RAF had ordered 500 Rolls-Royce Kestrel-engined two-seater Miles Masters, which had a performance rather closer to that of the front-line fighters, and these were the main aircraft which undertook a role similar to that of the Harvard in the United Kingdom.

Some senior RAF officers who had experienced personally the shortcomings of inadequately-trained pilots in the 1914-18 conflict, had recognised clearly the need for these Operational Training Units at an early date. One such was Air Vice-Marshal Sholto Douglas, who in 1938 held the post of Assistant Chief of Air Staff. In his auto-biography *Years of Command* (Collins, 1966) he wrote: "We had had to devote precious time and effort in the squadrons to giving them their final training, and no matter how hard we tried, they were still only half trained when they went into battle. As a result of that we suffered very heavy casualties. I was determined that that should not happen again and when my chance came as a senior officer on the air staff, I pressed hard for the formation of those initial training units."

Douglas was surprised to find Air Chief Marshal Sir Hugh Dowding, Commander-in-Chief of Fighter Command, and a man known to have a great regard for the welfare of his pilots, raising some quite strenuous objections to the formation of OTUs. His reason was that he did not want his front-line squadrons depleted in either men or aircraft – and he knew that was where OTU material would be drawn from. The scheme went ahead in spite of Dowding's objections, although the great fighter leader was later to appreciate its benefits. But he had delayed its implementation, with the result that during the Battle of Britain, 10 July to 31 October 1940 – the supply of pilots presented an acute problem. In consequence training had to be restricted to the minimum, some pilots departing their OTUs with as little as ten hours flying time on Spitfires or Hurricanes.

Wing Commander H.L. Thompson in *New Zealanders with the RAF* (NZ Govt. Printer, 1953) noted: "There were only three fighter opera-tional training units at the time. Nevertheless, during the lull between Dunkirk and the start of the German attacks they worked intensively, an RAF report noting that 'Maximum output was helped by the keenness of the pupils; some New Zealanders who had been trained on Gordons and Vincents in their own country, reached Hawarden one evening, spent the night on Spitfire cockpit drill by the light of torches, and began flying the following morning.'"

By coincidence, it was two New Zealanders who were instrumental in getting the OTUs up and running once the Air Council had decided to go ahead against Dowding's objections. They were Air Vice-Marshal C.T. MacLean, who laid the groundwork of 23 (Training) Group in 1940, and Air Vice-Marshal Keith Park, who was responsible for the Group's vigorous expansion in 1941. Park, who had been so successful in his handling of 11 (Fighter) Group during the Battle of

Britain, had been pushed sideways into training following tactical conflicts with Air Vice-Marshal Trafford Leigh-Mallory, AOC 12 (Fighter) Group during the Battle. That was a bonus for Mackie and the thousands of trainee pilots who were to pass through the OTUs after him, for they reaped the benefits of Park's brilliant administration.

Where only months before fighter pilots had been rushed into battle with perhaps only ten hours of operational training, Mackie was to complete his course at 58 OTU, Grangemouth, with 40 hours and 10 minutes experience aloft in Spitfires. Further, having gained an 'Above Average' assessment for the course, he would be asked to stay on at the OTU as a staff pilot, and gain an extra 30 hours and 15 minutes of Spitfire experience before being posted to an operational squadron. Few pilots arrived at their first squadron with 70 hours plus of Spitfire time in their logbooks, and Mackie would never deny the advantage which that additional experience gave him.

Although Grangemouth opened, originally for night-fighter training purposes, in October 1940, staff and aircraft were in short supply. June 1941 was the first month in which the station worked as a full OTU, and Mackie arrived in time to join the 12th course, about half the pilots on which were Polish. Accommodation was inadequate, and the trainees lived in Avondale House, which had originally been allocated for the Women's Auxiliary Air Force staff. The huts intended for the pilots had been taken over for housing the school's permanent staff airmen, who had overflowed from the nearby Town Hall, which had been commandeered for the initial accommodation.

That all 38 forming the course would get through was no certainty. During the No.10 course, just a few weeks previously, five aspiring pilots had died either in mid-air collisions, through spinning into the ground, or by flying into high ground in cloudy conditions. It really was make or break!

Mackie's first flight at Grangemouth occurred on 17 September 1941, in a Miles Master (T8779) piloted by Flight Sergeant Eade; after 40 minutes on circuits and landings Mackie was sent off solo. On 20 September Warrant Officer Morfill* gave him a 'Spitfire test' in a Master, in which he had by then accomplished one hour and 25 minutes solo, and after a further one hour and 10 minutes solo, he took a Spitfire aloft for the first time. The date was 21 September 1941, the aircraft was a Mark I, N4851, and the flight lasted 40 minutes. From that tentative first flight was to develop two years of operational flying on Spitfires during which he would claim the destruction of 16 German and Italian aircraft.

---

* (Flt Lt P.F. Morfill, DFM; see *Aces High*, page 450.)

But all that was quite a way into the future when Mackie pressed the starter button in N4851 and for the first time experienced the crackle of a 1,030 horsepower Rolls-Royce Merlin's exhausts from the driver's seat. "What a marvellous machine! It seemed to be packed with power. Not so noisy as some of the other types. Smoothness and power, sleekness and manoeuvrability. In the air it seemed to have enough power to do anything. It flew like a dream in turns."

Mackie noted that after the Harvard, which was large and roomy, typical of American aircraft, the Spitfire seemed small, not exactly cramped, but leaving no room to spare in the cockpit. "At the same time one realised there was a sting in its tail – it was a real weapon itself. You had to come to grips with the fact that although it was a beautiful sleek machine, it was basically just a weapon."

He also discovered that tractability in the air was not necessarily a characteristic during takeoffs and landings. "They were a wee bit tricky taking off and landing. First of all, when a Spitfire is running straight and level on the runway the tips of the propeller are only six inches from the ground. So you mustn't get your tail too high. Visibility is not very good forward, when you realise you've got a 15 ft long bonnet sticking out in front of you. You can really only see either side when the tail is well up. So there is always that tendency to get the tail a wee bit higher and see directly ahead."

There were other little tricks to learn in this new high-powered aircraft, like counteracting the torque of the propeller with the rudder, and taking care not to drop a wingtip on landing. Unlike the Harvard however, the Spitfire did not display the same tendency to veer after touching down.

While part of each day was spent on theory in the classroom and Link trainer practice, the emphasis was now on flying and the skills that went with it, like navigation and gunnery. Even so, he was by no means in the air every day. During the six weeks of the course, which ended on 27 October 1941, he only flew on four consecutive days. The practice was, however, to make up to three flights in one day when scheduled for flying. More than once he logged more than three hours in the air in one day.

Whilst some attention was paid to formation flying, radio-telephone drill, instrument and cross-country navigation, most of his time aloft was spent on steep turns, aerobatics, gunnery practice, dog-fighting, stern attacks and the like.

He was critical however of the small amount of time devoted to gunnery practice. It was to be a continuing source of concern to him during his service career, that so much time should be spent honing the skills of pilots to enable them to get onto enemy aircraft, and that so little should be done to ensure they had a good standard of marksmanship once they got there. (This is a common criticism voiced by many pilots in later years. Certainly the RAF seems to have given much less consideration to air firing training than was the case in certain other air forces, such as the US Navy and the Luftwaffe. This seems to have been a 'hangover' from the inter-war years when Treasury pressures instilled an ethos of pilot flying skills above all else.) Certainly No.12 course at 58 OTU gained no impression that gunnery was a priority skill. Less than three hours of the 40 spent airborne during the course were devoted to actual firing practice – and to Mackie the cine-gun exercises provided as an alternative seemed to be of doubtful value in pointing up aiming faults. "We did have plenty of dog-fighting experience, mostly among ourselves," he said.

"The idea was for one to get on the other's tail and for No.1 to try and shake off No.2 and they try and get around onto his tail – and some very hairy flying went on in an endeavour to do that. We practiced stern attacks, attacking from above, below, formation dog-fighting. In general, we were kept very busy and because of our keenness we got very tired. I'm afraid not much attention was paid to theoretical subjects such as aircraft recognition. Ideal methods of attack and tactics in general were never really drummed home."

About halfway through the course Mackie and another pilot were chosen to deliver two new Spitfires from Grangemouth to Castletown, which was about 200 miles north on the Pentland Firth. It was this flight which indicated to the New Zealander the value of experience. For him, it could easily have been a one-way trip.

The new Spitfires were not equipped with radio, and before taking off the two pilots had agreed that they would run their engines at minus four boost, which would give 200 miles per hour at a certain height and ample fuel for emergencies. Mackie explained that excessive boost damaged the engine, and also used fuel at a great rate. "In a Spitfire you can vary your rate of consumption from 25 gallons an hour to over 100 gallons an hour. In other words, you can use everything up in 55 minutes if you go flat out."

When they got airborne, bound for Castletown, the other pilot, who was leading the flight, lowered his undercarriage for some reason, then put it up again. "This had me puzzled. I couldn't make it out. It sounded like, or I interpreted it, that perhaps we were going to land again. We had no communication. He didn't seem to make any signals, other than to lower his wheels and put them up again. He did this twice and I still didn't catch on to the fact that we had a problem. Anyhow, he then set sail in the direction of Castletown and away we went, but I found that I had to keep roughly plus-four boost in order to keep up with him. This also had me puzzled, as I knew that the consumption of the Spitfire would rise dramatically at that figure, compared with minus-four boost."

Consoling himself with the thought that the other, more experienced pilot was leading the way, and that he probably knew what he was doing, Mackie flew on. When he realised that they were still going to do the flight without any intermediate stops, he also realised that he was going to be desperately short of fuel – if he made it at all. The fact that they were flying over inhospitable country and that he had not had the chance to sort out an emergency landing ground did not help his anxious state of mind.

Fortunately they were able to go straight in to land at Castletown without the formality of doing a circuit. "By this time my fuel gauge was reading zero, and I have no doubt the tanks were near enough dry," he said. "Anyhow as soon as I put my hand on the undercarriage lever I spied that the landing wheel indicator lights were showing red, which meant that either one or both of them had not locked up in position. Suddenly everything clicked into place. One of my wheels was not in place and he had been trying to indicate that to me by lowering his undercarriage and retracting it again. I was having to use excessive boost to keep up with him on account of the drag of a wheel being partially down. It dawned on me there and then just how easy it would have been to come to grief through my sheer ignorance of flying and inexperience at the time. Of course, there would have been no problem whatsoever had we had the normal communication between aircraft – or if I hadn't been so damned dumb!"

Although the wheel had not locked up, it did lock down when Mackie activated the mechanism and he made a normal landing, returning to Grangemouth in a twin-engined de Havilland Dominie biplane flown by Pilot Officer Russel. Towards the end of the course Mackie sensed that the inadequacy of the gunnery section of the course could be a disadvantage. Dissatisfied with the amount of firing practice, he was also critical of the quality of the cine-gun exercises. "In general the results were very poor from the old 12mm cine-guns – oh, the results were terrible! They didn't seem to work half the time, and you were lucky if you saw anything on the film."

On his own initiative he persuaded one of the few pilots with whom he had struck up a friendship, fellow-Kiwi Russell Mathieson, to put in some extra dog-fighting practice with him. "I always maintain he was one of the best opponents for dog-fighting I've come across," he said. Mackie was a good judge of airmanship, for Mathieson was also assessed 'Above Average' when he left Grangemouth. He was one of the few chosen later to be an instructor at the Fighter Leader Training School at Milfield, Northumberland.

At his home at Mount Maunganui, on Anzac Day 1991, Mathieson recalled the occasion. "I had known Evan for quite a while and knew about his flying ability. I think he came over to me one day and said: 'Well, let's you and I have a dog-fight and see how we get on.' That's how it really came about. It was just arranged between the two of us.

"So up we went and I thought, well, you know, I wan't going to let Rosie, as we called him, get the better of me, because I had heard that he was fairly good up there, although I don't know what opinion he had of me. But he was determined that I was not going to get on his tail. And it was a sort of stalemate up there for over an hour – and quite an exciting stalemate – because we both learned to do things with our aircraft that we had never done before. We learned how to spin them upside down and how to flick-roll – all the manoeuvres you don't usually do, and the object was to make sure the other fellow did not get on your tail and get into a position where he could go ah-ah-ah-ah-ah over the R/T.

"Well, that never happened. I wasn't able to do it to him and he wasn't able to do it to me. And looking back, both Evan and I considered that of all our training, that was the icing on the cake for both of us, because it taught us to have the utmost confidence in our aircraft."

Mathieson was posted to 66 Squadron (which he would later command) on 18 October 1941, but Mackie was persuaded to stay on at Grangemouth as a staff pilot. He was not keen to miss the direct posting to an operational squadron that would be the lot of his fellow trainees, but there was an inducement. At the end of the next course he could pick the squadron for his next posting – provided he fulfilled the requirement and there was a vacancy.

Most of his time at Grangemouth during that November of 1941 was spent in leading formations of trainees on No.13 course, which included 13 New Zealanders. His work included leading formation cloud flying, and it was probably not difficult to find suitable conditions in the Scottish late autumn weather then prevailing. Mackie described formation flying as "another of our exercises which was useless as such, but it did improve one's ability to fly the aircraft and keep position – which was most important when going up and down through cloud."

Going through cloud, only the leader could pay attention to his instruments. "The remainder had to close in on him in what we call close formation. That would be, say, 12 feet between wingtips, so that he was well within sight but not too close for comfort. And we had to rely on his ability to fly accurately through that cloud. Anyone who lost contact had to sheer away, and whip over to instruments, because up until that point you didn't have your eyes on them. Hence the emphasis placed upon formation flying. It was the only way that squadrons could operate.

"You might want to take off where there is a ceiling of say, 4,000 feet. There might be thick cloud up to 10,000 feet. Obviously you don't want to fly all the way below 4,000 feet because it might lead you over enemy territory. To get up to a normal economical flying height you've got to get up through the cloud barrier – and that's how its done. You remain as a squadron."

He made his last flight at Grangemouth on 22 November 1941, well-versed in a role which would eventually become his frequent duty – leading formations as a squadron commander, and a wing leader. Generally, he had enjoyed his extra time at the OTU, valuing the additional Spitfire hours. Unlike most of his fellow trainees, he did not spend much time in their favourite pub in nearby Falkirk – alcohol held little interest for him then or later.

The RAF lived up to its promise, and Mackie was indeed allowed his choice of a squadron. He was formally posted to 11 Group Pool, but it was to 485 (New Zealand) Squadron that he went, at his own request. He had by then a total of 199 hours and 55 minutes dual and solo flying experience, and even though he had accumulated an extra 30 hours on Spitfires as a staff pilot, he was later to take a cautious view of that bonus. "That was little enough flying, when you look back, for the pupils to meet the enemy – who no doubt, in many cases, would have ten times that amount of flying behind them. Still, you had to learn, and no doubt some went into service with less flying than I did."

The fact of the matter was that they certainly did. Mackie had more experience than most greenhorn operational pilots and it was probably that, coupled with his natural ability, which saw him safely through those first most dangerous weeks with 485.

Squadron Leader Harvey Sweetman*, who had been on the No.1 Spitfire course at Grangemouth, wrote from his Auckland home in February 1995: "On looking back, our training was most skimped. I ended up with a total of 14 hours on Spitfires and ten hours on Masters. We had no instruction on air-firing at all, and very little squadron formation. I wholeheartedly agree on Rosie's observations on inadequate training!"

---

* (Sqn Ldr H.N. Sweetman, DFC; see *Aces High*; page 578.)

CHAPTER FOUR

OPERATIONAL FROM THE UK – 485 SQUADRON

Mackie's biggest fear on joining 485 (New Zealand) Squadron at Kenley on the southern outskirts of London, was that he would not measure up. Despite the training he had received, he was aware that a pilot on his first operational flights was most vulnerable.

"You only start to learn once you get on a squadron," he said. "Everything you have done until then has prepared you for it. If you haven't taken it in, or can't comply in some respect, well, you're the loser. I was very keen to comply, not only for the squadron's sake but also for my own – to learn what I could, as soon as I could."

485 Squadron, motto "Ka whawhai tonu" – "We will fight on", began forming at Driffield RAF station in Yorkshire on 1 March 1941. The first New Zealand fighter squadron in the United Kingdom, it was partly manned by experienced aircrew drawn from RAF squadrons and declared operational on 12 April 1941, under Sqn Ldr M.W.D. Knight of Dannevirke.

When Mackie joined in early December 1941, the squadron was commanded by Sqn Ldr E.P. 'Hawkeye' Wells*, who had taken over from Knight on 11 November 1941, and was flying Spitfire VBs. The squadron had been at Kenley, in 11 Group, Fighter Command, under the command of Air Vice-Marshal Trafford Leigh-Mallory, since the previous October. The intensive operations of the summer and the autumn had tailed off, and when Mackie joined only occasional operations were taking place, a situation which would prevail until the spring of 1942.

It was a good time to join an operational squadron (for the first time), since he was able to get a lot of patrol flying experience without being exposed to enemy action. He was assigned to 'B' Flight, led by Flt Lt R.H. Strang.

Mackie was first airborne with 485 on 5 December 1941, under-

---

* (Wg Cdr E.P. Wells, DSO, DFC & Bar; see *Aces High*, page 624.)

taking local flying to familiarize himself with the area. His first operational missions were a convoy patrol off Selsey Bill in the English Channel on 8 December, in company with Flg Off W.V. Crawford-Compton*, Sgt H.N. Sweetman and Sgt A.R. Robson, and later that day, an air-sea rescue patrol led by Wg Cdr J. Peel* and Sqn Ldr Wells.

The Spitfire VBs flown by 485 were not much different from the Spitfire Is and IIs that Mackie had trained on. They had the same airframes, but a more powerful engine – a 1,440 horsepower Rolls-Royce Merlin, compared with the 1,030 hp and 1,150 hp Merlins of the earlier models. Formation flying, camera-gun exercises and dog-fighting practice gave him plenty of opportunity to familiarize himself with the enhanced performance of the Mark VB, and there were occasional convoy patrols to bring home that there was still a war on. One such patrol, off the Thames Estuary on 16 January, gave him his longest flight to date – two hours 15 minutes airborne.

During December he had only one real opportunity to improve his marksmanship – 85 minutes of air-to-air firing at Bexhill range on Christmas Day.

The Mark VB was equipped with two 20 millimetre calibre Hispano cannon, each with a drum of 66 rounds, capable of firing at the rate of 720 rounds a minute. It also had four .303 inch Browning machine guns which fired at the rate of 1,100 rounds a minute. Effectively therefore he had 11 seconds of cannon fire and 20 seconds of machine-gun fire – but little opportunity to practice. During the first three months of 1942, apart from a cannon test off Beachy Head, he was allowed only two air-to-ground firing sessions on the Leysdown range.

On 25 January 1942 his flight commander, Strang, dived into the English Channel at more than 300 miles an hour from a considerable height, watched by his appalled flight. Kevin Wells in his *An Illustrated History of the New Zealand Spitfire Squadron* (Hutchinson NZ, 1984) surmises that since no contact had been made with the enemy, he had either omitted to turn on his oxygen supply, or the system had failed.

The result of Strang's unfortunate death was that Crawford-Compton, one of 485's more aggressive fighter pilots, was appointed OC, 'B' Flight, and Mackie became his No.2. His chances of seeing action were definitely improving!

A mission escorting a Wellington at a low level along the Channel coast on 8 February had an unfortunate ending for the young man from Waihi. The ground was covered with snow from a recent fall

---

* (Wg Cdr W.V. Crawford-Compton, DSO & Bar, DFC & Bar; see *Aces High*, pages 195-6); (Grp Capt J.R.A. Peel, DSO, DFC; see *Aces High*, pages 491-2).

and he happened to notice Hawkinge airfield as he flew over it at about 2,000 feet, only because its cleared runway contrasted with the white landscape. It was a fortunate sighting, for a few seconds later his engine stopped.

"The propeller went into fully-coarse pitch and it wouldn't take it. It stopped. Malfunction of the pitch-control mechanism," said Mackie. "So there I was with very little height and no motor. I immediately about-turned and headed for this aerodrome." In retrospect he felt he should have lost rather more height than he did by side-slipping. "Anyhow, I didn't, and this damned thing seemed to float and float and float. I think I was about halfway down the runway before it touched down. The tail wouldn't come down and I braked and ended up straight on my back. Rather ignominious."

However, had he not braked, he would have overshot the end of the runway. He put it down to inexperience, not appreciating that with the propeller blades edge-on to the slipstream they were not offering the same resistance as they would in fine pitch, which accounted for the higher than normal landing speed.

With only his pride damaged, Mackie extricated himself from the cockpit. With the benefit of the similar Tiger Moth experience in New Zealand he managed it without falling onto his head. Parachute tucked under his arm, he caught the train back to Kenley.

"There was an investigation, but no action taken, so it was conceded I wasn't too much to blame," he said.

Two days later, on 10 February, he spent 30 minutes on ground firing practice at Leysdown range, while just two days after this the novice was blooded. His first battle experience was dramatic. On 12 February 1942, 485 Squadron was one of dozens of RAF units hurled against the maelstrom of Luftwaffe fighters covering the up-Channel breakthrough by three German warships.

Adolf Hitler, the German leader, had decided that the fast, heavy-gunned 30,000-ton battlecruisers *Scharnhorst* and *Gneisenau*, and the only slightly less potent heavy cruiser *Prinz Eugen*, were needed to defend German-occupied Norway, and to threaten the Allied North Atlantic convoys, together with those now being despatched to North Russia in increasing numbers. For some months these vessels had been virtually trapped in the French Atlantic port of Brest, under almost constant air attack by the RAF.

Unwilling to risk an encounter with the Royal Navy's Home Fleet, based at Scapa Flow in the Orkney Isles, the German naval staff planned an audacious daylight dash through the English Channel. Air superiority over the ships at all times was essential if the plan, code-named 'Cerberus', was to succeed. General Adolf Galland, in command of the Luftwaffe's fighters, was responsible for the subsidiary operation 'Thunderbolt', which was to ensure a minimum of 16 fighters over the fleet at all times, that number being doubled for 20 minutes of each hour. A substantial reserve of aircraft would also be kept in hand to counter major attacks launched by the RAF. But the real card up Galland's sleeve was the new radial-engined Focke Wulf FW 190 fighter, which out-performed and out-gunned the latest Spitfire of that time. The FW 190 would be seen in numbers for the first time when they were used to protect these German warships, the first enemy fleet to challenge the superiority of the Royal Navy in the English Channel for nearly 300 years.

Were it not for the tragic losses incurred by the RAF and the Royal Navy, the 'Channel Dash' could best be described as a comedy of errors! In essence, practically everything went right for the Germans and practically everything went wrong for the British.

Surprise, another German prerequisite for a successful 'Cerberus', was complete. Although three large ships, escorted by six destroyers, sailed from Brest late on the evening of 11 February, they were not seen until 1035 hours next day, and by then they were only 90 minutes away from their most crucial part of the passage, the narrow Straits of Dover. Shore-based German radar operators calculated that their fleet was making 31 knots. Incredibly, although the British authorities were fully expecting the German warships to undertake a breakout from Brest and seek to force just such a passage up the Channel, the Germans nonetheless achieved the surprise that they so desperately needed. This was occasioned in no small degree by the failure of several radar sets, both airborne and ground based, which might otherwise have been anticipated to provide adequate early warning.

Until recently, history has credited Grp Capt F.V. Beamish* with the chance discovery of the German fleet steaming up the Channel. Not so, according to Air Marshal Sir Edward Chilton, a former Commander-in-Chief of Coastal Command, who has made perhaps the most penetrating study yet undertaken of this amazing event. "His research and authority are undoubted, his findings historically important," says 'Laddie' Lucas*, who published them in *Out of the Blue* (Hutchinson, 1985).

According to Sir Edward, the first sighting was made by Sqn Ldr R.W. Oxspring* and Sgt Beaumont, who had been despatched in Spitfires of 91 Squadron from Hawkinge at 1000 hours by 11 Group to investigate radar reports of enemy aircraft circling over small areas just north of Le Havre. "Sqn Ldr Oxspring reported the ships by

---

* (Grp Capt F.V. Beamish, DSO & Bar; see *Aces High*, page 119); (Wg Cdr P.B. Lucas, DSO & Bar, DFC; see *Aces High*. page 408); (Wg Cdr R.W. Oxspring, DFC & Bar; see *Aces High*, pages 476-7).

R/T to base at 1035 but for some reason no action was taken and the record of the transmission later vanished, although it still exists in the German records because they intercepted the transmission and expected immediate attacks to follow." Oxspring, unaware that he was likely to encounter any other British fighters in the area, was greatly surprised when he saw two other Spitfires in the mass of enemy fighters over the German ships.

The other Spitfires were flown by Beamish, commanding Kenley airfield, and his Wing Commander (Flying), R.F. Boyd*. Beamish, a notable leader during the Battle of Britain, was taking one of his 'Beamish Special' jaunts over the Channel. Wrote Terence Robertson, author of *The Channel Dash* (Evans Bros. Ltd., London, 1958): "These were 'special' only because Beamish, a senior officer to Air Vice-Marshal Leigh-Mallory of 11 Group, should have been behind a desk instead of a joystick. No-one, however, could keep Beamish away from his Spitfire for long and rather than have him break the rules, Leigh-Mallory had allotted him an allowance of flights each week. Like a drug addict, Beamish had to be weaned away from flying in excess by a gradual decrease of the dosage."

Finlay Boyd had been assigned the unenviable task of keeping his senior officer out of trouble.

"The weather was reasonable, with the overcast breaking a little, the wind was still moderate and visibility remained constant at five miles. Beamish knew of a possible Channel dash by the enemy, but on this morning both pilots were blithely unaware of the gathering climax below. They had just sighted a pair of Huns, and as Beamish described it later 'couldn't have cared less about Brest, battleships and breakouts'. With a joyful wave to Boyd, Beamish led the race into the attack," wrote Robertson.

"The Luftwaffe pilots cast hasty glances over their shoulders and retreated anxiously in the direction of Boulogne with the Spitfires close behind. Hunters and hunted lost height rapidly and almost before they could do anything about it, Beamish and Boyd were streaking across the bows of the great German armada.

"Both pilots lost interest in the Luftwaffe and gazed in open-mouthed amazement at the enemy fleet with creamy bow-waves pouring over the foredecks of the proud battlecruisers and the long lines of escorts bouncing at high speed against the choppy seas. They turned in a steep banking movement and headed for home on a reverse course, pursued by the Luftwaffe 'umbrella'."

It was at this point that Beamish became a victim of his own orders, according to Sir Edward. His research showed that it was Beamish

---

* (Grp Capt R.F. Boyd, DSO, DFC & Bar; see *Aces High*, page 144.)

who had issued the fateful 11 Group instruction restricting the use of R/T: "Hence Group Captain Beamish did not report the enemy ships until he landed back at 1125."

So, Oxspring, unaware that he was not to use his R/T to report the enemy, had reported the presence and position of the German fleet in plain language over the radio-telephone to Hawkinge at 1035 – a report disregarded by the British and noted by the Germans with concern. Following this, Beamish, who saw the German ships at 1042 according to Sir Edward, conscientiously obeyed his own orders and did not say a word to anyone until he landed back at Kenley 43 minutes later.

The advantage of the Beamish sighting was, of course, that after some cross-examination on the telephone from 11 Group Headquarters, he was at least believed – and the wheels of command began slowly to turn. Surely, even then, as in hindsight, it would have been difficult to see how an immediate alarm in plain language could have been disadvantageous to anyone except the Germans? It was 43 minutes before Beamish landed and telephoned his sighting. Forty-three minutes earlier and the first strikes against the German units could have been launched before they reached the crucial Straits of Dover. Later the German Naval Commander, Vice-Admiral Ciliax, commented: "Our passage through the Straits of Dover, the most crucial point on our route, was no more difficult than an exercise in home waters."

At 1130, after slowing to ten knots for a recently-cleared minefield, Ciliax's squadron increased to its full speed of 31 knots – although the Royal Navy was later to estimate that the big ships and their escorts went through the Straits at 27 knots.

At 1200 the Germans were in the Straits. Poor visibility and a smokescreen generated to port by the escorts made it difficult for the gunners of the Dover batteries to see the enemy. It was not until 1218 that the first of 33 nine-inch shells lobbed into the water a mile from the closest German ship. The rest never got any closer, as the Germans got further away.

At 1225 hours the first active response of Operation 'Fuller', the long-planned British reaction to a German Channel breakthrough, began. Six Fairey Swordfish biplane torpedo bombers of 825 Squadron, Fleet Air Arm, left Manston airfield led by Lieutenant Commander Eugene Esmonde. Their promised top cover of three fighter squadrons from Biggin Hill, and close cover by two squadrons from the Hornchurch Wing, had failed to arrive. It was to be the story of the day. Instead, when ten Spitfires appeared, Esmonde accepted them as the only escort he was likely to get.

At 1230 five motor torpedo boats and two motor gun boats from

Dover broke through the German escort screen and attacked the battlecruisers, without promised fighter cover and without effect. At the same time battery 'Siegfried', west of Calais, returned the fire of the Dover guns, sending 12 rounds into the English port.

At 1240 ten Hurricane fighter-bombers of 607 Squadron left Manston airfield, but failed to find the German ships.

At 1255 Esmonde led his fabric-covered 80-knot Swordfish on what was virtually a suicide attack, for the ten Spitfires had disappeared into a maze of dogfights with the German fighter umbrella. Esmonde and the other two pilots in his section managed to launch their torpedoes, although to no effect, before being shot down. It was at this point that FW 190s of III/JG 26 had broken through the Spitfire escort, and they quickly wiped out all the Swordfish as these headed into the wall of water thrown up by the big guns of the German ships. Of the 18 men involved, only five survived to be rescued from the sea; Esmonde himself was lost, and was subsequently awarded a posthumous Victoria Cross.

At 1318 eight cannon-armed Hurricanes, escorted by a squadron of Spitfires, left Manston, but again failed to find the enemy. Then came the turn of 485 Squadron and Evan Mackie. Having sighted the German ships, Beamish was determined to have a hand in their destruction. He and Boyd led 14 Spitfires aloft from Kenley at 1320 hours and rendezvoused at 1325 with 12 Spitfires of 602 Squadron. They were to provide cover for Beaufort torpedo bombers due over Manston at 1330. But the four Beauforts of 217 Squadron did not leave Thorney Island in Chichester Harbour until 1325, and there was no way they were going to be able to fly the 100 miles east to Manston, near the North Foreland, to arrive by 1330.

When the Beauforts failed to appear on time, an impatient Beamish signalled the Spitfires out of their orbit, and they formed up and headed to where the action was. 485 was led by Wells, and in his section were Plt Off J.M. Checketts*, Sgt W.M. Krebs and Sgt T.C. Goodlet. Flt Lt W.V. Crawford-Compton led Mackie, Plt Off H.N. Sweetman (newly commissioned), and Plt Off D.T. Clouston. The third section was led by Flt Lt G.A. Francis; in this were Plt Off R.J.C. Grant*, Sgt J.D. Rae* and Sgt J.R. Liken. Alan W. Mitchell in his *New Zealanders in the Air War* (George Harrap & Co, 1945) wrote an excellent description of the action which followed:

"The Spitfires flew across the Channel at 5,000 feet above a cloud bank and maintained this position until Wells estimated they were

---

* (Wg Cdr J.M. Checketts, DSO, DFC; see *Aces High*, pages 173-4); (Wg Cdr R.J.C. Grant, DFC & Bar; see *Aces High*, page 297); (Flg Off J.D. Rae, DFC & Bar; see *Aces High*, pages 508-9).

approaching the Belgian coast. He then led the squadron through a break in the cloud, and as they went down sighted four Messerschmitt 109s about 1,000 feet below. He detailed Compton and his flight to attack them.

"Executing a dive-turn, Compton, Mackie, Clouston and Sweetman went down on the German fighters, and in the melee which followed Compton blew the wingtip off one Messerschmitt. He had no time to observe the effect of this strike, however, for he was engaged in the pursuit of the remaining enemy aircraft. The Messerschmitts made full speed for the Dutch coast and the protection of the German defences, but Compton, not to be tricked by this ruse, led his section, flying at 200 feet, away from the coastal batteries, which sent tracers spurting after them.

"The New Zealanders re-formed over the sea, and in a few moments they sighted six more Messerschmitts. Compton immediately led an attack, but these Messerschmitts also sought the protection of the coastal defences. Once again the section re-formed, and they were gaining height when Compton heard Sweetman shout into the radio-telephone: 'Lookout, Bill. There's one on your tail!' Compton dived and turned and shortly after he did so he saw a Messerschmitt crash into the sea. It had been shot down by Sweetman and Clouston. Compton then attacked a Messerschmitt and, after firing three long bursts, saw it crash on the beach five miles west of Ostend.

"The section, having by this time exhausted all its ammunition, turned for England; but its operation was not entirely ended. Compton, Mackie and Clouston suddenly heard Sweetman reporting enemy aircraft, and they looked round to see him leading what appeared to be a flight of Messerschmitts. Although they had no ammunition they wheeled immediately as though to attack the Germans who, however, were not prepared to fight. They fled, leaving the unarmed Spitfire pilots chuckling to themselves.

"In the meantime Wells and the remainder of the squadron suddenly arrived over the German warships. They could see the *Scharnhorst*, the *Prinz Eugen* and the *Gneisenau* steaming at full speed, screened on either side by destroyers. Outside the destroyers were screens of E-boats, and the distance between the two E-boat screens was about five miles. It was a remarkable sight.

"Detailing Francis to lead his flight between the destroyers and the battlecruisers on the side nearest the Belgian coast, Wells took the 'lane' on the opposite side. Francis, followed by Grant, Rae and Liken, soon sighted four Messerschmitts flying in pairs, but the German fighters immediately flew off across the battlecruisers, seeking the protection of anti-aircraft fire.

"Then, as suddenly as anything can happen to fighter pilots, the four New Zealanders abruptly found themselves surrounded by about 30 Focke Wulf 190s, which were making one of their first appearances. Francis fired a ten-second burst at one and saw it crash into the sea. Grant and Rae selected two more and they had begun to attack when Grant suddenly noticed a third German wheeling to attack his tail. He turned sharply, out-manoeuvred the German, and shot it down with a ten-second burst.

"In the meantime Rae continued his dive on the pair of Focke Wulfs and fired long enough to see pieces fly from the tail of one before he had to break off the action. Liken had also been engaged, and the flight soon found itself, like Compton's, with no more ammunition. It returned to base without further incident.

"Wells and his flight, meanwhile, were flying down the lane between the battlecruisers and the destroyers in a vain quest for Messerschmitts. They flew to the end of the two lines of ships then wheeled and followed them, hoping that German fighters would appear. But they were unlucky, however, and with petrol beginning to run low in the tanks Wells decided to use up ammunition by attacking an E-boat. He selected the last in line of the outer protecting screen and led his flight down. The German sailors fired a frantic barrage, so heavy that Checketts, immediately following Wells, temporarily lost sight of his leader in the smoke from the bursting anti-aircraft shells. The E-boat was left in a sinking condition. Then, with all its ammunition used, this flight too returned to base."

In the midst of the many failures of that unfortunate action, 485 Squadron had done well. Its claim for four aircraft confirmed destroyed, two probably destroyed, and an E-boat either sunk or severely damaged, was the highest achieved by any fighter squadron that day. Beamish was happy too, because although he did not shoot down an aircraft, he at least had the satisfaction of raking a German destroyer from stern to bow with his Spitfire's cannon and machine guns.

For Mackie, his first chance to really mix it with the enemy had proved an interesting experience. He remembered conditions as being "really murky", although he got a good look at the awe-inspiring sight of the line of racing ships. "I actually fired at some 109s, but with no effect because of the conditions," he recalled.

That sortie was his second longest to date, two hours and five minutes. The squadron landed at Manston to refuel before going on to Kenley.

Meanwhile, all this action was not having the slightest effect on the German battle squadron, which was quite comfortably high-tailing it into the North Sea. On the British side, the inadequate response continued. More Beaufort torpedo bombers were despatched without fighter escort. Six elderly destroyers were rushed down from Harwich, also without a promised fighter escort. The Germans blasted one of the destroyers almost out of the water. And then to cap it all, three of the Beauforts attacked the British destroyers, rather than *Gneisenau*. Bomber Command struggled to get three groups of assorted aircraft into the air. The few that found the German squadron made individual attacks, mostly without fighter protection, because the action was by then too far out into the North Sea.

Untouched by torpedoes from aircraft, destroyers and motor boats, unmarked by bombs and only scratched by bullets, the three big German ships completed Operation 'Cerberus' successfully, but not entirely undamaged. *Scharnhorst* struck mines twice, and, *Gneisenau* once. All three incidents required temporary halts for emergency repairs, but the ships carried on.

When *Gneisenau* and *Prinz Eugen* came to anchor in the safety of the Heligoland Bight at the mouth of the Elbe, and *Scharnhorst* put into Wilhelmshaven, early on the morning of 13 February, Ciliax could finally relax. The great gamble had paid off, and *The Times* could thunder: "Vice-Admiral Ciliax has succeeded where the Duke of Medina Sidonia failed. Nothing more mortifying to the pride of sea power has happened since the 17th century."

It was not sea power, however, but air power that the Germans had feared. More squadrons of the calibre of 485 could have had a decisive effect that day, and poor Esmonde's sacrifice need not have been in vain. When the *Daily Express* published a photograph of 485 Squadron pilots walking back to their quarters after that 'Channel Dash' sortie with the caption: "Whatever questions may be asked, these men did a grand job for Britain," it was a pretty good indication to Mackie that he was with a group of pilots from whom he might learn much.

If there was one particular attribute which distinguished Mackie from most other fighter pilots it was his wonderful vision, his ability to see distant aircraft long before his fellow pilots. But it was not only the quality of his eyesight which made him outstanding, it was the manner in which he used it.

Mackie had had instilled into him during his training: "It is the one you don't see which will get you." When he joined 485 Squadron he found that some of the pilots, but not all, were as keen as he was to discuss flying and tactics and learn as much as they could of their new craft. Vision was a common talking point. Mackie never under-rated its importance, and proof of the fact that he had mastered the art of keeping a good lookout in the air was that only one enemy pilot was ever able to surprise him and hole his aircraft. About a score of British Commonwealth fighter pilots were credited with more air victories than Mackie, but many of them returned with badly damaged aircraft or were shot down, some several times. Mackie simply didn't allow that to happen to him or to his machine, and the main reason for this was his excellent vision and his superb lookout technique, coupled with flying skills. Once he had an enemy fighter locked in his vision he was determined that, if he did not shoot the enemy down, at least his opponent was not going to shoot him down.

Modest to a fault, as always, Mackie was careful to claim no false credit for the skills he developed, when recalling his early days as a fighter pilot; "I always knew, or at least I was given the advice and followed it, to look at each sector – not just glance around looking everywhere, you know, up and behind, not giving myself time to recognise anything. But look at a sector and decide whether there was or there wasn't something there. Then I'd look at another sector and do the same. And I found that the best policy if you really wanted to look at something."

He had not been on the squadron many months when he noticed that his shirt collars were too small. Through continually swivelling his head around to keep a good lookout when aloft, his neck muscles developed considerably.

Mackie was later to have three major criticisms of 485 Squadron. Two concerned situations which became evident to him only when he had experience on other squadrons. They were the retention of the line-astern formation, long after other units had adopted the much safer and more efficient 'finger-four' formation, and the 'cliques' that seemed inevitably to develop in single-nationality units.

The third criticism was a situation which soon became apparent to him, which was the reluctance of many experienced pilots in the squadron to impart their knowledge to the new arrivals; "Never enough time was devoted to talking about attacks. Everyone seemed too keen on enjoying themselves and relaxing, getting their minds off the job in hand while on the ground. They seemed to leave it until they got into the air.

"In retrospect, I think it would have been far better to have talked about it a lot more, with demonstrations by those experts in the field, with the object of generally making pilots more gun-conscious or firing-conscious. To point out the errors that could occur, and perhaps did occur. Not skiting or bragging about things that had been done, but if they had talked about it a lot more on the ground I'm sure a lot of people, junior pilots in particular, would have assimilated a lot of that stuff and in turn argued about it themselves, brought forth new ideas."

He said that the American aircrews in particular had the ability to talk about their combats – even though they were regarded as a loudmouthed lot. But in the British squadrons that sort of thing was frowned upon, not only in the mess, but to a large extent even at dispersal: "People tended to think it was taboo, only for when they were flying." To an extent he was undoubtedly correct. "No 'shop' in the Mess" was a standard RAF peacetime rule, which continued in many units well into the war.

Mackie did not subscribe to that view; he was too keen to learn. Luckily, he came across some like-minded junior pilots, including Marty Hume, Stan Browne* and 'Chalky' White. Hume and Browne would one day lead the squadron, and Leslie Samuel McQueen White, a rough diamond who would stamp something of his indelible character on them all, was to become Mackie's most devoted disciple.

"Several of us used to make a habit of discussing tactics, methods of attack and all that," said Mackie. "Myself and one or two of my cobbers used to get hold of these young pilots because after a month or two we were regarded as not exactly old hands, but we were looked up to a bit by the incoming pilots. They had no-one, really, to turn to to get a few clues other than the likes of myself, Marty Hume and a few others who were perhaps a bit keener and prepared to get out and take these jokers up and dogfight with them and demonstrate attacking methods. We explained a bit about gunnery which, when all's said and done, was what all our training had been directed at."

Stan Browne recalled those days vividly, at his Papamoa beach-side home in New Zealand in 1986: "As time went on I noticed that he (Mackie) devoured every scrap of information regarding our own and enemy aircraft. With other keen young pilots he would discuss air gunnery, tactics and squadron formations. Together Evan and I spent more time on air gunnery courses and cine-gun practice than the other pilots. Evan reckoned this avoided breaking up the 'drinking teams', to which neither of us had any aspiration. He was a perfection-ist in self-training and preparation."

Even in those early days it became apparent that Mackie would be one who would stand out from the rest, as Browne noted: "He was smooth and easy to fly with, knew where he was, and at de-briefing, despite flying relatively junior positions in the antiquated line-astern formations, he had a better mental picture of the relative position of the squadron and a clearer description, with no frills, of whatever action had occurred than most pilots."

His first impression of Mackie was one of a more-than-capable pilot who used his great physical strength to roll and turn his aircraft much faster than other pilots. He found him to be quiet, almost taciturn

---

* (Sqn Ldr S.F. Browne, DFC & Bar; see *Aces High*, page 153.)

in manner, but with a shrewd and accurate observation of everything and everyone.

By the time Mackie left the squadron a year later as a deputy flight commander, he had clearly made a strong impression on Browne: "To sum up, if I had to take part in a difficult action with the enemy and I was allowed but one companion, from all the pilots I have ever known Rosie Mackie would be my first choice," he said.

Marty Hume remembered Mackie's phenomenal powers of observation: "He had the ability to find and destroy enemy aircraft where others just simply couldn't find them." He regarded Mackie as a superb pilot, highly skilled in airmanship.

'Chalky' White owed a lot to both Mackie and Hume, and was the first to admit it: "Mackie and Hume taught me to fly operationally and Evan certainly showed me what a Spitfire would do, which was of great use later, more than once. I used to think, well, if it does those manoeuvres for him, it must do the same for me without falling to pieces."

White described Mackie as a "ham-handed" pilot – not in the clumsy sense, but in the strong sense. It was a description Mackie used of himself. "What I mean by that," said White, "he was a survivor, and when he moved back the stick, it really moved." He attributed Mackie's success and survival to his intellectual approach to air fighting: "Everything was worked out perfectly. He fought gentlemanly. He even gave the enemy a chance, although they had no chance with him." White was known never to pay a tribute lightly, yet he said of Mackie: "The most decent and honourable man I have ever met in my life and certainly the bravest, and the perfect fighter pilot."

In later years Mackie would marvel at the way the Kenley Wing was permitted to retain the line-astern formation for squadron patrols. At the time he had a very personal concern in the matter, for he was a No.2, and the life expectancy of a No.2 – and a novice No.2 at that – was short indeed.

Wing policy was for each squadron to fly its aircraft in three parallel lines, each line consisting of four aircraft following one behind the other – literally 'line astern'. Each four was made up of two pairs, each comprising a leader (No.1) and his wingman (No.2); the No.2 was expected to remain a comfortable distance behind his No.1 and to guard his tail – warn him of anything approaching from behind in an attempt to shoot him down. As well as protecting his No.1, the No.2 was also expected to protect himself.

"This was, in hindsight, a very unsatisfactory configuration," said Mackie. "To do all of those things the No.2 was fully occupied. He could do nothing else, other than weave back and forth, glancing over first one shoulder, then the other. Because aircraft have a nasty habit of appearing out of the blue, or out of the sun, in a split second. One minute they are there, the next they are not, and vice versa.

"Also, an enemy coming down to attack is not necessarily going to attack No.1. In fact, he is less likely to. He is going to attack the last one in the outfit, which is the No.2 – the position to which the new pilots were always allocated. Many would call them just gun fodder. They were there to be shot down before the No.1. That is exactly what they were. They could do nothing useful other than warn the No.1 that there was something coming down. Meanwhile, the No.1 was supposed to be looking further afield for the enemy, and watching where they were going."

This formation was maintained as standard for the 12 months he was with 485 Squadron. He accepted it, for he knew no better at the time, and it was not until he was posted to North Africa that he flew in the 'finger-four' formation which had long since superceded the 'line-astern' formation in many units. In the 'finger-four' configuration, each section of four aircraft flew in roughly the same position as the fingertips of an outstretched hand, relying on cross-vision to guard each other's tails. "You became reliant on cross-vision," said Mackie, "which makes sense, the more you think about it. None of this weaving all over the sky. It allowed everyone to be on equal terms without wasting fuel."

But all that was in the future.

After the 'Channel Dash' episode, squadron life reverted to the limited activity which had been imposed by winter – formation and cloud flying, aerobatics and cine-gun practice, with some high-level bomber escorts over France later in February. The 22nd of that month found him in a role with which he would become familiar – giving Air Training Corps cadets their first air experience. Mackie was a firm believer in encouraging those who did not fly to gain air experience – particularly his squadron's ground staff. Their excellent servicing, which kept his aircraft in a safe condition, was never far from his mind. They were there when he took off, and there when he landed. Whenever the opportunity presented itself he endeavoured to give those who wanted it, the bird's eye view to which he was now so accustomed.

A bomber escort to Le Havre at 10,000 feet on 26 March 1942, gave Mackie the chance to open his score against the Germans, and he seized it in no uncertain way. Sqn Ldr Wells was away having his tonsils removed, and Crawford-Compton, with Mackie tucked in close behind him, was leading 485 Squadron. A few miles west of Le Havre the squadron became engaged with a strong formation of Messerschmitt 109s. Crawford-Compton claimed one shot down, as did Sgt

I.P.J. Maskill. Then it was Mackie's turn, and he promptly showed the courage that was to sustain him through so many victories in the air.

Crawford-Compton commented in a contemporary newspaper report of the incident: "I shared one with Mackie, who made a wizard of a head-on attack against a Hun. I saw them firing like blazes at each other, and then I saw glycol streaming from the Hun after they had passed each other, so I gave the Hun a few seconds' burst. He went down in flames and crashed into the sea a quarter of a mile from the French coast."

More than 40 years on that first successful encounter was still fresh in Mackie's memory. "There was no hope of getting around behind him so I just went straight for him, firing as I went, in the hope that I would present as small a target as possible. He evidently had the same idea, because I could see his guns were firing. Anyhow, it was all over in a matter of seconds as you can imagine, with the converging speed being something in the region of 500 miles an hour. I felt no reaction on my aircraft at all so assumed that I had not been hit. Nor did I realise that I had hit him until, on glancing around after we had passed, I noticed that he was streaming what presumably was glycol."

It was after that head-on attack that Mackie realised that luck was an essential ingredient of a successful fighter pilot: "While skill plays a large part in these operations, luck must play an equal part, I'm sure of that. I broke right after the attack and luckily for me he broke the opposite way. We could easily have ended up by crashing into one another, either by maintaining our direction for too long – or we could have broken in the same direction, still resulting in a head-on collision. So that's where luck comes into it – the hand of fate decided there and then I wasn't to hit him."

He also now knew the meaning of fear. "When people say that they weren't scared, weren't frightened on facing the enemy in an aircraft, all I can say is that they are bloody liars or that they are stupid. Each and every one of us should admit to being scared out of our wits when you realise you are facing a fully armed machine intent upon one's destruction." And he knew the feeling of elation, curiously mixed with relief, that came from surviving such a confrontation, of still being whole and alive and flying. Mackie, modest as he would be later about his score, started with a claim for a half share in one Bf 109 with Crawford-Compton: "It was firing everything at me as it came head-on," read his combat report. "I went straight for it, head-on, firing all machine guns and cannon guns and just missed colliding as we came together, but pulling up above it." The report continued: "Flt Lt Crawford-Compton, having just disposed of one enemy machine, engaged this machine before Plt Off Mackie could turn round and sent it spinning down in flames to crash off Fecamp."

Other squadrons in the Kenley Wing also had a successful day, as the same newspaper account noted: "The New Zealand Squadron is operating with the same wing as the Australian and 'City of Glasgow' Squadrons. It is regarded as one of the best wings of the Fighter Command. On Thursday it accounted for seven out of eight planes destroyed, of which two were scored by Group Captain F.V. Beamish, DSO, DFC, AFC, formerly of Rugby football fame, and who is the inspiration and driving force of the wing."

But that report was a swan song for the tough and aggressive Northern Irishman. Two days later, on 28 March 1942, Beamish led 485 Squadron on a Channel sweep in company with seven other fighter squadrons – an operation in which Mackie did not participate. Beamish launched the Kenley Wing from 20,000 feet into a large force of FW 190s which was about to attack a lower Spitfire wing. In company with Grant and Liken, he set off after two absconding FW 190s but the trio was 'bounced' by another pair of 190s. Wells wrote: "Beamish must have borne the brunt of the attack and was last seen going down near the French coast." Mackie was involved in an air-sea rescue patrol in a vain attempt to find the Group Captain the next day. Fighter Command had lost one of its most brilliant leaders.

The first half of April saw Mackie involved in no fewer than seven cannon tests and two dogfight practices, one of them with Hume, which would have pleased him greatly, as would the air-to-sea firing at Leysdown range later in the month. Air-sea rescue and convoy patrols were interspersed with a 'Rodeo' to Le Touquet and a 'Circus' to Marquise. 'Rodeo' was the codename for purely fighter sweeps over enemy territory, while 'Circus' was the code for fighter-escorted daylight bombing attacks against short-range or 'fringe' targets in an effort to bring the German fighters up to engage.

It was little wonder that the ground staff had a high regard for the young New Zealander; on 19 April he spent three hours up in the station Magister, giving eight 'erks' a taste of flying. ('Erk' is RAF slang, not unkindly meant, for ground crew.) Much as 485 Squadron's pilots liked the chance of mixing it with the enemy, they got rather too much of a good thing on 26 April. From the unit's Operations Record Book: "Wg Cdr Loudon led the Wing off at 1710 to Mardyck and flew on to St. Omer. When some 15 miles inland from the coast some 50 e/a (enemy aircraft), mostly 190s, came down through a thin layer of cloud at 23,000 feet out of the sun on 485 Squadron, flying top squadron, in two formations of 20 and smaller formations from behind and above and from the flank. Wg Cdr Loudon, with 602 and 457 Squadrons, not seeing this, continued towards Adnig and

Ambleteuse. 485 found themselves at a numerical and tactical disadvantage and had hard fighting with the FW 190s, which pressed home their attacks. As a result of individual combats Plt Off Mackie, 'Yellow 4', probably destroyed one FW 190." In fact, Mackie's was the only successful combat report from an action which saw three of the squadron's pilots shot down. "We were attacked by FW 190s from all angles." He reported: "I fired at one but it dived away and I did not see the effect of my fire. Then a stream of tracers passed just under my port wing so I pulled up sharply and turned to see another Focke Wulf approaching. Gave it a long burst and saw it give out a cloud of black smoke as it went down. Closed in again to give several more bursts and could see liquid streaming from the starboard wing, but my windscreen fogged up as I pulled out of the dive. AA gunners scored a direct hit in my mainplane as I flew out over the coast," he ended, claiming one FW 190 "probably destroyed".

Recalling this combat, Mackie remembered that it was he who had first seen and reported the Focke Wulf formation. During his individual attack he lost contact with the squadron: "One moment the sky can be full of aircraft. Next minute you can look around and not a one in sight." Although he had not seen the last moments of the descent of the FW 190 he had fired at, "from the way the machine continued down without further manoeuvre, it seemed to me to indicate that it was out of the fight, that it would hit the deck." Having fired both cannon and machine guns for what seemed like quite a long time, he reckoned he was fairly well down on ammunition – and certainly in no position to hang around and try and make contact with the rest of the squadron. "Anyhow, there I was, all alone at 10,000 feet 50 miles or so inside France, so I decided to get right down on the deck and get out of France as fast as I could. This may or may not have been the right action. It's hard to say. At 10,000 feet one is very vulnerable to all sorts of Flak, medium and light, as well as enemy aircraft. Knowing that the 109 and 190 had superior straight-and-level speed I actually could have been prevented (from returning) by either one of these turning up.

"Admittedly the Spitfire was superior in manoeuvrability, which would mean I could have probably out-manoeuvred one enemy aircraft, but that would be no help to me in getting home if that enemy had plenty of fuel and one or two mates to call upon."

In less time than it took for this latter-day philosophising, Mackie was zooming across France at 500 feet, hell-bent for the Channel, home, and all the amenities that a permanent RAF fighter station like Kenley offered the front-line fighter pilot.

Just before he got to the coast he came across a real snag – an anti-aircraft gun post on top of a 500 foot knoll; "There was no way of avoiding this, so I adopted the same tactic as I did in my head-on attack the previous month on the 109 – namely, to go straight for it on the assumption that I would present, first of all, the smallest target, and secondly that I may be able to disable it in some way. I can distinctly see today the gun crew swinging their gun, which had previously been facing out to sea, around to my direction, and I could see by the smoke that they had begun firing. It was obviously something in the region of a 40mm Bofors, from the smoke, and from the hole it subsequently made in the leading edge of my port wing.

"I began firing, but I was unfortunately out of ammunition, although the camera-gun did continue to operate. And all I ended up with were some beautiful shots of this gun post on this hill on the beach!"

Realistic and professional as always, Mackie admired the gunnery of the Germans. Although the Spitfire wing was probably less than a foot thick at that point, they had managed to blow a gaping hole in the leading edge, just outside the port cannon. But that admiration came a little later – during the next minutes or so he was engaged in some violent low-level weaving. Water spouts ahead of him indicated that the gun crew had re-trained their weapon out to sea in the hopes of bagging the fast-disappearing Spitfire. "I managed to get back to base quite safely, once again very scared but quite a lot wiser than when I started out," he said.

485 Squadron lost three aircraft and two pilots on that day – Goodlet baled out over France and was taken prisoner; Pattison and Liken baled out over the Channel. Both were rescued, but Liken died of his injuries that night.

While escorting Bostons to bomb the Lille power station the next day, the 485 Squadron pilots again tangled with FW 190s. Mackie fired at several, but saw no results. On the return flight he stayed back to escort a damaged Boston, using up his ammunition in doing so, and eventually beat a hasty retreat. Palmer was not so lucky, being forced to parachute from his damaged Spitfire over France – 485's third pilot to be lost in three days.

What was to have been an "arranged" 'Circus' on 29 April, for the benefit of HM George VI during a visit to Kenley, turned out to be the real thing. According to Wells, His Majesty arrived too late to see the planned squadron formation take-off, but when he did arrive he was able to hear some very realistic language over the radio-telephone – quite different from the "proper" language which had been agreed upon! When the pilots landed from what had been a rather sharp engagement, Mackie was amongst those who met the King: "He said something about me being a long way from home, or something to that effect, but nothing that really stands out. He was rather shorter than I had imagined he would be."

During April Mackie had been transferred to 'A' Flight, commanded by Reg Grant. May brought a couple of 'Circuses', and 4 May found Mackie again flying ground staff around in the Magister – he was relaxing after a 'Rodeo' to Le Havre earlier that day. Two of 485's pilots did not have the same opportunity to relax, however. Johnny Checketts and Flt Sgt D. Russell were both shot down on that operation, baling out over the Channel. Both were rescued, but Russell died that evening from his injuries. Only three days earlier Plt Off J.R. Falls had baled out over France. So there were five fresh faces at dispersal – five fledglings who looked to the more experienced pilots for guidance. To Mackie, Browne and Hume, they did not look in vain.

Four days later Mackie was fleeing for his life from four FW 190s he had encountered whilst engaged in a close escort over Dieppe at 12,000 feet; "I can't remember whether I intentionally went into a spin, or whether it was inadvertent, when I tried to out-manoeuvre these 190s. But when I say I beat a hasty retreat at zero feet that means the odds had been too great and discretion was the better part of valour."

Even at this early stage of Mackie's operational career he had a well-developed sense of preservation. He could never see the point of placing either himself or his aircraft in jeopardy if he was not in a position to inflict some damage upon the enemy or assist the common cause. It was far better, he believed, to live to fight another day. For those very good reasons, discretion remained the better part of valour on several occasions during Mackie's war.

His flight commander was now Flt Lt R.W. Baker, who had succeeded Grant after the latter's promotion to lead the squadron. During air-to-air firing on Shoreham range Mackie scored 15 hits with cannon shells. While testing his resistance to gravity during local flying, he managed to pull 7.5 'G's on the accelerometer – and established the fact that he was very fit by not blacking out until there was a steady six 'G's on the meter.

An 'erk' who he had aloft in the Magister on 20 May during an army co-operation flight, got more excitement than he had bargained for when the engine stopped, but Mackie managed an uneventful 'dead stick' landing back at Kenley.

Perhaps Mackie's normally excellent rapport with his aircraft was in a state of temporary hiatus, for next day, 21 May, he botched another landing. The incident is not recorded in his logbook, and neither did he mention it to the author, but 485 Squadron's Operations Record Book is explicit: "21/5/42 – 1145 hours – Plt Off Mackie, returning from an anti-'Rhubarb' patrol, damaged his aircraft on landing at base, overshot and tried to collapse undercarriage, which, however, did not respond as quickly as pilot expected, and he only succeeded just before aircraft struck boundary fence – flying BM229." Rhubarbs – small-scale fighter or fighter-bomber attacks on ground targets of opportunity – and anti-Rhubarb patrols occupied much of the latter part of May.

Mackie was doubtful of the value of these Rhubarbs: "These missions were always rather dicey sorts of operations because one was always so vulnerable to light flak", and fellow-kiwi ace fighter pilot Alan Deere* described the Rhubarb as "that hated and useless operation."

Two more faces disappeared at the end of May when both Browne and Flg Off M.G. Barnett were forced to bale out over France. Both were to evade capture by the Germans and rejoined the squadron later in the year after making good their escapes.

On 4 June Mackie was appointed deputy commander of 'A' Flight "which gave me a little extra standing in the squadron and a little more freedom of action in that I was now leading a section of aircraft, and was on occasions given the flight."

A Rhubarb to Etaples on the French coast on 13 June in company with Hume convinced Mackie that these operations had little to recommend them: "The weather was very suitable for the occasion, in other words, 10/10ths cloud down to 1,000 feet and reasonably clear below that. We were flying almost on the deck and as fast as we could to avoid, as much as possible, the light flak." Even so, Mackie's aircraft was struck, the cooling system was punctured, and he was lucky to make it back to Lympne, the closest English aerodrome. Hume struck power cables during the same operation. Mackie saw strikes on two railway engines and goods trucks before he was hit, but commented: "It goes to show that they were not a very profitable type of operation from the results, this being quite typical." He left Spitfire 'G' at Lympne to be repaired and returned to Kenley in the station Magister, which Flg Off J.G. Pattison flew over to collect him in. Mackie was at the controls for the return flight – he never was a happy passenger!

Dr David Clouston later claimed that Mackie had saved his life at Kenley. Writing from his Wellington home in 1986: "One of my enduring memories is how Rosie's nightmares (the FW 190 had arrived) indirectly saved my life. His noises used to wake his room mate who, in the early morning of 13 June 1942, heard me crash out of an upstairs window to the path below. I would have died that night. After 12 months in 11 Group we all had some sort of twitch. Mine was sleepwalking!" Clouston, a Plt Off at the time, broke his jaw

---

* (Wg Cdr A.C. Deere, DSO, DFC & Bar; see *Aces High*, pages 216-7.)

and an arm in the fall. He said of Mackie's flying: "As a pilot, just like the rest of us, I suppose; we were not aerobatic specialists, just good workaday fliers."

485 Squadron moved to Ipswich on 15 June for a one week rest, and Mackie took advantage of the break to get in some air-to-air firing on the Orfordness range. Three percent of his cannon and machine-gun shells hit the drogue, which confirmed his opinion that his marksmanship was far from perfect, and that far more time and attention should have been devoted to such matters.

The squadron returned to Kenley on 22 June, a station Mackie was always pleased to be based at, as: "Kenley was a peacetime station, with a huge permanent mess hall with accommodation wings on either side. It was fully equipped with all the trimmings – a big lounge, snooker room, games room, bar. It had everything. It was a really comfortable station. The food was absolutely bang-on, comparable to a five-star hotel." After experiencing battlefield conditions in Tunisia, Sicily and Italy, he would come to appreciate the facilities of Kenley even more.

On 1 July Mackie flew a Spitfire IX for the first time. Variously engined with Rolls-Royce Merlins of between 1,515 hp and 1,720 hp, the Mark IX was nearly 50 miles an hour faster than the Mark VBs of 485 Squadron, and had a service ceiling of between 42,500 feet and 45,000 feet. He made a 'battle climb' to 40,000 feet during the 40-minute flight.

When he flew Sqn Ldr C.R. 'Killer' Caldwell* from Kenley to Northolt in the station Magister on 4 July, Mackie no doubt talked tactics with the Australian ace. Caldwell by then had a confirmed total of 20.5 claims against enemy aircraft whilst flying Tomahawks and Kittyhawks in the Western Desert. He had been based briefly at Kenley as a supernumerary, flying Spitfires operationally for the first time before returning home to lead the first Spitfire Wing in the Royal Australian Air Force. Caldwell ended the war as a Group Captain, having claimed a total of 28.5 victories.

485 Squadron moved to King's Cliffe in Northamptonshire on 8 July, for a rest. Rurally situated in Rockingham Forest, this airfield located between Peterborough and Leicester would, in fact, be the unit's home for the next six months. Mackie's logbook did not indicate much time for relaxation and recreation, however. On 12th and 14th he flew sector reconnaissances, while later on the latter date the squadron flew to Wittering, where Wg Cdr P.G. Jameson*, a New Zealander, led it on 65 minutes of combat practice with a squadron of Typhoons

---

* (Grp Capt C.R. Caldwell, DSO, DFC & Bar; see *Aces High*, pages 162-3); (Grp Capt P.G. Jameson, DSO, DFC & Bar; see *Aces High*, page 352).

at 15,000 feet. "The practice was found to create good experience for the new pilots," according to the Operational Record Book. "Cine camera gunshots were taken and some interesting data should result from those." It was probably Mackie's first meeting with Jameson, who had flown Hurricanes in Norway in 1940, and was one of the few survivors when the aircraft carrier HMS *Glorious* was sunk. At this time Jameson was leader of the Wittering Wing. He was clearly impressed by Mackie, whom he chose a few days later to accompany him on a Rhubarb over France.

Meanwhile, back at King's Cliffe, there was little rest for 485 Squadron. After the Typhoon practice Mackie flew back to King's Cliffe and then on to Kenley the same day. The next day he returned to King's Cliffe, and the following day he was scrambled for a patrol over that base. While airborne, the ceiling dropped to 250 feet, and he landed at Wittering, returning later in the day to King's Cliffe. There was a dogfight practice and low flying on 21st, and that evening he flew again to Wittering, where he made one dusk and two night landings.

22 July was to be an even busier day. Arriving at King's Cliffe from Wittering, he formed up with Wg Cdr Jameson, Flt Lt Baker and Sgt L.J. Montgomerie*, and took off at 1600 hours, headed for Martlesham Heath. The section left the Heath at 1615 on a Rhubarb over the Flushing/Woensdrecht area, attacking a locomotive drawing a goods train east of Goes. After damaging the engine with cannon fire they withdrew, and all four aircraft landed safely back at Martlesham, before continuing on to King's Cliffe the same evening. He flew a 70-minute convoy patrol from Docking the next day, returning to King's Cliffe before flying on to Wittering, making a dusk landing and staying there the night. 28 July saw him aloft over Norwich for 95 minutes on his first night patrol, and the month ended with a defensive patrol off Skegness, together with formation and cloud flying practice.

August was conspicuous for two reasons – the month marked Mackie's promotion to Flying Officer on 8th, and was also notable for the only occasion on which an enemy fighter managed successfully to draw a bead on his aircraft and hole it with machine-gun fire. His logbook entry on 19 August: "Fired at FW 190 – had extremely busy time – got two .5″ mg bullets in wing – refuelled at Lympne" has an almost aggrieved look about it!

The occasion was Operation 'Jubilee', the mainly Canadian raid on Dieppe in German-occupied France, from which much was learned, but at an enormous cost in lives lost. 485 Squadron had been re-positioned from King's Cliffe to West Malling, near Maidstone in

---

* (Flt Lt L.J. Montgomerie, DFC; see *Aces High*, page 449.)

Kent, on 16 August in readiness to contribute fighter cover over the raid on 19th. Strict secrecy was supposed to surround the operation.

All the station commanders, wing leaders and squadron commanders involved were briefed by Leigh-Mallory at 11 Group Headquarters on 18 August, and at the airfields that evening everyone was confined to camp, communications with the outside world being shut down. However, the German intelligence system proved too good on this occasion, and when the Dieppe raiders put to sea on 19th the enemy already knew that they were on their way.

The New Zealand Spitfires flew four patrols over Dieppe as part of a 12 Group Wing led by Wg Cdr Jameson, who flew a 485 Squadron aircraft on the first such sortie. The preparations made by the Germans were evident in the report in the squadron's ORB: "0745, took off from West Malling, 485 being the lowest of the three squadrons. On arriving over Dieppe at 3/4,000 feet each squadron was immediately attacked by e/a (enemy aircraft) in pairs and fours out of the sun. Jameson (Red One) got a 190 as did Plt Off Chrystall (Red Four) and one other was damaged. The wing leader and squadron commanders said they had never before experienced such an intensive battle with so many e/a."

Although West Malling was much nearer to Dieppe than was King's Cliffe, it was still a flight of about 100 miles, and Mackie had to put down at Lympne, near the Channel coast, to refuel after his one hour 45 minute sortie. His re-positioning flight to West Malling took ten minutes, and he was up again at 1120 to fly withdrawal cover at 9,000 feet. Returning direct to West Malling after a one hour 40 minute sortie, he refuelled and left the ground again at 1405, once more flying withdrawal cover, but at 10,000 feet this time. After a one hour 25 minute sortie he landed back at West Malling once more. The logbook entries show he was not in contact with enemy aircraft on the second and third sorties, indicating that by then Fighter Command had achieved some of the air superiority originally envisaged from the outset. Altogether Mackie had been airborne for five hours during the day.

Not since the Battle of Britain had air fighting been on such an intensive scale over Western Europe. Fighter Command flew more than 2,000 sorties during the day, and their efficiency was such that a military report commented: ". . . no enemy aircraft were allowed to interfere if they could be driven off and not many got through." 485 Squadron suffered no casualties, but the Command lost 91 fighters – 59 of them Spitfires – and six bombers for the claimed destruction of 96 enemy aircraft plus 39 more 'Probables'; Luftwaffe losses were actually substantially lower than this, at 48 – 23 fighters and 25 bombers.

For two days the ground crews had not had any hot meals – only sandwiches to sustain them while they worked hard to keep the squadron in the air. So pleased were the Kiwis with the magnificent effort of the "penguins" during 'Jubilee', that they clubbed together to give them a party at the end of the operation.

The squadron undertook a new duty on 20 August, flying rear support for Boeing B-17 Flying Fortress bombers from the newly-arrived first elements of the US 8th Air Force, which raided Cayeux on that date. The unit then returned to King's Cliffe on 21st, the servicing echelons travelling by road and rail.

Mitchell commented upon the next phase of 485's employment: "The squadron, during the period that Grant commanded it, entered on a somewhat less spectacular phase, chiefly because a later type of Spitfire was put into operations, the Spitfire IX. The New Zealanders, still equipped with Spitfire Vs, remained mostly on close escort duties and intruder patrols, but they took a fair share of the fighting whenever the opportunity presented itself."

According to Wg Cdr H.L. Thompson in *New Zealanders with the Royal Air Force, Vol.1* (NZ Govt Printer, 1953) the experiences of 485 Squadron during the last months of 1942 were typical of those of many squadrons with which New Zealand pilots were flying: "As part of Jameson's 12 Group Wing, the New Zealand Spitfires flew many sorties as cover for the Fortresses, Liberators, Bostons and Venturas."

Included in Mackie's lot were two night patrols over Cromer-Wittering-Boston during September, and some of his much-relished air-to-air firing, this time on the Cromer range. Of 400 shots fired at the target drogue, 62 registered, which was at least an improvement on the previous performance.

The English Midlands continued to attract airborne German intruders, and King's Cliffe was well-suited to counter any attention being paid to the cities in this region. Mackie was scrambled three times during September, recalled from two within minutes, but on the third made an interception at 22,000 feet.

A four-day engine course which he attended at the Rolls-Royce factory at Derby in early October was meat and drink to Mackie, with his abiding interest in things mechanical. Always meticulous in the maintenance of his machinery, rather more than most pilots, he appreciated the absolute precision and the fine tolerances within which Rolls-Royce designed and manufactured the V-12 Merlin engines which powered the Spitfires and many other types of aircraft. He was rather less satisfied after an air-to-air firing session later that month, when only 24 of 200 machine-gun bullets he fired hit the drogue target over the Matlask range.

Operation 'Torch', the Anglo-American invasion of French North Africa on 8 November 1942, which followed within days of the British 8th Army's victory at El Alamein, in Egypt, and was to spell the ultimate end of Axis presence on the southern side of the Mediterranean, also provided 485 Squadron with an excursion to Ireland. "We had somehow to conceal the concentration of shipping which from the beginning of October began to crowd the Clyde and other western ports, but also the actual sailing of the convoys," wrote Winston Churchill in *The Second World War, Volume IV* (Halstead Press, Sydney, 1951). "We were completely successful. The first of the 'Torch' convoys left the Clyde on October 22. By the 26th all the fast troopships were under way, and the American forces were sailing for Casablanca direct from the United States." 485 Squadron's chance to ensure that if enemy reconnaissance aircrew did get a glimpse of the invasion fleet, they did not live to tell the tale, came on 24 October. The squadron left King's Cliffe for Northern Ireland, staging through Hawarden, near Chester, and arriving at Kirkistown on the Ards peninsula of County Down the same day.

The next day, 25 October, a convoy of 42 liners, merchant ships and their escorts slipped down the Firth of Clyde, Algeria-bound. And as they steamed through the North Channel, that narrow gap between Ireland and Scotland, 485 Squadron pilots, Mackie amongst them, were flying a sector patrol high overhead. That convoy, which included four aircraft carriers amongst its protective force, was only one of several forming up and leaving at about that time for the 8 November landings.

At Kirkistown the squadron was admirably placed to patrol the North Channel and the upper Irish Sea. Almost immediately however, there was a need for patrols further north. On 26th Mackie flew northwest to Eglinton near Londonderry, and the next day he made a two-hour convoy patrol over the North Channel from there. Eglinton remained his Northern Ireland base until 12 November, several days after the Torch landings. He flew only six sorties, mostly convoy patrols, from there.

On 12 November the squadron left Eglinton for King's Cliffe, where it arrived the next day, after staging through Valley air station on the Isle of Anglesey – but not before the pilots had made the most of some "unaccustomed" shopping in the Irish Republic. They may not have tangled with the Luftwaffe during their Irish excursion, but an evening trip across the border had yielded whiskey, hams and other luxuries not readily available in England. There were not many empty nooks and crannies in the Spitfires when they landed back at King's Cliffe.

Mackie then did little flying until 29 November, when he checked that Plt Off M.G. Sutherland was properly strapped into the front cockpit of a Tiger Moth, and made a one hour 45 minute flight to the RAF Central Navigation School at Cranage, near Middlewich in Cheshire. Even allowing for that biplane's normally modest rate of progress, Mackie must either have had a strong headwind or made a diversion, to record an average speed of only 54.2 miles per hour over the 95 miles between the two points.

At Cranage, in Ansons piloted by Flg Off Douetil and Sgts Bentum and Thain, he completed five hours and five minutes of low-level map reading exercises over Cheshire and North Wales – and in typical Mackie fashion, topped the school's No.20 Course with a 96% pass.

He rejoined the squadron on 13 December and flew local patrols, formation and cine-gun practices, and one scramble. The only major activity that month occurred on 23rd when the unit moved to Coltishall, and flew from there to provide withdrawal cover for Ventura bombers returning from a raid on Den Helder.

Mackie was back in his element on Christmas Eve – during an air-to-air shoot off Skegness, when he shot the drogue away! He and White left King's Cliffe on 29 December for Martlesham Heath, on the east coast near Ipswich, and from here flew a Rhubarb towards the western Scheldte estuary. "On reaching the Dutch coast the weather seemed unsuitable, so after flying parallel with the coast for a few minutes they returned straight to King's Cliffe," recorded the ORB. Both Mackie and White were too pragmatic to take risks with little chance of reward.

On 2 January, 1943, 485 Squadron came back into the front line when it returned to 11 Group and established itself at Westhampnett in Sussex, near Chichester on the south coast. Little more than a fair sized grass meadow, according to 'Hawkeye' Wells, Westhampnett was a satellite of Tangmere, and 485 Squadron became a part of the Tangmere Wing.

In spite of its new front line position, 485 Squadron was unable to meet the superior enemy fighters like the FW 190 on anything like equal terms, because it was still flying the now outmoded Spitfire VB. As a consequence, it continued to perform secondary roles like air-sea rescue and coastal patrols, although some Rodeos, Circuses and diversionary sweeps were included in its itinerary.

Mackie had his last contact with the enemy as a 485 Squadron pilot on 13 January, when the squadron took part in a Circus as a 'bouncing wing', climbing to 26,000 feet. "Yellow section dived to attack a train just south of Conchil, but owing to windscreen icing little detail could be seen," recorded the ORB. "Flg Off Mackie fired a six-second burst."

Browne, recently returned to the squadron after escaping from

France, courtesy of the French Underground resistance movement and the Royal Navy, accompanied Mackie on one of his last patrols, from Selsey Bill to Shoreham on 14 January. Ironically, his last flight with 485 Squadron was a Rhubarb, one of those missions into which he had never been able to put his heart and soul. Accompanied by Plt Off G.J. Moorhead, he headed for Fecamp on 16 January, but owing to unsuitable weather, did not cross the French coast, and returned after 70 minutes.

Mackie did not have a lot to show for a year of operations in terms of results – a half share in a Bf 109, and an FW 190 probably destroyed. As with most fighter pilots, it had come down to what Peter Townsend* described as "time and chance". In practise, there had not been many occasions which offered the young New Zealander the chance to show what he could do. That would change with his next posting.

What he did have the opportunity to do, and it was an opportunity denied to many Fighter Command pilots, was to get plenty of flying experience in a variety of conditions, and some target practice. True, the target practice was always much less than he would have preferred, but it was a lot more than most had enjoyed. And he had 375 hours of Spitfire flying experience. By the time he was posted from 485 Squadron, Mackie was showing clearly some of the flying skills which would eventually place him head and shoulders above the majority.

Pattison, with whom he had flown during much of his time in the squadron, and who would later lead 485, described him as "a very sound, reliable pilot, who could be depended upon one hundred percent, particularly in a tight spot." He considered that Mackie was a more serious young man than many, who kept himself in top physical condition with early morning runs around the aerodrome. "This was his approach to life and flying – to do his very best by keeping himself in top form."

Johnny Checketts, who flew with Mackie from November 1941 until August 1942, and had plenty of opportunities to assess his abilities, described him as "an exceptional pilot and a first rate fighter pilot and leader." Writing from his home in the South Island in 1986, Checketts stated that Mackie was a splendid fellow, unassuming, almost shy, with a great sense of humour and a universal popularity. "I consider that he is one of New Zealand's unsung heroes, and I cannot understand why he was not given credit in this country for his magnificent war effort." Checketts, no slouch in the air himself, went on to command 485 Squadron and ended the war as a Wing Commander, claiming 14 enemy aircraft destroyed.

---

* (Grp Capt P.W. Townsend, DSO, DFC & Bar; see *Aces High*, pages 590-1.)

Sqn Ldr Grant's assessment, written in Mackie's logbook on the eve of his departure, was fulsome: "Flg Off Mackie has been with this squadron for some considerable time now and by his keenness and energy has done a lot towards helping his flight commander. He has been a good deputy and is a fine leader and definitely *above the average* as a fighter pilot." The underlining was Grant's and Mackie was to justify it.

While Mackie was passing through London in late January 1943, en route to the Middle East, he met up with Marty Hume and Johnnie Houlton* in the New Zealand Forces Club. Houlton, a fellow Kiwi, had flown with 485 Squadron during June and July 1942, before obtaining a posting to Malta. He had just returned from that besieged island, and Mackie listened eagerly as he described conditions in the Mediterranean area. It was with a hint of envy that Houlton outlined the situation which was to develop a few months later in his book *Spitfire Strikes* (John Murray, London, 1985): "Word was filtering back of the success already achieved by Evan Mackie. . . . 'Hap' Harrison, another ex-485 Squadron Sergeant, who had elected to go out to the Middle East theatre, was also beginning to climb the ladder; and they were certainly seeing more action than we were in the Tangmere sector in the first half of 1943." Houlton, who ended the war with claims for nine shot down, went on to fly Tempest Vs in 274 Squadron of 135 Wing on the Continent during 1945.

* (Flt Lt J.A. Houlton, DFC; see *Aces High*, pages 338-9.)

CHAPTER FIVE

NORTH AFRICA – 243 SQUADRON

On 23 January 1943, the first British troops entered Tripoli in Western Libya, three months to the day since the 8th Army had joined battle with Feldmarshal Erwin Rommel's Afrika Korps at El Alamein. Still far away on the western borders of Northern Tunisia, the Anglo-American forces which had landed in Algeria and French Morocco during November, had been brought to a halt in the mountainous border territory by rapidly-deployed Axis forces, and were held in a state of stalemate. With long, tortuous lines of communication compared with those of the Axis, who were supplied with relative ease over the short sea/air route from Sicily, the Allied air forces were also now at a disadvantage. Based on rough forward airstrips that all too often became morasses of mud, they found themselves outclassed by numbers of the latest Messerschmitt Bf 109Gs and Focke Wulf FW 190s, which were operating from excellent all-weather airfields around Tunis and Bizerta, manned by highly experienced pilots drawn from every main theatre in which German forces were operating.

Evan Mackie was not aware that it was to these very different conditions that he was on his way, when he was attached briefly to 122 (City of Bombay) Squadron on 24 January to gain experience on Spitfire IXs. At Hornchurch, in Essex, he made two flights in different aircraft – a 35-minute climb to 23,000 feet and 50 minutes of local flying and aerobatics. Added to his 40-minute battle climb to 40,000 feet back in July 1942, he now had two hours and five minutes in the type. From Hornchurch he was posted to Tunisia.

His odyssey to North Africa, and subsequently to Malta, Sicily and Italy, began on 1 February 1943, when he joined the transport *Monarch of Bermuda* in Liverpool, bound for Oran. She was carrying a large number of United States troops, mostly black, to support US II Corps in Tunisia.

"One of the duties for us few pilots was 'officer of the guard' at various times of the day and night," he said. "It was amusing. On night patrol we had to go up and down the various decks to make sure the black guard on each deck was on the job. Well, by the time we got to the bottom, having woken each one on the way down, the top ones were asleep again, dead to the world with their rifles at all angles. We realised it was a hopeless job trying to keep them awake – if we had been hit they would have been the first awake anyway."

Wg Cdr W.E. 'Smokey' Schrader*, writing from his Auckland home in February, 1995 recounted: "I travelled to Oran on the *Monarch of Bermuda* with Rosie, but did not get to know him. I went on to Malta and did not see him again until joining 486 Squadron in March, 1945. Again our relationship was fleeting. Not an easy man to get to know, as others have said."

Successfully eluding the prowling German U-Boats, *Monarch of Bermuda* slipped through the Straits of Gibraltar and arrived at Oran seven days later, to discharge her contingent of troops. She then back-tracked for 18 hours to offload her pilot passengers at Gibraltar, where Spitfire IXs, previously uncrated, were being assembled for them to ferry to North Africa. The aircraft were not ready, so Mackie and his fellow pilots had a week of leisure on The Rock, enjoying the sunny contrast to the grey English weather they had just left behind.

"It gave us time to explore the whole place, to climb The Rock and say hello to the rock apes. They're there all right, cheeky as one thing, grab your haversack if you turn your back." They saw the water catchment areas, and found The Rock to be a honeycomb of tunnels. "Gibraltar itself, the town, was very interesting. Mostly troops, but civilians came in from Spain every day and wandered off at night."

On 4 March they were allocated their Spitfire IXs, and Mackie found he was to lead a section of six aircraft to Maison Blanche, near Algiers. The Mark IX was in many ways similar to the Mark Vs that Mackie was used to, except for a more powerful engine – the Rolls-Royce Merlin 61. This engine developed 1,565 horsepower at 30,000 feet – a useful increase on the 1,470 horsepower Merlin 45 with which the Mark V was fitted. The increased power gave the Mark IX a climbing, diving and level flight performance almost identical to the FW 190; even better, the Spitfire's greatest strength – its ability to turn more tightly then the Focke Wulf – was further enhanced. As well as adding power, the two-stage supercharging to the engine increased the altitude to which the Mark IX could be flown operationally.

With fuel tanks topped to the brim for the two and a half hour flight, and guns loaded, Mackie led his section out onto the Gibraltar runway.

---

* (Wg Cdr W.E. Schrader, DFC & Bar; see *Aces High*, page 536.)

"In a fighter it is essential that you have good forward vision," he explained, "and the erks used to spend no end of time polishing up the perspex bubble hood as well as the main bulletproof windscreen in front. Well, mine was shining just like a new one.

"I took off along the runway and a great cloud of oil came out of the constant-speed pitch mechanism in the propeller. From then on I couldn't see a thing forward – everything was out the side. It got slightly worse as I went on because obviously there was a leak in the seal." Nevertheless, he led the section safely eastwards at between 8,000 feet and 10,000 feet, the mountains near Maison Blanche proving to be a good landmark to home onto.

The next day he flew Spitfire EN291 about 90 miles south-east to Setif, and left it there for some undoubtedly appreciative pilot. In the event Mackie was not to begin flying Spitfire IXs operationally until September, although 243 Squadron, for which he was bound, began replacing its Mark VCs with IXs in June. It would be whilst flying the Spitfire VC that he would claim more than half of his confirmed air-to-air victories, eight of them while flying the same aircraft.

13 March found the New Zealander back in Maison Blanche, thumbing a lift in a Douglas Dakota transport aircraft to Souk el Arba, via Setif and 'Tingley' – the latter airstrip having been named by Wg Cdr Piet Hugo* after the engineer who built it. Souk el Arba and Souk el Khemis were about ten miles apart, and some 60 miles west of Tunis. For the sake of convenience, the airstrips located here were named after London railway stations, that at Souk el Arba being Sloane Square, whilst the six strips around Souk el Khemis were named Paddington, Victoria, Marylebone, Waterloo, Euston and King's Cross. 243 Squadron was based at Euston, and it was there that Flg Off Mackie reported for duty. His arrival was not logged in the squadron's Operational Record Book, but he made his first flight, a 75-minute sector reconnaissance and cannon test, in a Spitfire VB, SN-E, on 15 March.

At this time 243 Squadron, together with 72,93 and 111 Squadrons, made up 324 Wing, which was part of Air Commodore K.B.B. 'Bing' Cross'* 242 Group in the North West African Tactical Air Force, under the overall command of the highly-regarded Australian-born Air Marshal Sir Arthur 'Mary' Coningham*. (The 'Mary' was a corruption of his early nickname 'Maori' from his early life in New Zealand).

---

* (Grp Capt P.H. Hugo, DSO, DFC & Bar; see *Aces High* pages 343-4); (Air Chief Marshal Sir Kenneth Cross, KCB, CBE, DSO, DFC; see autobiography *Straight and Level* Grub Street, 1993); (Air Marshal Sir Arthur Coningham, DSO, MC, DFC; see *Above the Trenches*, page 118).

The position had improved greatly since January, the 8th Army having reached Southern Tunisia, whilst Axis offensives against the Allied forces on the western border had been halted and reversed. The Allies were now firmly on the offensive, and close to gaining aerial superiority. The Wing was engaged in offensive patrols over the battlefront, and also provided escorts to medium bombers as the Allied ground forces prepared for the last big push in Africa. General Bernard Montgomery's 8th Army had won the Battle of the Mareth Line, and the German and Italian armies were being compressed into an ever-shrinking area of the Tunisian peninsula by the British and American forces.

243 Squadron had arrived in Algeria in December 1942, but it was not until 6 January 1943 that it obtained aircraft – mostly Spitfire VCs – and began to undertake shipping patrols over the Bone area. The following day the unit lost one pilot, but avenged this by the end of the month by damaging two FW 190s. It then flew sweeps, escorts and tactical reconnaissance sorties, which continued for the next two months. However it was not until 1 March that 243 recorded its first confirmed victory. That month it concentrated on ground strafing to good effect, but in April it would increase its score by shooting down German aircraft evacuating Tunisia.

Mackie was to make his name in his new unit because of his splendid physique and great strength – "easily the strongest man in the squadron" recorded the ORB.

James K. (Jim) Porteous, a New Zealander in 243, recalled that by March the squadron had had a bad time, and was reformed with a good Canadian CO, James Emslie Walker*, with Evan and himself as flight commanders: "I think the success of 243 Squadron was due to tight discipline by the CO. I had been a Flying Officer with 93 Squadron, and on my promotion to Flight Commander in 243 was invited into the CO's tent, and over a glass of whisky was read the Riot Act. He was Boss, and said so. No doubt Rosie was given the same treatment."

Harold C. Payne (always known as 'Mickey' in the squadron), an English Sergeant pilot, was recovering from a wound administered by an unfriendly Flak shell when Mackie joined 243: "Rosie Mackie was not a great communicator, and being in separate messes the personal touch was missing. However, I flew a number of times as his No.2 and well remember his laconic 'Watch my tail' expression. It was not an instruction or a command. He said it in a matter-of-fact way, almost as one would say 'let's go'. Watching his tail – and my own – and careering about the skies was a full time job and exhilarating. It was good flying with him."

---

* (Wg Cdr J.E. Walker, DFC & Bar; see *Aces High*, pages 613-4.)

Mackie's North African campaign was to be conducted in circumstances quite different from those to which he had become accustomed on the established English fighter stations: "Once we landed in North Africa we were in tents from there on. We had our own bedrolls with us. The aircraft were dispersed, not covered. They may have had camouflage nets on at times, but not many. Just dispersed around the ground – there's plenty of flat ground there!

"There was no problem to make an airfield. The airfields were made by the Yanks, merely by bulldozing a strip roughly 1,000 yards long and laying out what they called PSP – perforated steel planking, which all fitted together like a jigsaw, like a Meccano set, and made a mat the length of the runway. Of course, when you landed on it, it sounded like nothing on earth – like landing on a heap of tin cans!

"It stabilised the ground but it didn't diminish the dust, at the starting end anyhow. The dust was quite a problem. It must have been very hard on a lot of the motors, because it was never-ending dust. Of course, they had special air filters for the Spitfire V, the tropical model presumably – a special extra big filter underneath." (These were Vokes tropical filters, which gave the noses of the Spitfire Vs a 'pigeon-chested' appearance).

The squadron dispersal centre was a marquee, and the mess was a mile or two away, in some old buildings. It was probably there on 17 March that he met the Wing's senior officers for the first time – Wg Cdr George Gilroy* (who was just taking over command of the Wing from Grp Capt R.B. Lees) and Wg Cdr H.S.L. 'Cocky' Dundas*, the Wing Commander Flying. That night they and all the squadron commanders in the Wing were the guests of the 243 Squadron mess. Mackie was quick to form a high opinion of George Gilroy, whom he described as an aggressive and highly competent fighter pilot. Wg Cdr Gilroy was universally known in the RAF as 'Sheep', as a result of his occupation as a sheep farmer in the Scottish lowlands before the war. By the time he was posted back to the United Kingdom in November 1943, he had amassed a considerable total of aerial victories, and had been promoted to Grp Capt.

"We would follow Sheep Gilroy anywhere," declared Evan Mackie. "Sheep Gilroy was the most fearless fighter pilot I flew with in North Africa."

The New Zealander's good opinion was reciprocated by Gilroy, who was quick to see Mackie's leadership potential. Sensing a similar determination to down Axis aircraft, he gave Mackie every opportunity, advancing him within months to Squadron Leader, twice

---

* (Grp Capt G.K. Gilroy, DSO, DFC & Bar, DFC(US); see *Aces High*, page 284); (Grp Capt H.S.L. Dundas, DSO & Bar, DFC; see *Aces High*, page 238).

successfully recommending him for the Distinguished Flying Cross, and later as a Companion of the Distinguished Service Order.

March passed fairly quietly as Mackie settled into 243 Squadron's way of doing things. During his first six days he made four flights in SpitfireVBs, but from 21 March his regular mount was to be a Mark VC. There were some operational missions, like a close escort to Hurri-bombers in the Sedjenane area, and a high level sweep over Tunis, but mostly it was squadron training – combat drill, formation flying and weaving practice, as Sqn Ldr Walker welded his new pilots into an effective fighting formation.

On 4 April, after being scrambled to 17,000 feet, Mackie fired his guns in anger for the first time over North Africa – to no effect – at a Bf 109.

Later that day, while on a check flight, his airscrew jammed in fully-fine pitch. ". . . . which made it a bit awkward to fly," he recalled. "You had some control, but it was like putting your foot down in a motor car with the clutch slipping. Lots of revs and no pull. But I managed to get home."

The next day he flew withdrawal cover for B-17 Flying Fortress bombers of the USAAF over Tunis at 29,000 feet, followed by a sweep over Tunis Bay at 27,000 feet – after which he landed at Paddington. It was just ten minutes by Spitfire from Paddington to Euston airfield according to his logbook, about the same time as it takes between those stations on the London Underground!

7 April 1943 was one of Mackie's red-letter days as a fighter pilot. It began with an uneventful patrol over the Beja-Medjez el Bab area, and ended with him breaking his North African duck by blasting two Junkers Ju 87 dive-bombers out of the sky.

The Squadron Intelligence Officer, Flg Off Arthur Rawlinson, wrote the following account in 243's ORB: "12 a/c scrambled for a sweep over Medjez at 3,000 feet. Chuka 3, one of our forward visual control posts, reports hostiles coming in from the N/E, later reporting them as Stukas escorted by Me 109s. N/E of Oued Zarga 15 Stukas with an escort of at least three 109s are sighted flying below cloud. The Squadron, flying in the opposite direction, turns to port and attacks. The Ju 87s jettison their bombs as we close in and make off eastwards, trying to gain cloud cover. Too late. 243 Squadron gets in among them with devastating results – five destroyed, five probably destroyed, one damaged.

"Sqn Ldr Walker sends one down in flames which crashes three to five miles N of Oued Zarga, probably destroys a second, damages a third. Sgt R.C.Jacques, two 87s probably destroyed; Sgt G.O. McKay destroys one which crashes, probably destroys a second. Flg Off Mackie destroys two; the first hits the deck, the second enveloped in flames."

"Coinciding with this first major victory, the Squadron concert was held at 324 Wing in the evening – a most excellent performance – drums, accordion, violin and cornet," Rawlinson concluded.

Research indicates that II Gruppe, Stukageschwader 3, lost at least four Ju 87Ds during this engagement. Mackie's combat report read:

> I was Yellow 1, and airborne with the Squadron at 1639 hrs 7.4.43.
>
> When flying towards Medjez eastwards after Chuka 3 had reported Stukas in the area, I saw a formation of approx. 15 E/A flying west on our port side.
>
> At the time I was on the port side of the Squadron, and reported the E/A to the Squadron Commander. I turned to port, coming in behind and slightly below the enemy formation which was then flying at approx. 3000 ft.
>
> As I went in to attack I noticed 2 Me 109s with white spinners, slightly above the Squadron and flying across it.
>
> (1) The Ju 87s were flying in vics of 3, four vics fairly close together with the rear starboard vic lagging. Coming up from below, I attacked the starboard 87, of this vic, opening fire at approximately 50 yds, with cannon and M/G. I saw strikes on the wings and fuselage of the A/C. Large pieces broke away, passing on both sides of my A/C. The 87 went into a dive and was seen to crash by Sgt McKay who was my No.3.
>
> Claim: 1 Ju 87 destroyed.
>
> (2) After completing my first attack, I climbed into cloud and was flying approx. eastwards when I saw and attacked a second Ju 87 from the starboard quarter, opening fire from 50 yds range with cannon and M/G and closing in rapidly to dead astern. I saw strikes all over the fuselage and around the cockpit and engine. Volumes of black smoke issued from the engine which became enveloped in flames. I last saw the A/C in a steep dive flying eastwards.
>
> Due to the amount of cloud, I had become separated from the Squadron, so steered for base, landing about 1830 hrs.
>
> Claim: 1 Ju 87 destroyed.

The following day 324 Wing was visited by the AOC, Coningham, who brought personnel up to date on the Tunisian war situation. In a few weeks, he said, the Germans would be driven out; Typhoons were to operate in the area; passages home may be commandeered by 'sand-happy' warriors, some of whom had been in North Africa for two or three years.

On patrol over Medjez next day, Mackie and the CO jointly damaged a Bf 109:

> I was airborne at 1745 hours on 9th April 1943 from Euston aerodrome, Souk el Khemis. Near Medjez 2 Me 109s were sighted flying south and then east at 3,000 ft.
>
> I made a quarter stern attack on one of them with cannon and M/guns seeing strikes on the fuselage.

Claim: 1 Me 109 damaged.

(Shared with S/Ldr J.E.Walker, DFC & Bar)

Mackie kept up the pressure, consolidating his fast-growing reputation as a pilot to watch, when he destroyed a Bf 109 quite spectacularly just 24 hours later – a fact not missed by war correspondents in the area. A contemporary newspaper account, published back in New Zealand complete with his photograph, read: "A former Waihi goldmine electrician, now Flying Officer E.D. Mackie, of the RAF Spitfire squadron in Tunisia, destroyed three enemy aircraft in three days. His latest success was over a Messerschmitt 109, which was about 30 ft from him when he fired his cannons and machine-guns."

'I just could not miss it. I saw big lumps falling from the plane and black smoke pouring from its engine,' he said.

"Flying Officer Mackie returned to his base with his windscreen and parts of his plane smothered in oil from the Messerschmitt's engine. With two Junkers 78's *(sic)* shot down two days previously, Flying Officer Mackie has made a handsome contribution to his Squadron's total of 10 aircraft destroyed in four days without loss to themselves."

This action involved 12 of the squadron's aircraft. Four Bf 109s had been sighted below while the Spitfires were flying at 20,000 feet, and as they dived to attack, 12 more Bf 109s were seen above them – so it was 16 Bf 109s to 12 Spitfire VCs when battle was joined. Rawlinson takes up the story: "In the fight that followed the squadron destroyed four Me 109s and damaged one."

"Squadron Leader Walker set one on fire (this aircraft blew up in mid air) and damaged another. Flg Off Mackie got another 'flamer' and was so close to the aircraft that oil from it sprayed over his windscreen. Flg Off M. Graham* and Flg Off F.S. (Frankie) Banner* shared a destroyed. The squadron score mounts steadily."

---

* (Flt Lt M. Graham, DFC; see *Aces High*, page 296); (Flt Lt F.S. Banner, DFC & Bar; see *Aces High*, page 110).

Mackie's own account was:

> I was airborne with the Squadron at 1720 hrs on 10.4.43 on an offensive patrol of the Medjez area.
>
> Over Medjez at 1800, I attacked a Me 109, firing one long burst with cannon and M/Guns and breaking away when 10 yds astern of the E/A. I saw strikes and flashes from the tail, all along the fuselage; pieces dropped away from the E/A.
>
> My windscreen was covered with oil from the Me 109, which was seen by S/Ldr Walker, F/O Macdonald and my No.2 Sgt Hill to burst into flames, after black smoke in volumes poured out of it.

Next day Rawlinson recorded: "Pressmen descended on us. In the action above Flg Off Banner diced with death, two 109s on his tail making alternative attacks at ground level. He got in several bursts with machine guns only and had the satisfaction of seeing these 109s crash in flames behind him. When the journalistic 'twist' applied to Banner's escapade was revealed in a news sheet from the Press a few days later one long howl arose from the pilots' dispersal tent. Enough said."

Recognition of Mackie's increasing competency came on 12 April when he was promoted to Acting Flight Lieutenant and took over the leadership of 'A' Flight. Fellow-Kiwi Jim Porteous was leading 'B' Flight. To celebrate his promotion, he went out next day on an aerodrome patrol at 15,000 feet, and shared in the destruction of another Bf 109 over Beja with Sgt R.I. Hill, who was again flying as his No.2. Six 243 Squadron Spitfires led by Mackie had come across three Bf 109s, which fared rather badly, Flg Off Banner and Sgt G.T. Melville sharing a probable, and Plt Off C.W.J. Fearn being awarded a damaged. Mackie reported:

> Up: 0536. Down: 0632. 15th April 1943.
> From Euston – Aerodrome patrol.
>
> Six of us were patrolling over base at 15,000 ft, when control reported 3 bogies travelling towards Tabarka on a S/W course. Some time later they became hostiles and we were able to intercept them approx. 15 miles east Beja.
>
> I attacked one Me 109 from 250 yds using a deflection shot. I saw no strikes but two plumes of white smoke poured out of the A/C and I saw a piece fall off. I followed it down from 13,000 ft almost to ground level, firing 6 or 8 bursts, and saw it crash at J.4548 approx. spinning round on its starboard wing.
>
> Confirmed by Sgt Hill, my No.2 and Sgt Melville.

Claim: 1 Me 109 destroyed.

(Shared with Sgt Hill)

Later that same day Mackie had a crack at another Bf 109 during a sweep at 23,000 feet over the Pont du Fahs/Enfidaville area, but saw no results from his attack.

Sweeps and escort sorties in support of Mitchells, Bostons and Hurri-bombers took up the next few days, but his next opportunity to increase his score did not occur until 16 April, when the squadron, led by the CO, was on a sweep at 21,000 feet over Medjez. Four Bf 109s with mottled green camouflage, white spinners, white wingtips and white bands around their fuselages were intercepted, Sqn Ldr Walker damaged one, but Mackie made no doubt about his chosen victim:

Up: 1405 hrs. Down: 1535 hrs. 16th April 1943.
Aerodrome: Euston Souk el Khemis.

On patrol at 19,000 ft, 4 Me 109s were engaged by the Squadron west of Medjez-el-Bab. I fired at one using a full deflection from 200 yds range, seeing cannon strikes on the starboard wing and cockpit. Black smoke came from the E/A, which caught fire. I followed it down some distance and estimate that it would crash south of Medjez and just south of the river.

Claim: 1 Me 109 destroyed.

N.B. (1) S/Ldr Walker saw this E/A catch fire.
(2) P/O Grieve, his No.2, saw it crash south of Medjez to the south of the river.
Approx. pinpoint J.5631

Euston aerodrome was bombed that day, but no damage was caused. However the enemy returned next day. Intelligence Officer Rawlinson described the attack vividly in the ORB: "Famous last words – it's one of ours! When the first bombs exploded and the heavy and light ack ack batteries went into action there was a rush for whatever cover was available. Most of us lay prone and hoped for the best. Canisters of butterfly bombs burst in mid-air, raining down their anti-personnel bombs.

"Runways at Euston were hit, but were quickly repaired. Anti-personnel bombs with delayed-action fuses exploded through the night. In the morning, thankful for yet another lucky escape, tents were more widely dispersed and slit trenches dug. Slight damage to two aircraft."

Mackie's account was a little more graphic: "We were attacked by some type of German bomber one night. It scared the hell out of us. The only thing I could find to hide under was a motorbike." It was in the middle of the night and we were all in our tents. The next day a lot of us were quite busy making pits to put our bunks in, a bit lower down, out of sight, because in the morning there was a bullet hole in the top of my tent."

At about this time Mackie managed to wangle for himself a set of 12 special stub exhaust ports for his Spitfire VC, of the type then fitted only to Mark IXs. Standard Mark VCs were fitted with three exhaust ports each side, with two of the Merlin's 12 cylinders (which were arranged in a V configuration) discharging into each one. It was generally reckoned that by having a separate exhaust port for each cylinder the Merlin produced more horsepower. They improved the efficiency of the engine and were also aerodynamically superior. Most important, they gave the aircraft a few more miles per hour – and any sort of an 'edge' in performance was always welcomed by the Allied fighter pilots in Tunisia, since their aircraft were generally outclassed by their opponents' machines. Mackie was known to be very proud of his special exhausts.

Action continued unabated for 243 Squadron, with most aircraft in the air at least once a day, and sometimes on several sorties in the same day. On 18 April, Mackie claimed an FW 190 damaged. The squadron was on top cover escort when it encountered 16 enemy aircraft over Teboursouk and the base, mostly Bf 109s, but at least one FW 190. Although it was a reasonably satisfying scrap for the squadron (Flt Lt Jim Porteous claiming one Bf 109 destroyed and damage to two others, Flg Off K.F. MacDonald one destroyed and Sgt Hill one damaged) some Bf 109 fighter-bombers which had not jettisoned their bombs, penetrated to the Souk el Khemis airfields. The runways were untouched, but two aircraft were damaged.

Mackie's contemporary account of the incident was:

Up: 1624. Down: 1732. 18th April, 1943.
Aerodrome – Euston.

South East of Tebersouk *(sic)* the Squadron engaged Me 109s and FW 190s. I delivered an attack at 13,000 ft on a FW 190 from underneath and ahead at a range of 200 yds closing to 150 yds.

  I saw strikes in the centre section of the FW 190 underneath the cockpit. The E/A went into an absolutely vertical dive, nose downwards and I saw it in this position when it was 2-3,000 ft from the ground. The time was approx. 1640 hrs. If he crashed it should be within a radius of 5 or 6 miles from J.4005.

Claim: 1 FW 190 damaged.

Meanwhile back on the ground, life in at least one sense was not so very different from that on permanent RAF stations in the UK. They say that an army marches on its stomach, and in the RAF the ground crew obviously had a keen interest in their rations. Rawlinson recorded that on 21 April an airmen's mess meeting held in the parachute tent in the evening disclosed the fact that "in general, the food served up by the cooks is satisfactory. Representatives from various sections declared that if bully could be served on occasions in different ways for the midday meal the variety would be greatly appreciated."

Jim Porteous recalled that life in 243 Squadron in the first months of 1943 was difficult: "The winter was wet, and the airfield was some-times unusable. The Army engineers laid coconut matting with wire-netting over the top, but the Spits got caught up and sometimes overturned.

"We slept at the beginning under the wings of an aircraft on safari beds and sleeping bags carried with us in the aircraft. We had communal kitchens, with the Wing/Co, pilots and erks joining the queue.

"Sometimes the Germans threatened to break through, and we had the wonderful feeling of loading our adjutant and clerks onto trucks and sending them 50 miles back. Then we helped ourselves to stores!"

The situation improved greatly as the British First Army, US II Corps and General Montgomery's 8th Army joined up and pushed the retreating German and Italian forces even faster up the Tunisian peninsula into a trap from which most would have no escape: "Eventually we got so confident that we used our workshop diesels to run street lighting around the tents," wrote Porteous. "We were a wild mob.

"On one occasion when a hospital arrived nearby we sent a truck back to Algiers and stole the band instruments from the senior officers' mess so that we could invite the nurses to a dance. We were frustrated in this move. We got the band, and sent out the invitations, but the nurses (American) brought their own doctor boyfriends.

"Again, we sent a truck to Algiers to draw our liquor ration – gave the squadron number of a Desert Air Force squadron – sold the spirits to the Americans and thus had free beer. And sent another truck to draw our own rations!"

Porteous remembered Mackie as one of the few who maintained standards, in spite of the lack of water and proper toilet and ablutions facilities: "We had gone bush – sloppy clothes, hats etc., but Rosie maintained his Air Force uniforms to a greater degree than any of us. He insisted on keeping the wire in his hat and on many occasions wore his blues."

It had been discovered meanwhile that the Bf 109 shot down by Flg Off MacDonald on 18 April was a G-6 model, one of the first to be identified. The squadron's engineering staff promptly recovered this aircraft and prepared it for despatch to either the UK or USA for testing.

With the approach of summer, anti-malarial measures were now necessary. The pilots were required to take a five-grain quinine tablet each evening, and other personnel two mepacrine pills twice a week. The mepacrine could have unpleasant side effects, which was why they were not issued to pilots. They also tended to affect judgement of height and distance.

"Tents are sprayed daily. Very soon we shall be sleeping under mosquito nets. Everything possible is being done to keep us fit and free from malaria," noted Rawlinson.

The dosing had its humorous side: "The orderly officer on his rounds issuing pills is suddenly confronted by a mechanic, bent double under an aircraft supporting on his back a long-range tank, who asks whether or not he should drop the tank to swallow his pills!"

During a sweep over Tebourba/Mateur at 9,000 feet on 23 April, Mackie fired at several Bf 109s, but saw no results. 24 April was a fateful day for him – first success, and then a walk home. It began with a Rhubarb over the Pont du Fahs-Bir Meherga road during which he shot up five lorries and three staff cars, also obtaining strikes on others: "Fired 300 rounds cannon – several flamers – not much flak" he recorded in his logbook.

Flg Off Banner, probably on the same low-level mission, had the misfortune to strike the ground with his aircraft's propeller, bending the tip of each blade back about nine inches – and the good fortune, and even better airmanship to nurse his aircraft safely back to base.

Later that day, Mackie and the pilots of the remaining eight service-able aircraft were scrambled to patrol over the Medjez/Pont du Fahs area at 7,000 feet. It was a patrol from which only six aircraft would return.

The ORB recorded that Flt Lt Mackie had attacked a Bf 109, was hit, called up to say he was west of the lake and would 'Rosie aircraft' lead him home? "The phone rings," Rawlinson wrote. "The C/O picks it up while the rest await the news expectantly. Flt Lt Mackie is safe and on his way to rejoin us. Someone is willing to wager that he will not return unless he brings with him his stub exhausts. We know Mackie too well. The bet is not taken."

Mackie's logbook record reads: "Fired at Me 109 from close range – hit by another Spitfire from above – damaged airscrew – crash-landed at J645090."

He later recalled the occasion: "On the second trip I was right over the battle line. It was fairly late in the evening. It was not exactly dusk, but the light was fading. I was leading two sections of three. I was on the bottom, and the three were staggered above, you see. And I got into a position where I was firing at a Hun right over the battle line.

"I was firing and I was well within range and I was really scoring hits – and the next thing another Spitfire from above came down and knocked my propeller blades forward.

"The other section leader, the English one, you'd think butter wouldn't melt in his mouth – I could see what was wrong from his point of view. He had probably lost sight of me for the moment, saw this Hun, and thought: Hah, here we go – and he went! Whereas, really, he should have been keeping his eye on me, seeing where I was. But nevertheless, it happened.

"He landed back in our lines and reckoned he had been hit by flak. But I knew what had happened to me. I was out of balance. The whole plane nearly shook to pieces. I had to throttle back immediately. The motor kept going at very few revs and I was only at 1,500 feet, right over the battle line, and I think everything in the creation of cats fired at me.

"The tracer was so heavy. In failing light they thought I was a sitting duck. But I was going so slow that not a one hit me.

"Anyhow, I had to do a 180-degree turn in the middle of this and get back into our own lines, or where I knew the land was occupied by our boys. And I had just enough power in a shaky form to carry out a regular wheels-up landing in, would you believe, a field of wheat in Tunisia. I never even knew it grew there! But I mowed down 30 feet of it in one fell swoop.

"I got out unharmed, and the first two on the job were two boys from Waihi. As far as I can remember they were Jack Cornthwaite and Ron Spiers. I was a bit shaken. I stopped the night with them, and the next morning I borrowed a spanner and took off my special little stub exhausts, which at the time were just coming into use. I got the first set and nobody else had them. So I took them off, put them in a sack, and arrived home by Army truck the following day."

And the record book duly noted, on 25 April, 1943: "As forecast, Flt Lt Mackie returned with his stub exhausts at 1600 hours." Rawlinson also noted that the New Zealander had jettisoned his oil-covered hood before landing near the headquarters of the 1st Armoured Division.

Although exasperated about being brought down by the actions of one of his own pilots, Mackie did not make a big thing of it. "I could see it from the other bloke's point of view. He, in all good faith, was firing away at this thing, and he was lucky to be able to get in and crash-land. But that's another of my lives which, like the old cat, well and truly went by the board."

Mackie was given a new Spitfire VC on his return, and the machine was promptly fitted with the stub exhausts. Rolls-Royce Merlin engines had by now developed a tremendous reputation among Allied aircrew for reliability, even under extreme conditions such as sometimes existed in North Africa. For instance, Mackie would fly his new Spitfire VC, serial JK715, coded SN-A, without a single falter from the engine, for the next 180 hours, almost up to its first major overhaul.

He once told his Tauranga fishing partner, Leo Quinn, that when he and his wingman were flying over an area of desert, they were 'jumped' by German aircraft. As Leo remembered it: "The wingman pushed his throttle through the gate and could not release it, although he was not supposed to use the engine on boost for more than 30 seconds. Evan told me that his wingman used up petrol for 90 minutes duration in 30 minutes, and finally landed his Spitfire 'deadstick' at their base airfield after running out of petrol. The engine was removed, stripped, and the engineers could find no discernible signs of wear, even though the Merlin had been running for 30 minutes on full boost. Evan said that gave the pilots even more confidence in the reliability of their machines."

Early on 26 April, eager to see how his new Spitfire performed, Mackie was up for a 20-minute cannon test. A Boston escort to Jebel Mansour at 7,000 feet followed and then, perhaps still not happy with the way his guns were calibrated, he made a second cannon test flight.

Mackie continued to place a great deal of importance on armament accuracy. He was convinced that the RAF gunnery courses were inadequate, and that more time and trouble should have been taken over teaching fighter pilots the finer points of deflection shooting. He would sometimes persuade a fellow pilot to fly out with him on practice sessions low over the desert, so that he could fire at the shadow cast by the other aircraft.

There was little more galling to Mackie than to have to write in his logbook: "Fired at Me 109 – saw no results." It is a tribute to the effectiveness of his constant self-improvement philosophy that the "Fired – no results" entries were made only nine times up to 10 September 1943. By then he would have claimed 12 enemy aircraft, so he had a more than even chance of scoring every time he fired at that stage. He was to do far better.

That 26 April in Tunisia ended for Mackie with a tactical reconnaissance escort south of Tunis at 10,000 feet, and a pep talk to the squadron by Air Commodore Cross*, who landed his personal Taylorcraft at Euston to discuss the Tunisian situation, which he estimated would be over within a fortnight. The ever-observant Rawlinson, with his almost Boswellian recording of squadron events, noted in the ORB: "Flt Lt Mackie, the strong man of the squadron, swings the AOC's prop and away he goes after a very short run."

Mackie's new Spitfire was blooded the very next day. He took part with 11 other pilots in a freelance sweep over the front. At 15,000 feet 18 Axis fighters were intercepted over Tunis, and six more east of Pont du Fahs. Mackie attacked two, seeing hits on one and getting a good burst into the cockpit of the other. It went down in flames, and was seen to crash south-east of Tebourba by his wingman, Sgt D.J. Schmitz, RCAF. It is believed that his victim was probably Uffz Heinz Hoffmann of I/JG 53, who baled out to become a POW.

> Up: 1125. Down: 1243. 27th April 1943.
> Aerodrome – Euston.

> The Squadron was patrolling east of Medjez at 9 to 10,000 ft when 18 bandits were reported near Tunis at 15,000 ft, and at the same time another 6 bandits were reported to be east of Pont du Fahs at the same height.

> Whilst orbitting S.E. of Medjez at 11,000 ft, Yellow 3 sighted and reported 6 A/C 2,000 ft below slightly west of us.

> I dived and attacked one Me 109 without seeing any results. I then attacked his No.2, using cannon and M/guns. After manoeuvring for a short time, I was able to fire a long burst from 200 yds closing to 150 yds, in a quarter astern attack.

> I saw strikes all around the cockpit, the E/A rolled over on its back and I saw it crash approx. 6 miles S.E. of Tebourba, and burst into flames.

> Claim: 1 Me 109 destroyed.

> Sgt Schmitz, Flt Lt Mackie's No.2, saw the Me 109 in flames before it crashed. He also saw it hit the ground.

---

* (See autobiography *Straight and Level* by Air Chief Marshal Sir Kenneth 'Bing' Cross, KCB, CBE, DSO, DFC, with Professor Vincent Orange; Grub Street, 1993.)

Mackie recalls: "From this point onwards the tempo was on the increase as the German forces became more or less bottle-necked in the Cap Bon peninsula and nearby area, with the 8th Army and the First Army converging on them.

"On 28 April, on a freelance sweep at 9,000 feet I damaged another Me 109 and fired at two others – saw no results."

Up: 0819. Down: 1000 hrs. 28th April 1943.
Aerodrome: Euston.

During a sweep over Medjez-Pont du Fahs, 20+ Me 109s were intercepted S.W. of Tunis at heights varying from 9-12,000 ft.
  During the engagement I fired at three different 109s.
  After firing a burst using cannon at the first 109 from 200 yds range, Sgt Payne, my No.2, saw strikes on the tail unit.

Claim: 1 Me 109 damaged.

"On 29th we fitted long-range tanks and did a long-range channel sweep outside Tunis Bay, because it was known at that time that the Germans were starting to evacuate the peninsula both by sea and air.

"Some of the squadrons were very fortunate in encountering transport aircraft obviously evacuating key personnel, and of course they were just decimated."

It was the first time that the squadron had flown with the 30-gallon overload tanks. The last pilot to land had been up for two hours 58 minutes, and fuel remaining varied between ten and 31 gallons. Jettisoning of the tanks went without a hitch.

Evidence of the pilots' keeness in 243 was indicated by expressions of exasperation on 29 April, when Marauder bombers which the squadron was airborne to escort, failed to rendezvous – "A waste of time, petrol and everything else!"

Rawlinson was in top form describing the events of 30 April. The day began on a down beat, when he recorded: "Nearly 100 per cent of ground crew personnel today suffering the unpleasant after-effects of taking mepacrine tablets." But then things improved: "Three rings on the Ops phone – the AOC, Air Commodore Cross, wishes to speak to Sqn Ldr Walker. The CO is not available. Could the AOC speak to Flt Lt Mackie? He is still airborne. (He is actually away on his second sortie of the day, cover for a shipping reconnaissance at 14,000 feet over Cap Serrat/Bizerta.) Will he ring the AOC when he lands? We suspect the inevitable.

"When Flt Lt Mackie picks up the phone it is to receive the AOC's congratulations on being awarded the DFC. Good show, Mackie! We adjourn to the bar to celebrate the first DFC earned in the squadron. During the evening many guests arrive to offer congratulations and drink his health – Wg Cdr Dundas, Sqn Ldr Wilf Sizer* of 93 Squadron, the CO of 72 Squadron (Sqn Ldr Daniel*), Flt Lt 'Butch' Lyons, New Zealand friends of Mackie and so on.

"The month closes with the squadron totals – 21 destroyed, 8 probably destroyed, 27 damaged."

Mackie's DFC was awarded effective from 28 April 1943, and back in New Zealand the press made the most of it, publishing the citation and his photograph. "Flying Officer Mackie set a courageous inspiring example in the North African operations and showed himself to be a skilful leader possessed of great tenacity. He has a tally of five enemy aircraft destroyed, four of them within 11 days in April, 1943."

Another contemporary newspaper account touched on his forced landing: "Mackie had a lucky escape when he collided over the enemy lines, but he managed to 'stagger back' and spent a night with the 8th Army. It was a narrow escape." The account also referred to his previous service with 485 Squadron: "He was always regarded as one of its best pilots. His physical fitness was a byword. The squadron is delighted to hear of his success."

Mackie was very happy with 243 Squadron, revelling in its cosmopolitan character, which he considered to be far more effective than single-nationality squadrons: "The CO was Canadian, there were three New Zealanders, there was another Canadian, there was an Argentinian, British, Scots, and possibly one or two others I can't think of at the moment. It was the happiest squadron I had ever been on.

"After being on the New Zealand squadron (485) I realised, looking back, that it's not the best combination. We'd got so much friendly rivalry and chiaking amongst the different nationalities on this squadron that it really made it. There were never any arguments – it was all good fun type of thing. A very good spirit. A great competitive spirit. Which is really what made the Air Force – the spirit of competition where you tried to do better than another squadron or another individual.

"If it wasn't for that and the recognition you got for it in the way of decorations etcetera, I don't think it would have been what it was. It had its place, all that sort of thing, in creating competition, spirit." He added that, while he did not want to be critical of 485 Squadron, it had tended to be "cliquey". "I've heard it said that the Canadian ones, and other ones, tended to get in their own group and try and

---

* (Wg Cdr W.M. Sizer, DFC & Bar; see *Aces High*, pages 549-50); (Sqn Ldr S.W. Daniel, DFC & Bar; see *Aces High*, pages 208-9).

remain that way. Whereas in these mixed squadrons everyone was equal.

"The Group Captain (George Gilroy) was a Scot, a real Scot. 'Cocky' Dundas (the Wing Commander Flying) was a typical English boarding school boy, you know, cricket and that type of thing – but oh, we had a lot of fun."

Flg Off Rawlinson, writing up the ORB on 5 May, sets the scene for the final push to defeat the German and Italian armies in North Africa. "Escape-aid boxes for all pilots arrive. Squadron on Boston escorts. In the morning the CO addresses a few quiet words to those present in the officers' mess. The final big assault is to commence at dawn tomorrow. The programme is amended – the bombers, with fighter escort, are to blast a way for the Army.

"Dawn readiness for us. By 0500 hours the IO (Intelligence Officer), EO (Engineering Officer) and the Adjutant are at dispersal. Pilots and crews, as usual, have been there some time already. We watch the sun rise – a beautiful morning – our task is to escort Bostons – this we do all day. No Bostons are lost – all our aircraft return safely.

"We try to visualise the effect this continuous bombing will have on the enemy. How long, we ask ourselves, will he be able to stand the strain? A few days hence and Tunis may be in our hands. Of one thing we feel certain – that the Hun will never be able to evacuate his troops as we did at Dunkirk."

By the end of that long day the squadron had successfully escorted six bombing missions. Gilroy, as always, led by example and headed the six aircraft of 'B' Flight on one escort.

Air Chief Marshal Tedder, the Air Commander-in-Chief, Mediterranean, noted that his forces flew a total of 2,000 sorties that day. During one of them Mackie's aircraft developed flap trouble and he landed at Paddington airstrip to have it adjusted before returning to Euston.

It was at this stage of the battle that the forward control concept, fine-tuned by the Americans to integrate air strikes closely with ground attacks, came into its own. The bomb-line was shifting so rapidly as the Allied troops moved forward that the squadrons were warned of the fact while still airborne.

Mackie was full of admiration for the precision of the ground/air co-operation: "They were all American troops and they had a forward control unit, a mobile van, which was right on the job. And he was invaluable. He was an ex-flying man normally, who would tell us, warn us, of any aircraft which were in sight, which way they were going, etcetera. The unit was even able to ask the squadron to do particular jobs, like 'beat up that house over there', a certain house that was giving trouble, or some strongpoint."

At 1010 am on 7 May news that Tunis had fallen reached the squadron, which then learned that Tebourba had been captured and that the Americans had taken Ferryville and were attacking Bizerta.

Later that day a sweep over Tunis and Bizerta at 10,000 feet was planned, but the names of Mackie and Sgt Day were missing from the 12 pilots on the operations board. Mackie had already flown a sweep at 16,000 feet over the battlefront, and a Mitchell escort over Tunis Bay that day, but he was still keen to go. Rawlinson recorded: "12 aircraft plus Flt Lt Mackie and Sgt Day (Jack 'Ferdi' Day), who ask to be allowed to fly so as to get in one more smack at the Hun before it is too late, are airborne to strafe the beaches at Protville. One small single-funnelled boat at K0585 on the beach well and truly strafed, three persons aboard being killed." Mackie logged himself as one of those involved: "Shot up small ship."

He added decisively to his score the following day: "On 8 May I destroyed an Me 109 which had just shot down one of our aircraft. Unfortunately I was unable to warn the pilot that he was being fired at. He was intent on firing at a Hun. There was another Hun intent on firing at him, and he set him alight, and that's when I saw him. So although I promptly dealt with that 109 in the appropriate manner it seemed like the score was just about even." The crash was verified by his No.2, Sgt Eddie East.

Up: 1305. Down: 1454. 8th May, 1943.
Aerodrome: Euston.

The Squadron was patrolling at about 11,000 ft over Cap Bon Peninsula, Me 109's were reported below. Yellow section was ordered to go down and intercept.

As Yellow 1 I first saw one Me 109 flying west across the road near K7383. My section lost height going out to sea and then flew S.W. along the coast, keeping 5 Me 109's in sight.

When approaching the sands at K3572 I was flying at 1,000 ft and saw 2 Spitfires to port, overshooting me, and presumed it was Yellow 3 and 4.

I saw Yellow 3 (P/O McKay) open fire at an Me 109 which crashed in flames in the hills at K5368 from a height of 200 ft. At the same time I saw a 109 attack Yellow 3 from port. Before there was time to warn him that he was being attacked his a/c was aflame. The port wing blew off, the Spitfire crashing in flames from a height of 100 ft in the same area.

I closed in on this Me 109, opened fire from astern at a range of 100 yds and saw the 109 crash near the K5368. My No.2, Sgt East, also saw this e/a crash.

I chased another Me 109 out to sea but was unable to draw within range.

Claim: 1 Me 109 destroyed.

Rawlinson recorded that in fact the squadron did a little better than even – actually getting three for two: "Sgt East . . . also saw one of our pilots send another Me 109 crashing into the ground in the same area. The pilot, whom we are almost certain was Plt Off MacKay (*sic* – G.O. McKay, a Canadian recently commissioned) was himself shot down in flames almost immediately afterwards from a height of 100 feet by another Me 109. Flg Off (Michael) Graham damaged a 109 which was finished off by Flg Off Bishop as it got on the tail of a Spitfire and shot it down. We can only assume that this was Sgt (V.O.) Young.

"Three 109s were destroyed, but Plt Off McKay and Sgt Young did not return.

"Outside dispersal Reginald Forsythe entertained us at the piano with sweet music – the sun shone brilliantly – a lovely day – but uppermost in our minds was the fact that two of our pilots were missing and one would never return."

"Taking it all round our losses were very low," said Mackie. "We continued to harass those evacuating troops right up to the day it was considered the North African campaign had been completed, in other words, 10 May. We used long-range tanks and patrolled the area outside Tunis Bay in the hope of catching more transport aircraft. Unfortunately, we did not."

Operational flying from Euston airfield ceased after 11 May, and next day a ground party moved off to Le Sebala II, an airfield about eight miles north-west of Tunis, where the squadron would next establish itself.

On 13 May the last groups of Axis troops gave up the fight. General von Arnim, who had replaced Rommel as the leader of the German forces in North Africa, surrendered 238,000 of his troops, German and Italian.

Sqn Ldr Walker and Flt Lt Porteous visited Le Sebala II, which was still under construction, on 14 May. Satisfied that arrangements for the squadron were satisfactory, they drove into Tunis in their Hillman car, left it unattended for a few seconds, and returned to find it stolen!

There was a 'liberty run' into Tunis that day for most of the squadron, according to the Operations Book: "Cars and motorcycles in various states of disrepair began to appear on the camp site. Trophies of this campaign are eagerly sought after by many: German helmets, rifles and badges being popular acquisitions."

By 16 May the squadron, complete with ground staff and its 13 Spitfire VCs, was established at Le Sebala II. Operational patrols, mostly coastal, began the next day, and on 20th the squadron took part in a victory flypast over Tunis – 12 aircraft, plus Sqn Ldr Walker and Flt Lts Mackie and Porteous, at 800 feet.

Another move, 15 miles to the north-east, saw the squadron ensconced on Mateur airfield, south of Bizerta, on 25 May. Pilots prepared to go on leave, mostly to the aircrew rest camp at Tabarka. Meanwhile at Mateur the squadron headquarters staff began preparations for the next campaign. A new staffing establishment was introduced, reducing the strength of the unit to 189 personnel; aircraft were given a new grey/olive green camouflage and trucks were loaded and re-loaded.

"In short, the squadron is being prepared to move at short notice, whither we know not," notes Rawlinson. "Not many of us will be sorry to shake the dust of North Africa from our feet forever."

The signing of war risk insurance forms for officers' kit indicated that a journey over the sea was imminent. On 1 June Sqn Ldr Walker, Flt Lts Mackie and Porteous, and Flg Offs Graham, MacDonald and Rawlinson travelled to Grombalia to hear Prime Minister Winston Churchill and Foreign Secretary Anthony Eden speak to the RAF.

Rawlinson faithfully recorded the event: "An audience composed of personnel from the fighting forces listened intently to speeches by the two politicians, who were accompanied by Air Chief Marshal Tedder and AVM Coningham.

"The PM's four-engined three-finned aircraft excited considerable attention. We learned that it was a 'York', evidently a combination of a Lancaster, Manchester and a Flamingo. Sumptuously furnished, it took off soon after the meeting dispersed. Rumour had it that it was to fly non-stop to the UK."

News on 1 June that Sqn Ldr Walker, Flt Lt Porteous and Flg Off Graham were to be taken off operations caused a stir throughout the squadron, wrote Rawlinson: "Flt Lt E.D. Mackie, DFC, becomes our new CO. Flg Off MacDonald becomes 'A' Flight commander, Flt Lt G.E. Gruwys taking over 'B' Flight." (Eddie Gruwys joined the squadron that day.) "Farewells are said in both officers' and sergeants' messes, Wg Cdr Gilroy in the officers' mess in great form."

Things were beginning to go the way Gilroy wanted them in 324 Wing: "I couldn't rely 100 percent on the original intake, but chaps came to us like Mackie and Monty Rose* of Malta, on whom you could rely 100 percent and so you kept an eye on them.

"Conditions were fairly tough and some squadron commanders

---

* (Flt Lt E.B. Mortimer-Rose, DFC & Bar; see *Aces High*, page 453.)

Cdr E.D.Mackie, DSO, DFC & Bar, DFC (US).

Top left and right: Robert and Katherine Mackie, Evan's parents.

Above: Although dating from about 1950, this photograph of Waihi depicts the town's main street much as it was in Evan Mackie's formative years during the 1930s.

Top left: Evan Mackie's expertise in photography has him about to give himself and pet cat a ride in the family wheelbarrow.

Top right: 41520 LAC Mackie, E.D. at the commencement of his flying training at 4 Elementary Flying Training School, Whenuapai, Auckland, in March 1941.

Middle: Evan's pride and joy in 1938 was his new Standard 8, purchased from Reg Willis on Waihi's main street.

Bottom: Passing-out parade at 4 EFTS, Whenuapai, in June 1941. Evan Mackie is in the second rank, immediately behind the Sergeant, and in the front left centre of the photo.

32 Service Flying Training School, Moose Jaw, Canada, in summer 1941. Evan Mackie is seen here with one of the school's North American Harvard advanced trainers, in, on, and in front of the aircraft

Top: Aviation cadets hard at their studies at 32 SFTS. Evan Mackie (left) is seated with his friend, G.E.'Bill' Jameson, later to become the RNZAF's top-scoring night fighter pilot.

Above: No.12 Course at 58 Operational Training Unit, Grangemouth, Scotland, in autumn 1941. The names indicate a high proportion of Free European graduate pilots – Poles and Czechs in the main. Back row from left: Sergeants Aldcorn, Bentley, Eby, Etienne, Ballantyne, Seifert, Lipinski, Gardner, Ford, Jaworowski, Beyer, Pegrum, Gretkifrewicz, G.R.Smith; Centre row: Sergeants Napier, Jones, Mount, Novak, Baycroft, Piercy, Holmes, Buettel, Szwaba, Stryjecki, Reid, Sullivan; Front row: Pilot Officers Duggan, Sly, L.R.G.Smith, C.D.A.Smith, Mathieson, Coldbeck, Muszel, Tomanek, Sawirk, Kowalski, Mackie, Mears. Sly, immediately identifiable in his dark blue Royal Australian Air Force uniform, would be killed on 8 May 1942 as a Flt Lt, when leading a reinforcement flight of Spitfires into Malta. Jim Ballantyne, RCAF, also served on Malta in 1942, where he claimed five and one shared victories. He was killed in action by flak over France on 8 March 1944.

Left: Evan Mackie practising Morse code at 32 SFTS.

Top left: Almost operational! Pilot Officer E.D.Mackie in his new officer's uniform, resplendent with the coveted 'Wings' badge.

Top right: Evan Mackie in the cockpit of his Spitfire VB whilst with 485 (New Zealand) Squadron a Kenley, in early 1942. The aircraft has a rose painted beneath the windshield.

Above: Some of the notable New Zealand pilots serving with 485 Squadron at the time of the 'Channel Dash' operation in February 1942. L to r: Harvey Sweetman, David Clouston, B.E.Gibbs, Reg Grant (7.5 victories), M.Shand (almost hidden), E.P.'Hawkeye' Wells (12 victories), I.McNeil, Bill Crawford-Compton (20.5 victories), Johnny Checketts (14 victories) and R.W.Baker. All apart from Baker survived the war.

p left: A 'readiness' section newly-returned from a sortie are met by other members of the unit and a number of admin officers. In the background is a presentation Spitfire VB, 'Auckland I'. Pilots are, m the left: D.G.E.Brown, A.R.Robson, J.J.Palmer, T.C.Goodlet, Bill Crawford-Compton, Stan Browne rtly hidden behind Crawford-Compton's left shoulder), four non-fliers, and n A.G.Shaw, Evan Mackie and H.R.Leckie.

(Sport & General via Mackie family)

p right: 'B' Flight, 485 Squadron, Kenley, spring 1942. L to r, standing: Sgt Jack Rae, Sgt A.G. w, unidentified, unidentified, Flt Lt Bill Crawford-Compton, Plt Off Evan Mackie; kneeling: Sgt j.E.Brown, Plt Off David Clouston.

(Sport & General via Mackie family)

ove: 485 Squadron disperal hut at Kenley. Seated, Marty Hume (left) and L.P.Griffith; standing, from left: Evan Mackie, A.R.Robson and J.J.Palmer.

Top: HM King George VI visits 485 Squadron at Kenley on 29 April 1942. L to r, in 'Mae West' life jackets, being interviewed by the King, are Stan Browne, B.E.Gibbs, J.R.C.Kilian and Evan Mackie.

(Associated Press via Mackie fam.

Above left: Stanley Browne served with Evan Mackie in 485 Squadron in 1942, until shot down over France on 31 May. He evaded capture and is seen here after his return to the squadron at the end of the year. Like Mackie, he then went out to North Africa, where he served with 93 Squadron during the spring of 1943. He returned to 485 Squadron late in the war as commanding officer.

(Sport & General via Mackie fam.

Above right: On 5 December 1943 Evan Mackie and Lt Albert Sachs, SAAF, claimed three Messerschmitt Bf 109s shot down. Two of these were credited to Sachs, who then collided with a Focke Wulf FW 190 and had to bale out. Sachs is seen here with his replacement Spitfire VIII, on which the triangular 92 Squadron badge can be seen on the cowling side, ahead of the cockpit.

(Imperial War Muse

p left: Two views of Spitfire VC SN-A, JK715, in which Evan Mackie accomplished 180 flying hours ween mid April and October 1943 with 243 Squadron, and in which he claimed eight of his victories.

p right: Sent off in time for Christmas, 1943, from 243 Squadron, this greeting was overtaken by nts, for by December Evan Mackie had already been gone from the unit for two months.

ve: The team who Evan Mackie joined on reaching 244 Wing in late October 1943. L to r: Sqn Ldr Turner, 417 (RCAF) Squadron – soon to become Wing Leader, Sqn Ldr P.H.'Hunk' Humphreys, Mackie would replace as CO of 92 Squadron, Wg Cdr W.G.G.Duncan-Smith, Wing Commander ing) – about to depart to command 324 Wing, Grp Capt Brian Kingcome, commanding officer of Wing, Sqn Ldr Lance Wade, 145 Squadron, and Major M.'Manny' Osler, 1 SAAF Squadron.

(Imperial War Museum)

Top: Sqn Ldr Mackie (seated centre) with pilots of 80 Squadron in front of the unit's dispersal hut at Volkel in spring 1945. A propeller blade above the door advertises the venue as 'Spud's Speakeasy'; 'Spud' was Mackie's predecessor, Sqn Ldr R.L. 'Spud' Spurdle.

Middle: 80 Squadron's mighty Hawker Tempest Vs on patrol.

Bottom left: Evan Mackie banks his Tempest W2-A, to lead his section down to investigate a possible target.

Bottom right: On 9 April 1945, 80 Squadron caught a number of Arado Ar 96 trainers in the circuit a Fassberg airfield, identifying them incorrectly at the time as Messerschmitt Bf 108 liaison aircraft. The were shot down, two of them by Evan Mackie; the second of these is seen under attack, as recorde by his gun camera.

Top: Evan Mackie's gun camera records a typical attack on MET – Motorised Enemy Transport.

Above left: The Wing Leader's personal aircraft. This is Evan Mackie's Tempest V, carrying his initials EDM, seen shortly after VE Day, 8 May 1945. The aircraft was SN228, which carried the crest of 122 Wing at the top of the tail fin, a Wing Commander's pennant, and 25 victory crosses on the cowling ahead of the cockpit.

Above right: Evan Mackie as Wing Commander (Flying), 122 Wing, with his Tempest V carrying his initials in May 1945.

Left: The splendid Mackie physique is demonstrated during a welcome brief leave in Cannes, South of France, in early June 1945.

Top left: The German yacht *Ryhr*, in which Evan Mackie and Pat Jameson spent many happy hours sailing whilst based at Kastrup, Denmark.

Top right: Evan Mackie on the foredeck of *Ryhr* in Copenhagen harbour, early summer 1945.

Above: Pat Jameson, relaxing on *Ryhr*, shows in his face the strains of a long, hard personal war, which included surviving the sinking of the aircraft carrier HMS *Glorious* five years earlier in June 194

Top: Wg Cdr Evan Mackie weds Sgt Marjorie Dear, WAAF, at Garston, near Watford, Hertfordshire, on 18 February 1946.

Above: At her new home in New Zealand, Marjorie Mackie poses with the still-pristine Standard 8 in early 1947.

Left: Evan and Marjorie Mackie with son Brian in the early 1950s, at home in Otorohanga.

Top: One of 92 Squadron's Spitfire VIIIs, this one JF476, QJ-D. The squadron badge can clearly be seen on the nose. The unit code letters are painted in a dark colour, while the individual aircraft le is in white. *(Imperial War Muse*

Middle left: Sqn Ldr Evan 'Rosie' Mackie at the height of his success, seen here with Spitfire VIIIs his 92 Squadron. *(Crown Copyright via Mackie fa.*

Middle right: New Year 1943-1944 in 92 Squadron was also marked with a unit-produced card.

Bottom: Mackie (fifth from left, front row) with his pilots of 92 Squadron in early 1944. Second fro left, leaning on the wing, is the very successful Canadian flight commander, J.F.'Stocky' Edwards. *(via Cedric Y*

Top: A group of pilots of 122 Wing with a Hawker Tempest V at Volkel, Christmas 1944. In front of aircraft, from 6th left, are Sqn Ldr K.F.Thiele, 3 Squadron, Sqn Ldr A.E.Umbers, 486 (NZ) Squadron, Sqn Ldr E.D.Mackie, 274 Squadron (supernumary), Flt Lt H.A.Crafts, 274 Squadron and Sqn Ldr R.F. Wardle, 80 Squadron.

Above left: Squadron commanders at Volkel with their Wing commanding officer, winter 1944/45. L to r: Sqn Ldr Evan Mackie, 80 Squadron, Sqn Ldr K.F.Thiele (an ex-bomber pilot with DSO, DFC & Bar) 3 Squadron, Grp Capt 'Pat' Jameson, 122 Wing, Sqn Ldr D.E.'Spike' Umbers, 486 (NZ) Squadron.

Above right: 122 Wing's Wing Commander (Flying), R.E.P.'Boy' Brooker. Evan Mackie would take over this officer's role, following Brooker's loss in combat late in the war.

Top left: "Just another fishing trip!" Evan Mackie and his regular fishing partner, Leo Quinn, are seen here in 1983 or thereabouts. Evan holds an 89lb 14oz yellowtail kingfish, whilst Leo demonstrates another of a 'mere' 39lb 13oz.

Top right: The competition never had a chance, as Evan and Leo share a cheque for $200 for catching the heaviest fish in one of the contests they entered.

Right: One of the last photos of Evan Mackie before his death from cancer in Tauranga Hospital on 28 April 1986.

couldn't cope. Mackie was so keen and popular I promoted him. He was a chap I knew I could depend on. Ultimately I managed to get all the squadrons commanded by chaps who were reliable," he recalled.

The same day that Mackie was promoted to the command of 243 Squadron, another New Zealander in 324's sister Wing, 322, was promoted Wing Commander, Flying. He was Colin Gray*, formerly CO of 81 Squadron. Gray, already one of the highest scorers in the RAF with 22½ confirmed victories, would go on to take his total to 27½.

Early in June Grp Capt Piet Hugo (322 Wing), Colin Gray and 'Sheep' Gilroy (who had just been promoted as Grp Capt also) flew from Tunisia to Malta, which had now been revealed as the next base for 242 Group elements.

As Gray related in his book *Spitfire Patrol*: "We landed at the main airfield, Luqa, and were met by the Air Officer Commanding, who was none other than Air Vice-Marshal Sir Keith Park*, the previous commander of 11 Group in Fighter Command during the Battle of Britain. Sir Keith insisted on personally driving us around his parish in his red MG, and we were most impressed by his efficiency and his knowledge of everything that was going on." Park, a New Zealander, made his fellow countryman particularly welcome and personally showed the wing leaders their respective new homes. Some of Gilroy's 324 Wing would be based on Hal Far airfield and Hugo's 322 Wing on Takali.

---

* (Wg Cdr C.F. Gray, DSO, DFC & 2 Bars; *see Aces High*, pages 298-9); (Air Chief Marshal Sir Keith Park, GCB, KBE, MC, DFC, DCL; see *Above the Trenches*, pages 296-7).

CHAPTER SIX

SICILY AND ITALY – 243 SQUADRON

On 5 June 1943, 243 Squadron's ground staff left Mateur and headed south towards Sfax, a port about 150 miles south of Tunis, from where they would sail to Malta. The squadron camped that night at 2030, after covering 160 miles, moving on next day to camp five miles outside Sfax. All motor transport was loaded on ships the following day, and on 8 June squadron personnel boarded LST 401 – motto: "Anytime, anywhere, any place." While the ground component of the squadron was on the move, the pilots camped on the beach at La Marsa, spending most of the time swimming and sunbathing. Ground personnel disembarked at Malta on 9 June and set up shop at Camp 25 on Hal Far airfield. 243 Squadron aircraft arrived on the island fortress in spectacular manner two days later, when Plt Off Mervyn Burke, a Tasmanian, undershot on landing. His Spitfire crashed into stone walls, somersaulting and disintegrating, leaving its occupant with severe head injuries. Two months later Burke would rejoin the squadron, fit and well.

Hal Far airfield was at the south-east corner of the island, almost on Malta's south coast, and about five miles due south of Valetta, the capital. Luqa (or Luca) airfield lay on high ground a mile or so inland from Hal Far, overlooking the Grand Harbour and the Three Cities. The third important airfield, Takali, was on a cultivated plain between Rabat, the ancient Maltese capital, and Valetta. One of the most remarkable dispersal strips ever devised had been created originally as a link between the airfields at Luqa and Hal Far. Famous among all who served on Malta as the 'Safi Strip', it was a track winding through the grey rock, small terraced fields, carob trees and scrub. Many tons of bombs were dropped on the strip, and it was often considered an adventure to travel the length of it unless guided by someone who knew all the shelter holes.

The two Spitfire wings had now left Air Cdr 'Bing' Cross's 242 Group and transferred to the Desert Air Force under Air Vice-

Marshal Harry Broadhurst*. Very experienced in tactical operations, Broadhurst had led his Western Desert Air Force in support of the 8th Army through the Libyan and Tunisian campaigns. (Retitled Desert Air Force, it remained a part of the North-West African Tactical Air Force – itself soon to be renamed Mediterranean Allied Tactical Air Force – under Coningham's command).

Reminiscing about the transfer of command, Gilroy recalled Broadhurst asking Mackie, when he first met him on Malta, how he liked being in the Desert Air Force. Mackie's laconic reply (after two months in Tunisia) was; "Oh, I'm no snob, Sir!"

Mackie certainly appreciated Malta following his Tunisian experiences: "After the primitive living conditions in North Africa, in other words, the excessive heat, and I mean excessive heat, the dust, the flies, the tucker – which was quite palatable, but we didn't see bread the whole time we were there, it was all biscuits, hard tack, tins, meat and veg and the like – lack of water. Not that we complained. We all took it in good part.

"But getting to Malta and into those cool stone, concrete or whatever they were, buildings – there seemed to be an abundance of nice fresh water, and the coolness and cleanliness of the place. It was a real pleasure to sit down to a meal in a mess with no flies and things like that, with the Maltese staff waiting in the mess. I really enjoyed the few weeks that we had there."

It needs perhaps to be added that conditions had resumed this comfortable level only very recently. During the siege period, which ended only at the start of 1943, conditions had frequently been as primitive, and food very much shorter than it had been in North Africa.

The new theatre brought a change of tactics: "We had to alter our tactics completely because we were over enemy territory for one thing, and we had rather a large stretch of water to get back across if anything did happen to us," said Mackie. "In other words, we, approaching Sicily, would be at least at 20,000 feet to 25,000 feet in the hope of catching them either coming up to catch us, or to see something below."

Sir Keith Park lost no time in making it clear to the Wing's personnel that top-class maintenance of all mechanical and ancillary equipment was vital for their new over-water role. Within hours of 324 Wing's aircraft landing, he had pilots and ground staff assembled in a cinema to congratulate them on their success in Tunisia. Rawlinson recorded: "He goes on to impress us all with the

---

* (Air Vice-Marshal H. Broadhurst, DSO & Bar, DFC & Bar, AFC; see *Aces High*, pages 150-1.)

importance of keeping all equipment in 100 percent serviceable condition. Guns, dinghies, parachutes, compasses, radio sets, engines must be on the top line. He declares that the Malta air-sea rescue service is the best in the Empire. We sincerely hope that it is."

13 June was spent swinging compasses, testing cannons and repairing 'Mae West' life jackets. Dusk landings and night flying ended at midnight without incidents. On 16th, 12 aircraft went out on the squadron's first operational patrol from Hal Far – and Sir Keith would not have been impressed when he was told that two of them returned with engine trouble.

18 June saw Mackie involved, unsuccessfully, in an attempted air-sea rescue. He observed an Allied pilot climbing into his dinghy ten to 15 miles south of Palazzollo, Sicily, orbited and gave Malta Control a 'fix'. Later he and Sqn Ldr Boddington* (242 Squadron) led eight aircraft out and again found the dinghy. They orbited at heights varying between 100 feet and 3,000 feet, the pilot waving and appearing unhurt. The ORB notes that the pilot was not able to fire signal distress cartridges "but, with the use of flurescine, pilots were able to keep him in sight much more easily. Four other aircraft relieved us on patrol." Mackie and Boddington set out once more to locate the dinghy, Mackie carrying with him a spare 'Mae West' with an additional supply of signal cartridges – but they failed to locate it.

"With all the white horses, it was probably a fluke that I saw him at all," said Mackie. "The dinghies were yellow, but they were only a pinpoint when you were looking at them from a few thousand feet. However, that's the fortunes of war."

At this point Rawlinson confirmed Mackie's score as seven destroyed, one probably destroyed and two and a half damaged. Mackie commented: "I was never a great one for claiming probables and damaged. You either got them or you didn't. As far as a probable was concerned, it was a bit of an unknown quantity and I can't see much place for them in the records."

It was undoubtedly "best bib and tucker" for all the squadron personnel on 20 June when the top brass called. Rawlinson, in the ORB noted: "From 1050 to 1130, ACM Tedder and AVM Park were with us at dispersal. Various points of interest were discussed, the ACM being careful not to reveal plans of future operations, at the same time being greatly interested in our surmises as to where we would strike next. On their departure, AVM Park complimented the squadron on the appearance and layout of material at dispersal."

The next visitor was of even greater rank. "At 1730, HM the King drove through the aerodrome. Those who were able lined the

---

* (Sqn Ldr M.C.B. Boddington, DFC, DFM; see *Aces High*, pages 135-6.)

perimeter track, giving three rousing cheers as His Majesty passed by." King George VI took the opportunity of his Malta visit to invest Park with the insignia of the KBE, which he had been awarded the previous November.

Next day the first of 243 Squadron's Spitfire IXs was received from 72 Squadron. Mackie flew a 40-minute air-test in one on 30 June, and was up twice in a Mark IX on 2 July (a scramble from which he was recalled after ten minutes, and a 60-minute patrol north of Malta at 20,000 feet), but he then reverted to his tried and trusted Mark VC, SN-A.

23 June saw the squadron's pilots attending a demonstration on the re-arming of Spitfire VCs and IXs, on the CO's instructions. Armourers explained in detail the finer points of cannon and machine guns, and the pilots then re-armed the aircraft themselves. 'B' Flight pilots were instructed to re-fuel and re-arm their own aircraft for a week, on landing from practice flights.

Involving the pilots with servicing normally carried out by the erks was typical of Mackie, whose philosophy was that a pilot should understand precisely how his aircraft functioned. He believed that a pilot who understood the mechanics of aircraft had a better chance of coping with a malfunction. And, with a typical Kiwi disregard for 'side', he probably also did it deliberately to get the pilots and the ground staff, normally separated in different messes, working alongside each other to enhance squadron camaraderie.

Throughout his RNZAF service, Mackie was forever conscious that his social background was much more basic than those with whom he was forced to mix as he was promoted. In the air he could more than hold his own with all who flew with him, but social occasions like wing and group dinners pointed up the fact that most of his fellow officers came from what the English called the 'middle' or 'upper' classes – and that by English standards, the man whose family lived in a miner's cottage in Waihi was definitely 'working' or 'lower' class. Without doubt, the distinction was felt much more by Mackie than by the officers in the units in which he served. It was, nevertheless, to be one of his principal reasons for deciding not to accept the permanent RAF/RNZAF career offered to him at the end of the war.

With his technical working class background, he had a natural empathy and rapport with his squadron's erks, the technical ground staff on whose mechanical expertise the pilots relied so totally. He appreciated that without their skills, 243 Squadron could never have achieved its record – and he was determined that all his pilots should appreciate that too. Hence, pilots would re-arm their own aircraft!

Visits by top brass were not over. On 24 June the officers and airmen of 243 and 72 Squadrons assembled near the windsock on Hal

Far to hear an address by Sir Archibald Sinclair, the Secretary of State for Air. "On behalf of His Majesty's Government, we were thanked for our services in North Africa," Rawlinson recorded.

Three days off operational flying followed, and pilots occupied themselves by cleaning and polishing their aircraft. The pilots were also photographed in civilian clothes, in the hope that the 'snaps' would be useful for creation of false identity cards to facilitate escape, should they be unfortunate enough to be shot down over enemy territory.

After the squadron had flown bomber cover over Comiso airfield, Sicily, on 29 June, the pilots returned to news that seven bags of mail were on their way that day. "The effect is most noticeable," wrote Rawlinson. "Spirits rise, conversation becomes animated, a general feeling of satisfaction is apparent as soon as mail is distributed and devoured. There can be no doubt as to the tremendous effect on morale that news from home has on the squadron. The more we get and the quicker we get it, the better for everyone."

The intelligence officer commented at this time that squadron personnel missed much by their enforced separation, due to accommodation difficulties. There were two officers' messes and two NCO's messes. In contrast to Mackie, who had welcomed the change of lifestyle on Malta, Rawlinson records that some officers found life in the home station style "a bit of a bind."

And so June came quietly to an end. The squadron had seen few enemy aircraft; the only major incident had been Burke's undershoot, and there was, Rawlinson noted, nothing much to report for the month. However, July was to be something else.

Operation 'Husky', the invasion of Sicily, had been the subject of intensive planning by General Dwight Eisenhower and the British commanders in the Mediterranean (Air Chief Marshal Tedder, General Alexander and Admiral Cunningham) during the past few weeks, and the balloon was about to go up.

Heartened by their success in subduing the Axis-held island of Pantelleria (150 miles north-west of Malta, mid-way between Sicily and Tunisia) solely by naval and aerial bombardment, the Allied leaders hoped to knock out the Luftwaffe and Regia Aeronautica on the Sicilian airfields and achieve air superiority before their troops landed. In fact, the subjugation of Pantelleria had been so successful that Eisenhower was already asking if something similar could be done about Sicily, leading Tedder to see the Pantellerian campaign "becoming a perfect curse to us in this manner."

The task of reducing the Sicilian airfields had begun on 15 June and continued steadily with raids by Allied heavy bombers. The last serious attempt by the Luftwaffe to interfere with Allied air operations occurred on 5 July. That day 243 Squadron had entered the fray in earnest: "Wg Cdr Dundas, briefing the squadron in dispersal, informs us that the 'show' starts today. Nine Mark VC and three Mark IX a/c provide cover over Catania while Fortresses operate. All a/c have 30-gallon overload tanks.

"As the Fortresses were turning to starboard out to sea, six Me 109s were met at 23,000 feet three miles N/W of Catania. A general dogfight ensued.

"Sqn Ldr Mackie's guns functioned intermittently, but he succeeded in setting one Me 109 on fire, and when chased by others dived out to sea and evaded them," the squadron intelligence officer recorded.

But that wasn't half the story, according to Mackie: "As so often happens in these mixed-up situations, one moment there are perhaps Spitfires and enemy aircraft all around you. The next minute you look around and you might not see an aircraft in the sky.

"In this particular case I looked around and all I could see were five or six 109s, all intent on my destruction. There wasn't a Spitfire in sight! I did all I could do, which was to keep turning, in very tight circles, to the point of stalling, knowing that the Spitfire will out-turn the 109. I also knew that a Spitfire could rarely out-dive a 109, but I had no options. I was maybe 100 miles from home, petrol running low, no other aircraft in the vicinity.

"Although I called the rest of my squadron I got no reply. In any case my attention was fully taken up in the evasion of the enemy aircraft – several of which fired at me, although I had no opportunity to fire at them. So I took the only alternative and did a power dive, twisting, turning, speed goodness knows what, terrific forces being exerted on the stick – I had to trim out from one manoeuvre to another on account of the speed."

Thus Mackie edged his way home from Mount Etna, over the water, in the general direction of Malta. "I got down to sea level with many sighs of relief and thought I would be right from there on, but to my amazement a line of bullets splashed in the sea, just off my port wing. Obviously a 109 had followed me down and fired at me when he was probably still out of trim and not following a true flight path. I turned, but I couldn't see anything, and I later found that he took to his scrapers from there on."

Mackie's low-level flight back to Malta was at first punctuated by huge splashes caused by big guns fired at him by the Axis coastal defences on Sicily. "I was trying to be as obscure as I could," he recalled. "I know I passed over a three-masted sailing ship and gave it a little peppering with .303 as I went over the top." He arrived safely back on Malta – in his own words: "One very relieved pilot."

In the dogfight Flg Off Banner also claimed a Bf 109, Flt Lt

MacDonald a probable, Flg Off S.I. Dalrymple a damaged, while Sgt D.J. Schmitz claimed damage to a Macchi MC 202. Mackie's combat report read:

> Up: 1010 hrs. Down: 1150 hrs. 4th July.
> Aerodrome: Hal Far, Malta.
>
> I was airborne at 10.12, and leading the Squadron to cover the area over Catania. As the Fortress bombers turned to starboard I saw approximately 6 Me 109s at 26,000 ft, which attacked myself and my No.2. After evasive action I found myself in a suitable position to attack a 109 which was approaching from starboard. I fired three deflection bursts, the last from approximately 70 yards range. I saw cannon and M/G strikes all over the cockpit and fuselage. The E/A immediately burst into flames. I last saw it at 25,000 ft going down vertically in flames with black smoke pouring from it.

> Claim: 1 Me 109 destroyed.

Mackie's victim may well have been Leutnant Herbert Broennle of II/JG 53, an Eastern Front Knight's Cross holder with 58 victories. His Bf 109 'Black 8' was damaged in combat with a Spitfire over the Catania area at this time, and as he attempted to return to base, the engine seized and he crashed vertically to his death. However, II/JG 77 and I/JG 53 also lost aircraft on this date, whilst 43, 111 and 126 Squadrons also made claims over Sicily during the day.

Mackie obviously had his eye in, and within little more than a week he would seize every opportunity offered him by German and Italian pilots to take his score more than half way towards its final total.

The next day, 5 July, Wg Cdr 'Cocky' Dundas and Mackie led seven Spitfires from 243, covering B-17s at 23,000 feet over Gerbini airfield. They encountered 20 Bf 109s at 24,000 feet and 30 more at 22,000 feet over the Ragusa area. The top layer of enemy aircraft made dive attacks, and Mackie was able to claim another 109 destroyed:

> Up: 1030 hrs. Down: 1210 hrs. 5th July.
> Aerodrome: Hal Far, Malta.
>
> Whilst Fortresses bombed Gerbini, the Squadron covered the area, being intercepted by 30+ Me 109's at 22,000 ft, 20 Me 109's at 24,000 ft, which approached from the S.E. as we neared Ragusa flying at 23,000 ft on a northerly course.

The top layer of Me 109's made diving attacks on the Squadron and a general melee resulted. Some time later I saw an Me 109, 6,000 ft below me flying N.W. I dived from 18,000 ft, closing to line astern and fired cannon from 100 yds range, breaking off to port to avoid collision. Just before I broke away I saw cannon strikes on the fuselage and wings. The E/A rolled on its back, and went down streaming glycol. I saw it crash and burst into flames just north of Palazzolo. F/Sgt Towgood, my No.2, also saw the 109 crash.

Claim: 1 Me 109 destroyed.

(Flt Sgt D.J.Towgood was a fellow New Zealander).

This was the only claim for a 109 by a Spitfire that day. III/JG 53 fought B-17s, P-38s and Spitfires and lost two aircraft, from one of which a Luftwaffe 'Experte', Oblt Franz Götz baled out. Stab and I/JG 53 also lost two Messerschmitts, reportedly to Spitfires, over Passero, and JG 77's Kommodore, Major Johannes Steinhoff, crash landed after being hit by a Spitfire.

According to Tedder, the big Luftwaffe fighter formations encountered by 243 over Ragusa were "the last serious attempt to interfere with our air operations . . . by D-Day, 10 July, the enemy did not have a single airfield in Sicily fully operational."

There seemed to be no end to the 'brass hats' visiting 243 Squadron. On 7 July Rawlinson recorded: "About half past three General Alexander, accompanied by AVM Park, visited dispersal, chatting pleasantly with our CO and other pilots."

Next day the squadron provided cover for 50 Liberators bombing Catania.

Shipping assembling at Malta had disappeared by the morning of 9 July: "Putting two and two together," wrote Rawlinson, "we surmised that 'The Day' had arrived." Eight of the squadron's Spitfires patrolled over a convoy, and the returning pilots reported three large and three small troopships. The squadron's last patrol over the invasion convoy returned to land in the dark at 2100 hours, and Mickey Payne recalled the pilots talking of hundreds of ships battling their way through stormy seas.

That night British and American airborne troops were parachuted onto key points in Sicily, and the next morning the seaborne invasion forces hit the beaches. With Mackie leading 'A' Flight and Grp Capt Gilroy leading 'B' Flight, 12 of the squadron's aircraft patrolled over shipping off Syracuse and in the Gulf of Noto – but some, including Gilroy, allowed enthusiasm for the job to override caution, and were forced to land on the Safi strip due to fuel shortage. This must have been critical, for Safi was less than two miles from Hal Far!

Indeed, Flg Off L.J. Connors did not even make the island. His Spitfire hit the sea a quarter of a mile from Hal Far's runway, and although Connors was seen swimming strongly for the shore, he never made it. Mackie took off as soon as his aircraft was refuelled and made an unsuccessful 25-minute search for the missing pilot.

Later that day he made two further patrols over the invasion beaches, spending a total of five hours in the air without encountering enemy aircraft. That day Allied forces captured Syracuse, Pachino, Gela and Licata.

A fighter-bomber raid on Gerbini next day by two squadrons of Kittyhawks was escorted by ten of 243's aircraft, and the squadron was north of Vizzini at 12,000 feet when two Macchi 202s were sighted at 9,000 feet: "These were chased, Sqn Ldr Mackie damaging one," according to the record book. Mackie reported:

> Up: 1820. Down: 2000. 11th July, 1943.
> Aerodrome: Hal Far, Malta.

> On the way to base after Kittyhawks had bombed Gerbini we were flying south at 12,000 ft, when 2 Mc 202s were sighted north of Vizzini travelling S. to S.E.
> We dived on them. I attacked one from astern firing cannon and M/Guns from 150 yds range. I myself saw no results from the attack.
>   N.B. (1) S/Ldr Mackie's No.2, F/Sgt Welch saw a cloud of white smoke issue from the E/A which turned sharply and dived away.
>   (2) F/Sgt Towgood saw a red flash under the fuselage of the E/A.

> Claim: one Mc 202 damaged.

The Macchi 202 Folgore (Lightning) was a low-wing monoplane fighter powered by an 1,175 hp Daimler Benz DB 601 engine, capable of speed of 309 mph at sea level and 370 mph at 16,400 feet in the later IX/XI series. Probably the most successful Italian fighter to see extensive wartime service, its performance was similar to that of the Spitfire VC being flown by Mackie at the time – but its two 12.7mm and two 7.7mm machine guns were no match for the 20mm cannon with which the Spitfire was equipped.

The tactics used by the Italian pilots gave the men from 243 Squadron something to think about: "They're a crazy lot, the Italians," Mackie recalled. "You don't know whether they're doing aerobatic manoeuvres or what, but they're all over the place. I never really had a ding-dong go with one to see how their machines performed, but they were all over the sky."

In action the next day (12 July) Mackie's perception of the Italians was reinforced: "Enemy tactics in this engagement were head-on attacks and stall turns," Rawlinson recorded of a scrap between the squadron's 12 Spitfires and three Macchi 202s north of Lentini. The Italians quickly decided that discretion was the better part of valour, against such odds: "I was chasing one and he was heading for home downhill and I wasn't gaining on him with normal boost, so I did what you can do in emergencies and that was put the throttle through the gate into extra-rich," said Mackie. "I did that with mine and the whole thing started to vibrate. I thought, hello, I'm being fired at, so I immediately throttled back again, and he got away. If I hadn't done that I think I might have been just gaining on him, because he was taking no evasive action other than straight for home."

He claimed a probable:

Up: 1430. Down: 1625. 12th July 1943.
Aerodrome: Hal Far, Malta.

After patrolling N. & S. inland of Augusta and Syracuse, I led the Squadron northwards decreasing height from 15,000 ft to 10,000 ft. North of Lentini 3 A/C were reported travelling in the opposite direction and slightly below us.

I attacked one of these Mc 202's from astern and saw cannon strikes on the fuselage from 200 yds range. The E/A half rolled and dived, and I followed, still firing. I last saw the Macchi in a vertical dive at 5,000 ft, white smoke pouring from it.

One mile from the coast and east of Mass Reitano, I saw on the ground a fire, and white smoke which was not observed before the attack.

Claim: One Mc 202 probably destroyed.

N.B. The fire and white smoke near Mass Reitano were noticed by several pilots who state that they did not see fire and smoke on the ground before the attack.

The number 13 is considered unlucky by some, but Mackie had already shared in the destruction of a Bf 109 on 13 April, while 13 July was to prove an even more successful day for him.

During an early morning patrol over one of the Sicilian landing beaches codenamed 'Acid', with eight Mark VCs and four Mark IXs,

Mackie surprised 12 unescorted Ju 87 'Stuka' dive-bombers flying south in line abreast. These were from the 121° Gruppo Tuffatori of the Regia Aeronautica, which had anticipated being escorted by three MC 202s and three MC 205s. However, the fighter pilots had not been able to find their charges, and had strafed ships off the invasion beaches instead, leaving the dive-bombers to their fate. Mackie turned the squadron, which had been flying north, to port and then led his pilots in a diving attack from astern. It turned out to be something of a 'turkey shoot' for 243 Squadron, with five of the Ju 87s being claimed destroyed, and the others all damaged. Mackie claimed two, and Sgt Jacques, Plt Off E.A. Lawrence and Flt Sgt H.C. Payne each claimed one destroyed; Mackie, Plt Off C.E. Gregory, Plt Off Lawrence, Flt Sgt Payne, Flg Off Dalrymple, Wt Off I.N. McLaren and Plt Off M.D. Einhorn each claimed one damaged.

216ª Squadriglia of the Gruppo lost seven Ju 87s, the last of which may have fallen as it struggled away from the engagement, for one further claim was submitted for an aircraft of this type by Flg Off Cyril Bamberger* of 93 Squadron, whose unit was patrolling in the Catania area at this time.

But that was not all, as the ORB revealed: "Hearing an RT message that trouble was afoot further north, Flg Off Banner led his Spitfire IXs towards Catania where four Me 109s in line astern were seen in the circuit. After probably destroying one 109 and damaging another, a Do 217 preparing to land at the aerodrome was the next to receive Banner's attention. Severely damaged by Flg Off Banner, the bomber was finished off by his No.2, Sgt P.J. Davoren, and it crashed into the sea half a mile from Catania.

"Six destroyed, one probably destroyed and eight enemy aircraft damaged represented a very satisfactory sortie."

Grp Capt Gilroy recalled that day well: "We were each leading squadrons – Ju 87 dive-bombers were seen at the same time as troop-carrying aircraft were landing at Catania – Catania being well-defended. I thought I had better take my squadron to cope with the important transports, and gave Mackie the chance of the 87s. That he did so well we never saw 87s again. Their few minutes finished the dive-bombers and probably finished the reinforcements coming into Catania."

Mackie's claim for the Ju 87s:

Up: 0650. Down: 0835. 13th July, 1943.
Aerodrome: Hal Far, Malta.

I was leading the Squadron on a patrol over the "ACID" beaches.

---

* (Flt Lt C.S. Bamberger, DFC & Bar; see *Aces High*, page 109.)

We were flying northwards at 14,000 ft when about 12 unescorted Ju 87s were seen to port at 10,000 ft, flying southwards in line abreast from some 3 miles S.W. of Gerbini.

We attacked from astern having come out of the sun. I made attacks on three E/A.

N.B. (1) I attacked one Ju 87 from astern firing from 100 yds range, and giving it another short burst from 60 yds distance. Its bomb was jettisoned. The 87 disintegrated in mid-air.

Claim: One Ju 87 destroyed.

(2) I attacked another from astern at 50 yds range. This A/C burst into flames.

Claim: One Ju 87 destroyed.

(3) Using M/Guns only I attacked a 3rd E/A from 60 yds range. This E/A started to stream glycol.

Claim: One Ju 87 damaged.

"Between the lot of us we seem to have either destroyed or damaged practically all of them, so it was just one of those lucky moments," he said later.

The 13th which was to prove so unlucky for the enemy was not yet over. Later that morning, Wg Cdr 'Cocky' Dundas led 12 of the squadron's aircraft (ten Mark VCs and two Mark IXs) out on a patrol over the 'Acid' beaches, when between eight and 12 enemy aircraft identified as MC 200s were seen dive-bombing two cruisers about ten miles north of Augusta.

According to the ORB: "Wg Cdr Dundas sent one crashing into the sea, Sqn Ldr Mackie claimed another, his third destroyed today, while Sgt 'Jock' Melville and Flt Lt Gruwys each damaged an MC 202 which attempted to interfere with our Spit VCs attacking the MC 200s." Mackie's claim:

Up: 1120. Down: 1310. 13th July, 1943.
Aerodrome: Hal Far, Malta.

Patrolling over the "ACID" beaches at 14,000 ft in a northerly direction, 8 to 12 A/C were observed heading southwards at 9,000 ft in the direction of two cruisers. We were 10 to 15 miles north of Augusta and although we flew to intercept these aircraft at maximum speed, we were still some 5 miles away when they dive bombed the cruisers and made off towards Catania. We gave chase. After some manoeuvring I got behind one E/A, now identified as Mc 200's and closed to 100 yds firing Cannon and M/Guns. Pieces broke off the E/A which began to emit clouds of black and white smoke. The starboard wing was almost shot away. I saw the E/A crash into the sea from a height of 1,000 ft.

Claim: One Mc 200 destroyed.

N.B. F/Sgt Towgood saw two E/A crash into the sea, one of which was a Mc 200 shot down by W/Cdr Dundas.

The victims on this occasion were not in fact Macchi 200s, but Reggiane Re 2002 fighter-bombers of the 5° Stormo Assalto, two of which were indeed shot down, Sottotenenti Arduino Vidulis and Dante Bartolucci being lost. The Re 2002 was a type unknown to Allied fighter pilots at this time, and on the few occasions when such aircraft were encountered, they were never to be correctly identified.

Mackie's fine performance that day attracted the attention of Wg Cdr H.L. Thompson, author of the official history *New Zealanders with the Royal Air Force*. Thompson noted the scarcity of enemy aircraft soon after the Sicilian landings and went on: "During the early stages, however, there was considerable activity on the part of the Luftwaffe and Squadron Leader E.D. Mackie, Flying Officer S.F. Browne, Flight Sergeant N.D. Harrison and Flying Officer G.G. White were among those engaged in combat.

"Squadron Leader Mackie, who led a Spitfire squadron on patrol over the beaches and shipping, continued a remarkable run of success. Within a matter of weeks five enemy aircraft destroyed, one probably destroyed and two damaged. One morning when his squadron destroyed seven Ju 87 dive-bombers, his own score was three."

A high-level view of the Stuka action is provided by 243 Squadron's Sgt Pat Davoren, writing from his home in Victor Harbour, South Australia, in 1987: "I was one of four Spit IXs doing top cover to six Spit VCs led by the CO on a sweep over Sicily on the most successful trip.

"We were all amazed when the bottom section reported eight or ten Ju 87 Stukas travelling east towards the coast. After warning the top section to keep a good lookout for fighters, Rosie led them to attack. It was my most memorable sight of the war with the top cover having a 'wide screen' view of the action.

"We could see the smoke from the cannons and then the 87s started to go down. The radio was pretty hectic. A Jamaican pilot, Ned

Lawrence, said: 'I've got one! I've got one! I've got one!' 'So what, I've got two!' from Rosie slowed up the noise."

Davoren's section went on to Catania, where as already mentioned, he shared in the destruction of a Dornier Do 217 bomber: "When I got back to the dispersal at Malta it was all excitement, with an Air Marshal calling in to check on the afternoon's events."

Writing from his home in Cheshire, Payne recalled returning to Malta after his own successful part in the 'Stuka shoot': "When I returned to Hal Far with my No.2 a few minutes after the CO I found him talking to Spy (the squadron intelligence officer, Flg Off Rawlinson) and as I approached the CO turned and said: 'How many did you get?' to which I replied: 'Two'. With a vestige of a smile he said: 'About time!' and went on reporting to Spy." It was a typical illustration of Mackie's taciturn nature and dry sense of humour.

(Payne was eventually credited with only one Stuka from the shoot. He went on: "That miserable old devil Spy reduced that to one destroyed and one damaged later, and I had to tell him that next time I would bring back the German pilot's number, rank and name!")

A party of eighteen 243 Squadron ground staff left Malta by sea for Comiso airfield in southern Sicily that day, and next day, 14 July, two Dakotas carried 324 Wing personnel and squadron intelligence officers, plus two jeeps to Comiso. The Spitfires of 243 followed the transports into Comiso and later that day made their first operational patrol from there. "Thick clouds of fine red dust. Flies and mosquitos eager to land and infest cuts and scratches – and succeeded," remembered Payne. Comiso strip was only 30 miles from the Gerbini airfields, which would not be captured until 21 July.

For the next week their work consisted mostly of patrols over Catania at between 12,000 and 14,000 feet. The remainder of the squadron's ground personnel arrived on 20 July, and camped in a nearby olive grove.

25 July found Mackie, Flg Off Banner and Intelligence Officer Rawlinson scouring the Sicilian countryside on behalf of their squadron. They had received 'inside' information that there were 25 wireless sets at a certain German headquarters – enough for one for each section: "After taking every wrong turning except the last one, the HQ was located at Donnafugata Castle," recorded Rawlinson. "No radios, however, could be found, but stationery of all descriptions was found in plenty, and brought back to the station, together with an Auto Union car in excellent condition."

Mackie was to have good cause shortly to reflect on such acquisition of vehicles surplus to establishment. News that Mussolini had resigned spread through the squadron like wildfire the next day: "Everyone was convinced that Fascism had 'had it' and that with concentrated bombing, Italy would soon be out of the war," read the observation in the record book. Meanwhile, the war went on, with the squadron escorting 20 Warhawks on an armed reconnaissance during the day.

The last few days of July were occupied escorting aircraft from 239 Kittyhawk Wing, led by the New Zealand Wg Cdr R.E. Bary. Based at Pachino airfield from 17 July, the Kittyhawk fighter-bomber wing had soon made its presence felt. On one occasion Bary led his pilots against enemy positions south-west of Catania, the Allied forces signalling their appreciation. Wg Cdr Thompson noted in his history: "Top fighter cover for the operation had been provided by Spitfires of No.243 Squadron led by Squadron Leader Mackie." Truly a Kiwi effort!

On 30 July the squadron moved about 30 miles south-west to Pachino, on the southernmost tip of Sicily. With Mackie leading, the 12 aircraft touched down at 1940 that day. Rawlinson takes up the story: "In the small hours the wagon containing pilots' kit makes its appearance, having been fired on three times by an American guard. Most of us by this time are half asleep and not at all inclined to hear a full description of the incident, but we gather that several good hearty strips were 'torn off' the guard by the scared occupants of the three-tonner."

Sgt Payne was amongst the pilots led by Mackie that day and he recalls his arrival there: "This was the first time the squadron had operated from a 'dust' strip about 800 yards long. The airfield at Pachino had been ploughed up then prepared by Royal Engineers assisted by members of No. 3201 RAF Servicing Commando Unit, who came ashore immediately behind the assault troops.

"I tell you this because Sqn Ldr Mackie was most concerned at the time the squadron would take to take off and form up, if we waited for the thick clouds of dust to clear after each pair took off. The strip was only wide enough to take off in pairs. Valuable fuel would be used in forming up – thus the CO's concern. The only possible solution was to set the gyro and take off into the dust!"

Payne claimed that they were eaten by flies and mosquitos at Pachino, but a compensating luxury was the plentiful supply of grapes and melons around their dispersed aircraft.

It was while at Pachino that Sgt Pat Davoren discovered that Mackie did not take kindly to incompetence in his pilots – and incompetence included running short of fuel. "I was flying in a Spit IX with one or two others over the toe of Italy at some 25,000 feet when I felt my oxygen tube come undone. I called up and told Rosie I was going down to fix it. I dived down near his section, fixed it, and throttled on to catch up with the top cover.

"I flew around at the height I had left them, but could not find them. After a while I realised I had used up quite a bit of fuel and throttled right back and tried to make the most distance I could. I passed over Catania and my motor cut and I proceeded to Lentini East, which was the nearest strip, eight to ten miles away.

"I followed the drill and kept close as I turned in, only to be too close. The side-slipping turn did not write off enough height, and as usual had allowed the speed to build up. I was left to do the last bit of the turn with 180 or more on the clock, so the only choice was to delay my final turn and when I was off the end of the strip do a very tight last 90 degrees to get my speed off.

"Anyway, it worked. On arriving back at Pachino I was very pleased with myself, having got away with my forced landing. Rosie wanted to know what had happened, and on telling him he raved on a bit. I don't know whether he was relieved I hadn't pranged, or what, but he told the rest of the pilots standing around to go and check their equipment, and that was the end of the matter. He never held it against me. A very peaceable gentleman."

Mackie was made a substantive Flight Lieutenant on 8 August. "The rule of the Air Force," he said, "seemed to be that, certainly up to Flight Lieutenant, you advanced one rank each year, unless you had 12 months in the rank above, in which case you became substantive in the rank below." It was just two years since he had been commissioned as a Pilot Officer.

Escorts to medium and Kitty-bombers continued out of Pachino, and news that 90-gallon overload tanks were to be collected had pilots guessing as to possible destinations. On 18 August 'B' Flight was escorting Kittyhawks when the formation was surprised by FW 190s. Flt Lt Eddie Gruwys, the flight commander, baled out into the comparative safety of a cactus patch, but Sgt R.C. Jaques went down in flames and was posted missing. Gruwys was then rested, Flt Lt Barry taking over his flight.

Mid August also saw some other postings when Flt Lt MacDonald, the 'A' Flight commander, was promoted to lead 93 Squadron, whilst Cyril Bamberger from that latter unit moved to 243 to take his place at the head of 'A' Flight. Flt Lt M.R.B. Ingram*, another New Zealander who had only been with the unit a few weeks, was also promoted, going to command 152 Squadron.

The Sicilian Campaign ended on 19 August, Mackie and his squadron then becoming involved mainly in air tests (he made one in a Spitfire IX) and combat drills until 29th, when the squadron moved north to Panebianco airstrip, ten miles south of Gerbini.

"When the opportunity presents itself pilots wander around the

---

* (Sqn Ldr M.R.B. Ingram, DFC; see *Aces High*, page 350.)

aerodrome examining the many types of pranged enemy aircraft, including an Me 210 which we found closely guarded," recorded Rawlinson. (The Me 210 was a largely unsuccessful twin-engined heavy fighter, designed to replace the Messerschmitt Bf 110. It had to be fitted with leading-edge slots to overcome a distressing tendency to spin at the slightest provocation, and a marginal increase in speed – by about 40 mph to 385 mph maximum – appeared to be its only advantage over its predecessor. The aircraft seen was probably one of the few Me 210As operated by III/ZG 1 in Sicily.)

The time for sightseeing was limited. The squadron was now really on the move as Air Chief Marshal Tedder positioned his forces to support the impending Allied landings in Italy.

A new squadron 'readiness' board, prepared largely by the combined efforts of the CO, LAC Lines and Plt Off E.A. Lawrence, had been completed but would not be in use for a few days: "We now possess a very fine board," wrote Rawlinson. "Pilots on and off the state, serviceable and u/s aircraft can be seen at a glance." LAC Lines was responsible for the lettering, while Plt Off Lawrence, having carved a Spitfire then displayed on the CO's car, had directed his artistic talents to carving and colouring the squadron crest.

On 30 August 243 Squadron moved 12 miles north-east to Catania aerodrome, near Sicily's east coast, and on 2 September made a five-mile south-west quickstep to Cassala strip, where it was almost as handily placed to cover the embarkation of some units of the 8th Army from Augusta the following morning.

As the landing craft ploughed across the narrow Straits of Messina on 3 September, towards Reggio on the southern tip of Italy, 243's Spitfires flew patrols high above them. On the first 90-minute patrol Mackie chased an inquisitive Ju 88 up to 29,000 feet, which was well within his Spitfire VC's 37,000 feet service ceiling. The Ju 88 escaped, enemy aircraft otherwise proving to be scarce.

Patrols over the Straits and Reggio, where the Germans and Italians who had managed to escape from Sicily were harried by the 8th Army yet again, began in earnest on 4 September. Mackie led his squadron aloft four times that day and was in the air for five hours 45 minutes, going as far north up the Italian coast as Palmi, at 5,000 feet.

The Italian Government had made secret approaches to the Allies, seeking terms for an Armistice, the basis of which had been agreed by 3 September. Formally, this was not due to be announced until late on 8th, but it was not in the event to end the fighting here. Well aware of what was afoot, the Germans had sought to establish them-selves throughout the country in a position where they could immediately assume control, and this they did from the moment of the announcement.

Meanwhile, 5 September saw the squadron making another Reggio/ Palmi patrol, and the following day it was off to Falcone aerodrome, 50 miles north on Sicily's north coast. It was from there, during the next week, that the unit would provide high-level cover over the Allied landings at Salerno.

These sorties over 175 miles of the Tyrrhenian Sea could be made only with the aid of 90-gallon drop tanks, and they tested the pilots' faith in their Merlin engines to the utmost.

On 7 September all pilots in 324 Wing attended a briefing by Grp Capt Ronnie Lees, its former CO, to learn about Operation 'Avalanche', as the Salerno landings were codenamed. "A wealth of information was admirably imparted to an attentive audience," Rawlinson recorded. The route was to be from Milazzo, over Stromboli to Cap Palermo, and then north-west to 'Peaches' beach.

Mackie, the perfectionist, flew a one-hour air test at 21,000 feet on 9th, and then, apparently still not happy with his aircraft's performance, had it up for a second ten-minute test the same day.

On 9 September, two separate fleets carried the US Fifth Army north for the Salerno landings. The British divisions of that army sailed from Sicily, while the American contingent sailed from Oran – and as the two fleets converged on the Bay of Salerno in the early hours of that day, RAF Beaufighters based in Sicily, together with Spitfires and Lightnings fitted with long-range tanks, gave them close and high cover.

"In those days it was considered to be rather a feat to be flying single-engined aircraft over such a distance, expecting action at the far end and returning over the same stretch of water," said Mackie. "We naturally had to fly at a reasonable height in case the Germans decided to intercept us from the mainland, and at the same time conserve fuel in case we were in action over the beachhead.

"I think 243 was once again first on the job. We arrived there just as day was breaking. We were allowing ourselves 30 minutes over the patrol line – the patrol line being from Salerno to Agropoli. That was the stretch the American forces had chosen to invade."

Mackie said that while opposition on the ground was stiff, there was little enemy air activity: "It was really quite picturesque up there, to see the gaggle of ships assembled in the harbour, destroyers and patrol boats whizzing around with their wakes. But at least we were on the job, and ensured that the Army and Navy was allowed to get on with its job."

The 90-gallon drop tanks extended the range of the Spitfires by about an hour and, while they increased drag, did not affect the handling of the aircraft to any extent. "To start with we jettisoned them once they were empty, but after several trips we realised opposition was not up to expectations, so we retained them until the time came when we had to drop them." Patrols from Sicily over the invasion beaches were usually from two hours 25 minutes to two hours 50 minutes in duration, wrote Mickey Payne.

On his second patrol over Salerno on invasion day, 9 September, Mackie fired at a Bf 109 but saw no results – an exercise which he repeated, albeit at long range, during his second patrol on 10th. But on 11 September there was no mistake, and he was able to write: "One Do 217 destroyed" in his logbook. It was his 13th victory, and the only twin-engined aircraft he would bring down. The Do 217 was being employed at this time to launch new Fritz X radio-controlled glider bombs, which were directed at the Allied shipping in Salerno Bay. These aircraft operated from bases in Southern France. These bombs were to inflict such severe damage on the battleship HMS *Warspite*, that she was forced to abandon her bombardment and withdraw; she would be out of action for six months.

Mackie's claim read:

Up: 0830. Down: 1035. 11th September, 1943.
Aerodrome: Falcone, Sicily.

I was leading the Squadron on a patrol of the beaches between SALERNO and AGROPOLI. We, in the Mk V's were flying at 12,000 ft (Mk IX's at 15,000 ft), when control reported 8 FW 190's bombing from 10,000 ft. I saw one bomb burst behind a ship, but no FW 190's. Looking upwards I noticed either a Ju 88 or a Do 217 at 15,000 ft, flying northwards. We jettisoned our 90-gallon tanks and gave chase. The Mk V's, unable to catch this E/A, returned to resume patrol over the beaches, whilst Blue section in the Mk IX's continued the chase.

When flying southwards resuming our patrol I noticed another bomb burst in square EASY 4, towards the southern end of the beach, and spotted a Do 217 at 16,000 ft, 3,000 ft above me, turning to port and making off E.S.E. just north of LICATA Point. I climbed after the E/A which then dived. I fired two bursts but saw no results, and broke as enemy fighters were reported behind us and above. The E/A went into cloud and I followed. During the chase in and out of cloud I fired several bursts, experiencing return fire. After seeing strikes along the fuselage, I saw pieces break away from the E/A. The E/A went down in a spiral dive and crashed, east of MONTESANA (*sic*) at approx. T5188, where it burst into flames.

Claim: One Do 217 destroyed.

Sgt Davoren claimed an FW 190 probably destroyed ten miles north-west of Montesano at about the same time.

In sorrow and anger Rawlinson recorded the death of a former 243 Squadron flight commander on the same day: "Sqn Ldr MacDonald of 93 Squadron was shot down and killed by American ack ack gunners at Battipaglia. While recognising the skill of the USA gunners, we deplore the fact that their aircraft recognition was of a very low category."

Mickey Payne recalls a particular quirk of Mackie's during these long-distance patrols: "Whether it was to keep us on our toes, to practice tight formation, or to amuse the CO I do not know, but he would order the squadron to close formation, three fours, line astern, on our way back to Sicily, and fly directly over the active volcano, Stromboli, through the smoke. The No.4s would swear that they could feel the heat and smell the sulphur fumes. Perhaps it was the CO's way of keeping the formation tight and providing a little light relief!"

Mackie noted that during the week of long-range patrols there were no engine failures or troubles – "Which speaks very highly of the ability of the ground maintenance crews." Payne retained an excellent grasp of the development of the Salerno invasion, and sets the scene for the squadron's next move: "For the first few days at Salerno the ground forces were holding on by the skin of their teeth, and on 12 September a number of heavy German counter-attacks began, which caused great anxiety.

"The American Air Force commander thus thought it would be a very good idea and a morale-builder for the ground forces if Spitfires were to land at Salerno instead of returning to Sicily. Allied airfield construction engineers were ordered to make four landing strips, one close to each of three rivers which crossed the plains of Salerno, and a fourth near the temples of Paestum. They worked under fire.

"The strips were small and built on friable soil, and could be used only in fine weather – an electrical storm made our strip useless at the end of the month."

Rawlinson recorded in the ORB that the Dakota in which pilots' gear, spare pilots and some ground staff were transported from Sicily to Italy was provided with fighter cover by their own squadron. "On 13 September 243 Squadron landed at Paestum, and upon landing was 'welcomed' by FW 190s," wrote Payne. "The speed with which we fell into any ditch, depression or any other cover, however small, was commendable. Thankfully no damage was done, but it was quite a welcome.

"After our next beach patrol on the same day we landed at a similar strip, Tusciano, about three miles from the front line."

With the death of Sqn Ldr MacDonald fresh in their minds, the pilots requested, before they left Paestum for Tusciano, that American ground control be advised that there were clipped-wing Spitfires in the squadron, just in case these might be mistaken for the square wingtips of Bf 109Es. (By late 1943 many Spitfire Vs had their wingtips removed to improve performance and manoeuvrability at low altitude when engaged in ground-attack work. It seems that by this date some of the unit's aircraft had been so modified.)

In setting up shop on Tusciano airstrip, 243 Squadron believed that it had made history. For the first time an RAF unit would operate in front of its own artillery. Not that 243's pilots were told that before they got there.

Payne carries on the story: "Our CO, Rosie Mackie, and the rest of us were very unhappy and somewhat annoyed to find that British 25-pounders were sited in olive groves on the sea side of our strip, and were firing continuously over our strip whilst we were in the circuit. Disconcerting, to say the least!"

The landing at Tusciano was probably the most nerve-wracking the squadron's pilots had yet faced, recorded the ever-observant Rawlinson: "All around the landing strip, some 200 to 300 yards away, 25-pounders were in action. We learned later that the gunners did not (theoretically) fire when aircraft passed in front of their sights.

"Coupled with the flashes and reports of the 25-pounders, a rather wide circuit brought our aircraft almost over the front lines, but in spite of these distractions all our pilots landed safely, thankful that they had not been mistaken for Me 109s."

Payne remembered that representations were made to the Wing Commander, Cocky Dundas, who had also been on the receiving end of this barrage, and who went to see the Lieutenant Colonel in charge: "The gunner was flabbergasted and found it difficult to understand our request, when he had orders to fire continuously. His reply, according to the Wing Commander, was: 'Certainly not. Who the hell ever heard of a Spitfire being shot down by a 25-pounder?'

"The Spitfire wings crammed onto the beachhead whilst a bitter battle waged with the best of German troops. We were very lucky that the German gunners put only a few rounds around our ears, and our own gunners never got any Spitfires!" (Davoren's account of this episode recorded that the Lieutenant Colonel detailed one of his officers to take Dundas to their mess, where he was given a couple of stiff whiskies and told that he and his pilots were perfectly safe, as the gunners had not shot down a single Spitfire in the entire war.)

What few tents the squadron had, were pitched that night at the south end of the runway, near 324 Wing headquarters. The squadron messed with the Wing, and lost no time in digging slit trenches.

"We turned in, but sleep was well-nigh impossible, the 25-pounders going into action periodically," wrote Rawlinson. "A unique experience, we decided. for an RAF unit to be in front of our own artillery. Most of us lay awake watching the vivid flashes of the guns, followed by the scream of the shells on their way to greet the Hun. With each round from the battery directly behind us the tent shuddered slightly.

"Enemy aircraft raided us, dive-bombing and starting a fire at the end of the 'drome."

Rawlinson noted that the squadron's 'A' party, which had arrived from the beach during the afternoon, had pitched camp some distance from the landing ground and closer to the front line: "Mortar shells burst near them, a Jerry machine gun rattled away, shells whistled overhead in both directions. About 0400, somewhat shaken, they made their way through the fields to spend the remaining hours of darkness with us in the orchard."

Next morning 243 Squadron flew its first patrol over the Salerno area from Tusciano, which was situated about eight miles south of Salerno. On 16 September Mackie began flying Spitfire IXs irregularly, alternating them with his trusted Spitfire VC, SN-A.

Rawlinson noted on 16th that intense shelling by the 25-pounders made lighter the work of the guards as they passed from tent to tent rousing out the pilots for the dawn patrol. "A visit to the 25-pounder troop in the next field reveals that they are ranging 6,000 yards – as good an indication as any as to the position of the front line."

One of the few instances of enemy aerial activity recorded was a series of raids on the landing ground by FW 190s on 20th.

On 27 September the weather gave its first intimation that it too would prove a difficult enemy during the coming winter. While the squadron was away on patrol, a thunderstorm rendered the Tusciano landing ground unserviceable, and Mackie diverted his Spitfires to Paestum. The departure from Paestum to Tusciano later that day was a disaster. Possibly Paestum's earth runway had also been affected by the downpour, because two of 243 Squadron's Spitfires collided on take-off, and a third lost power soon afterwards, and crashed into a tree. Mackie, with remarkable restraint, considering what he must have felt, described the incident in his logbook as a: "very shaky do!!"

On 1 October the squadron provided top cover while Mitchells bombed Benevento, whilst later in the day news that Mackie had been awarded a Bar to his DFC came through, coupled with the award of the DFC to Flt Lt Bamberger, the 'A' Flight commander. Mackie's citation read: "Acting Squadron Leader Mackie, who is in command of his Squadron, has shown himself to be an exceptional fighter pilot, whose fine fighting spirit, personal courage and determination have been an inspiring example to all. He has destroyed 12 enemy aircraft."

That evening they celebrated in the mess, with Grp Capt Gilroy the guest of honour. The CO and some pilots of 43 Squadron were also entertained. As well as the DFC awards, they were celebrating the fall of Naples to Allied forces that day – and probably also the capture of the Foggia airfields, the main landing grounds in southern Italy, by the 8th Army on 27 September.

Bamberger, relatively recently joined from 93 Squadron, had an interesting view of Mackie at this time: "The picture I have of Evan Mackie is of an Australian sheep farmer or miner. He was not a typical New Zealander. Rosie was proud of his physical strength and frequently put it to the test, arm-wrestling, lifting heavy weights, etc. He used this very impressive physical side of his character to establish himself as a leader, and from my recollections it was reasonably effective. It was not an ideal approach (everybody is different) for whilst this aggressive leadership produced results for Rosie in the air, it may have led him into scrapes on the ground and to some lack of squadron discipline.

"Rosie and I must have been complementary to one another for I cannot remember us ever having a row, although very different in character. I was much quieter (probably duller) and liked everything to be well-organised. I have an impression, nothing more, that when in the air Rosie always looked after No.1."

Wg Cdr Thompson notes at this stage that five New Zealanders were leading fighter squadrons in Italy: "They were Squadron Leaders E.D. Mackie, M.R.B. Ingram, E.L. Joyce*, R. Webb and D.F. Westenra*. All achieved a good record of service. Mackie, for example, was credited with the destruction of no fewer than 16 enemy machines when he completed his second tour of operations in February, 1944," he wrote.

By early October the beachhead was consolidated, but it had been a close-run thing. When the squadron landed at Tusciano on 13 September, Sgt Davoren recalled: "An American Major came up to us and said: 'We are definitely going to stay. We have too much ashore not to stay.' That was news to us!"

Mackie remembered: "The beachhead itself was in danger of becoming no longer a beachhead. The Hun made a serious attempt to overcome it, but evidently was not able to assemble enough forces. Certainly, there was not much opposition from the air, and we saw to that. Much as we would have liked to have seen more aircraft to engage in combat, they were not on the scene. The few that did appear got the hurry-up."

---

* (Sqn Ldr E.L. Joyce, DFM; see *Aces High*, pages 365-6); (Sqn Ldr D.F. Westenra, DFC & Bar; see *Aces High*, pages 626-7).

During its stay at Tusciano the squadron remained under canvas – an increasingly uncomfortable situation as winter advanced. "Aircraft were serviced outside, just a tent for a mess," said Mackie. "The tucker, of course, was still hard tack. We had forgotten what bread tasted like."

The squadron had also forgotten what fresh meat tasted like, and Mackie set out to rectify that. 'Mickey' Payne recalled the incident which, he said, showed the CO's concern for his troops "who had eaten nothing but compo rations for months.

"With a small party and a three-tonner he discovered a lost cattle-beast and shot it, and we all had fresh meat. As the dreaded word 'looting' occurs to me, perhaps this incident should not be printed! However, it showed the CO's concern for his men."

Amidst the mud and slush and dripping tents of Tusciano there were some lighter moments, recalled Payne: "Pat Davoren and I, and other pilots, probably Flt Sgts Glyn Evans and Brigham, a New Zealander, went to a landing strip where American squadrons were based and took with us our pooled precious bottle of whisky to see what we could get in exchange.

"After refusing an offer of clothes, a sergeant came up with the idea that, as we were pilots, what about a brand-new P-40 with just about 120 hours on the clock? They had just been equipped with Spitfire IXs. What a splendid bargain!

"We even discussed the possibility of putting in an extra seat so we could take up the ground staff.

"Back to Rosie Mackie, bubbling over with enthusiasm, but back came a very firm: 'No!', because he thought it would be just another aeroplane for the overworked groundcrews to service. So we returned with our whisky and settled for a couple of tins of coffee, four of milk powder and some sugar. Ah well, he was the boss!"

And it was at Tusciano that 324 Wing's Wing Commander, Flying, the irrepressible Cocky Dundas, was constrained to comment on the adjacent 25-pounder batteries: "I calculated that there must be almost as much metal as fresh air in the sky through which we had to fly when landing and taking off."

Winter was now definitely settling in. The Tusciano landing ground was unserviceable due to wet weather throughout the first week of October, but Rawlinson recorded one bright spot on 8th: "Bread was served for lunch for the first time since the squadron landed in Italy."

Tusciano remained unserviceable until 12 October, when the Spitfires were flown to their new base, Capodichino, about five miles east of Naples: "Billets are found on the second floor of a lunatic asylum, over a unit of the King's Dragoon Guards," noted Rawlinson.

Mackie was to make only one more operational sortie with 243 Squadron – his only one from Capodichino – and he made it worthwhile.

"Airborne at 0545, six Mk Vs, the CO leading, patrolled along the line of the Volturno River. Having been relieved by Spitfires of another squadron, the flight was flying westwards towards the river mouth when two aircraft were seen at 8,000 feet flying in the opposite direction," recorded Rawlinson. "The flight turned, followed them, and on close investigation identified them as Me 109s, each carrying a bomb. Sqn Ldr Mackie made a quarter-stern attack from 150/100 yards on one, which he damaged, while Sgt Davoren chased one for over 45 miles without being able to overhaul it."

Davoren, who had already made a name for himself on 15 September by being the first Italian-based Allied fighter pilot to down an enemy aircraft (a FW190) was flying as Mackie's No.2 that day: "We ran into a couple of 109s during a recce. Rosie and I chased them and he managed to get a burst into one of them before they broke into cloud.

"It was a magnificent shot around the cockpit and motor, but it didn't go down. I called him up and went above the clouds where they appeared, but I couldn't catch them."

Mackie's formal account of the encounter was:

Up: 0545. Down: 0705. 15th October, 1943.
Aerodrome: Capodichino (Naples).

I was leading 6 Spitfires on a patrol of the VOLTURNO RIVER area. We had been relieved by more Spitfires and were flying westwards towards the river mouth, when 2 A/C were seen flying in the opposite direction at about the same height 7,000 ft. We turned and followed them as they weaved. A close investigation proved them to be Me 109s each carrying a bomb which I did not see jettisoned. I attacked one E/A from quarter astern at a range of 250 yards, firing several bursts. I saw cannon strikes on the port side of the fuselage, and around the cockpit. The E/A climbed into cloud and I lost contact with it.
Time of attack – 06.45 to 06.50 hrs.

Claim: One Me 109 damaged.

N.B. Cannon strikes also seen by three other pilots.

Mackie's posting from 243 Squadron on 12 October, 1943, happened suddenly – so quickly, in fact, that he did not have the opportunity to say goodbye to all the squadron personnel. It seems that this may have been caused by personality differences in higher quarters, which had begun more than two years previously, and in which the New Zealander was a convenient pawn.

In 1941 Gilroy, then a Squadron Leader, had been on the same station as Sqn Ldr R.B. Lees (then commanding 72 Squadron) and Grp Capt Harry Broadhurst (who had earlier in the war commanded 111 Squadron). At the same time, Gilroy recollected later, he and Lees had both made Broadhurst aware of inadequacies in 111 Squadron. Clearly, said Gilroy, this rankled with Broadhurst.

Two years later Broadhurst, as an Air Vice-Marshal, arrived to become Air Officer Commanding, Desert Air Force. When RAF units were concentrated on Malta in June 1943, in readiness for the invasion of Sicily, two Spitfire Wings were transferred from Air Cdr 'Bing' Cross's 242 Group to Broadhurst's Desert Air Force – and one of those Wings was 324, with Grp Capt Gilroy in command. "Having to take me with 324 Wing's record of over 300 confirmed victories in Tunisia, it took him almost three months to get rid of me," wrote Gilroy. "Mackie's engineer officer's vehicle was only one lever."

The Group Captain's premonition of a plan to get rid of him was confirmed long after the end of the war: "I was interested to read in a book by the man who was given my Wing, that he had been promised it by Broadhurst in Malta. He was a Broadhurst favourite from the UK." (Grp Capt W.G.G. Duncan-Smith*.)

According to Gilroy, in correspondence with the author, Broadhurst decided to get at him through Mackie. A convenient opportunity occurred through the acquisition of an Army vehicle by 243 Squadron personnel in Sicily. If Broadhurst could show that one of Gilroy's squadron commanders had condoned the improper acquisition of transport, that would be a black mark against Gilroy, reasoned the latter.

What actually happened is not at all clear, and neither is it clear which of several vehicles was involved. There was a jeep which had been lost during the landings on Sicily, and recovered by 243 Squadron personnel from below the surface of the sea. Cyril Bamberger wrote: "I have a photograph of Rosie and myself with a super Mercedes car at Catania airfield in Sicily." Mackie himself recalled a "numbered Citroen car". Pat Davoren referred in correspondence to an RAF van, and Flg Off Rawlinson, in the squadron's Operations Record Book, records himself, Mackie and Flg Off Banner returning from Donnafugata Castle with "an Auto Union car in excellent condition", whilst in Sicily.

---

* (Grp Capt W.G.G. Duncan-Smith, DSO & Bar, DFC & Bar; see *Aces High*, pages 236-7.)

Gilroy reflected on Broadhurst's apparent attitude to transport, and confirmed the Mercedes: "At HQ, Malta, I do remember him (Broadhurst) saying to us: 'We'll get plenty of transport vehicles in Sicily' – which remark made me give little attention to the recovery of a broken-down, abandoned vehicle repaired by Mackie's engineer officer – Mackie himself had no use for it as he had a Mercedes staff car!"

Mackie's recollection was that a numbered Citroen car had been found abandoned near one of the airfields they were using in Sicily: "The boys said: 'What say we tow it in and get it going?' Which they promptly did, and used it as squadron transport until they came and took it off us."

There had been enquiries made about the Citroen while the squadron was still in Sicily: "That's where I couldn't evade the issue," said Mackie. "I had to tell the Army officer where we had got it, and that was that. I was hoping that was the end of it, but it turned out it wasn't, quite."

The Citroen and the jeep eventually arrived with the squadron ground personnel at Tusciano. "It was at this particular date that the Army's ponderous wheels finally caught up with me," Mackie recalled. "I was accused of appropriating this Army vehicle. I'd never driven the thing myself. I knew the boys had it. But the Army was adamant that someone must pay the price. And the outcome was that the Air Force officer in charge had to be punished in some way because his conduct had been prejudicial to good order and discipline."

Payne remembers the incident as having an effect on the squadron. "A vehicle was acquired by some members of the squadron and there was certainly some trouble about it. I cannot remember a court martial charge, but I do remember a Squadron Leader coming to investigate the matter, and a great feeling of unease about the squadron."

Whether Mackie was formally court-martialled cannot be established. He himself remembered some sort of disciplinary hearing, but could not recollect the details.

Air Cdr H.A. Probert, MBE, of the RAF Air Historical Branch (now retired) advised; "The proceedings of nearly all the wartime courts martial were destroyed many years ago, and even if they had been retained, it would be illegal under the Rehabilitation of Offenders' Act to make them public. Nor were details of courts martial normally recorded in the Operational Records Book, except insofar as the fact that one had taken place might be mentioned. Regrettably, therefore, I can think of no way of ever substantiating the circumstances under which Mackie was put on trial."

The only official record relating to the incident is in the 324 Wing

Operational Record Book at the Public Records Office in Kew, London. The entry for 12 October, 1943, reads in part: "Flg Off (A/Sqn Ldr) E.D. Mackie, DFC, relieved of command of 243 Squadron and relinquished the rank of Squadron Leader on posting to Wing HQ, supernumerary." (The 'Flg Off' ranking is wrong, for he had been a substantive Flt Lt since 8 August, 1943, and the entry also failed to mention the Bar to his DFC.)

In Gilroy's view, AVM Broadhurst had then achieved the desired effect; he had proved that Gilroy had not been exercising effective control over his staff. Having done that, the AVM obviously saw no point in keeping the promising young New Zealander out of action for a day longer than necessary.

On 3 November, 1943, Flt Lt Mackie was posted to 92 (East India) Squadron to command, and Gilroy was posted to No.1 Base Personnel Depot pending return to the United Kingdom. His place was at once taken by the man Broadhurst had promised the Wing to – Sqn Ldr (A/Wg Cdr) Duncan-Smith, who was at the time Wing Commander, Flying of 244 Wing (of which 92 Squadron formed a part), and who became A/Grp Capt commanding 324 Wing.

"It was obviously a put-up job," Gilroy was to write later. "What was one vehicle against the peace of mind of a chap giving his utmost? The proof of that was that he was given a squadron that needed him straight after."

Bamberger recalled: "Rosie left 243 Squadron in rather a hurry and apparently under a cloud – I was not privy to the reason why. His tour as squadron commander was incomplete and he was not promoted. Gossip, as I recollect at the time, suggested he had become unpopular with AVM Harry Broadhurst – maybe something to do with looting – Broadhurst was an expert."

Davoren undoubtedly spoke for the rest of 243 Squadron when he wrote: "It wasn't taken very seriously by the squadron, and in any case he went straight to 92 and apparently for the rest of the war it had no influence on his record."

That view is supported by Grp Capt W.G. Abel (Retd), secretary of the Royal Air Force Staff College at Bracknell, who wrote: "Lots of funny things happened under the stress of war – a court martial for such an incident seems somewhat inappropriate, but possible. If in fact a court did convene and hear the evidence it must have dismissed the charge (probably conduct prejudicial to good order and Air Force discipline) because the court would be unlikely to order Mackie's transfer to another squadron – that would be for his AOC to decide. Clearly Mackie was 'untainted' by the proceedings – and so I should hope – but we don't know the real circumstances."

Mackie took the whole thing philosophically: "Anyway, his punishment for me was to post me to an Air Force unit operating on the other side of Italy. It was, in fact, their crack squadron, No.92, the highest-scoring squadron in the Royal Air Force at the time, just approaching its 300th victory and just equipped with Spit VIIIs. As far as I was concerned, the punishment was promotion."

Neither did Gilroy suffer from his brush with Broadhurst. On return to the UK he was given command of RAF Wittering, from which flew two groups of USAAF P-38 Lightnings: "I had been given the US DFC at Salerno – perhaps that encouraged them to give me Wittering," he wrote. Gilroy ended the war as a Group Captain commanding the Newcastle sector – all the fighter stations between the Humber Estuary and the River Tweed.

There can certainly be no doubt that Evan Mackie had made his mark on 243 Squadron.

Davoren: "I joined 243 at Malta before the Sicily invasion and soon learned from the pilots the great praise they had for him as a fighter pilot – so much so that I gained the impression they figured if they didn't do any good in a scrap, Rosie could be relied on to get one or two and keep up the prestige of the squadron, a belief I always held."

"I very nearly wrote to Evan to see if he would request me to join 92. Rosie must have had a profound effect on me as I notice from my logbook that I only knew him for four months and as a Flight Sergeant had very little to do with him – no common mess, etc."

Payne: "I found Rosie Mackie a very determined, courageous, aggressive man in the air who thought it his duty to lead his squadron efficiently and shoot down as many enemy aircraft as possible and cause as much disruption to the enemy wherever they could be found. His standards of operational flying were exacting and he expected the best from us all."

Porteous: "Rosie Mackie was a determined character. As a fighter pilot he was quick. He could always pick up a target ahead of me, particularly if it was below us, and he gave us all confidence."

Gilroy: "Morale, all through, was a vital factor and Mackie kept us all at the top. Amongst those of us who are left, he will never be forgotten."

Mackie had an equal regard for 243 Squadron: "The only regret I had, and probably still have to this day, is leaving 243," he said shortly before he died. "I had been with them for so long and, you know, you get used to various personnel and you are reluctant to move away."

But moved he was, and so quickly that Davoren noted sadly: "He left without saying goodbye to the Sergeant Pilots." Perhaps Mackie did not have the social skills to deal with the distasteful situation and the farewells entailed. The squadron Operations Record Book for 6 November, 1943, recorded simply: "Sqn Ldr Mackie leaves for 92 Squadron, 244 Wing, his score being 13 destroyed, two probables and 5½ a/c damaged. He was replaced by Major Langerman." Rawlinson, for once, did not wax eloquent.

CHAPTER SEVEN

ITALY – 92 SQUADRON

When Mackie was flown in a Dakota transport eastwards across Italy, from Capodichino to Foggia on the Adriatic coast, on 22 October, 1943, one of the 'plum' fighter posts in the Royal Air Force was awaiting him. He was about to become commanding officer of the 'crack' 92 (East India) Squadron.

92 Squadron would end the war having claimed 317 enemy aircraft destroyed, making it one of the two top-scoring units of the RAF during World War II. In a way it was fitting that a New Zealander should command the unit, for Air Marshal Sir Arthur Coningham, commander of the Mediterranean Tactical Air Force, had become the squadron's second CO during 1918, when it was flying SE 5A biplane fighters in France, near the end of the First World War.

Reformed immediately after the outbreak of World War II, the squadron had got away to a good start in the new conflict when Wg Cdr (then Flt Lt) Robert Stanford Tuck* claimed a Bf 109 and two Bf 110s shot down whilst leading a patrol over the Calais/Boulogne area during the Dunkirk evacuation on 23 May 1940. From that day until the end of the year, the squadron's pilots claimed 128 enemy aircraft shot down while operating from the famous Biggin Hill fighter station. By the time the unit left England for the North African theatre in mid-February 1942, its pilots had notched up their total of claims to 193½ destroyed.

Fighting with Coningham's (later AVM Broadhurst's) Western Desert Air Force, 92 Squadron was credited with a further 79 destroyed. Sqn Ldr Neville Duke*, who subsequently became a test pilot on the Hawker Hunter jet fighter, in which he was to gain the

---

* (Wg Cdr R.R.S. Tuck, DSO, DFC & Bar; see *Aces High*, pages 594-5); (Sqn Ldr N.F. Duke, DSO, DFC & 2 Bars; see *Aces High*, pages 234-5; See also *Test Pilot*, Neville Duke's autobiography, published by Grub Street, 1992, and *The War Diaries of Neville Duke*, edited by Norman Franks, published by Grub Street, 1995).

World Air Speed Record in 1953, was a flight commander with 92 during the Tunisian Campaign, and increased his personal score to 22 destroyed whilst with the unit.

The squadron's score increased steadily during sorties from Malta and Sicily; 92 had followed 243 Squadron to Italy landing there a day later on 14 September, 1943.

During the Sicilian and Italian landings 92 Squadron, like Mackie's 243 Squadron, was usually early on the scene, flying beachhead patrols. When Mackie left Gilroy and 324 Wing to join Grp Capt C.B.F. (Brian) Kingcome's* 244 Wing, 92 Squadron's score was getting close to 300, and there was a good deal of speculation about which pilot would claim the sweepstake for the 300th victory.

Mackie was posted as CO of 92 on 3 November, 1943, arriving at the squadron's base, Foggia No.7, Zanotti/Triolo landing ground on 6 November to take over from Sqn Ldr P.H. 'Hunk' Humphreys. (The Squadron Intelligence Officer was Flg Off J.G. Cornish.)

Mackie wasted no time in taking over Spitfire VIII JF570, coded QJ-A, as his personal aircraft, and familiarising himself with what was considered by many pilots to be the best version of the Spitfire to be produced. 7 November saw his first flight in the Mark VIII, and after 45 minutes of local flying he was up again the same day (typical Mackie) on a 30-minute cannon test, to ensure that his armament was accurately calibrated and working properly.

The Spitfire VIII was (with the Mark VII which immediately preceded it) the result of an extensive redesign for high altitude operations. It was the first Spitfire variant intended from the outset to make use of the two-speed Merlin 60 series engines, and first entered service in August 1943 with 145 Squadron in Italy. In comparison, the Mark VC which Mackie had flown for most of his Mediterranean service, was basically a developed Spitfire II, which had first entered service in 1940. The Mark IX which he flew in his last days with 243 Squadron was really only a higher-powered Mark V. It had preceded the Mark VIII in service (and was always greatly to outnumber the latter model) because it required much less reworking of the production line, while offering a performance not greatly dissimilar. External differences between the Mark VIII and the earlier versions included a longer nose, a larger vertical tail surface area, symmetrical underwing radiators, and (in flight) a retractable tailwheel.

A comparison with the Spitfire VC may be made as follows:

---

* (Grp Capt C.B.F. Kingcome, DSO, DFC & Bar; see *Aces High*, pages 377-8.)

	Mark VC	Mark VIII
Engine power	1,470 hp	1,710 hp
Top speed	374 mph at 9,000 ft	408 mph at 25,000 ft
Service ceiling	37,000 ft	43,000 ft

Mackie's first operational sortie in the Mark VIII was a Sangro River patrol on 11 November, which set the pattern for much of the next two months.

His first social engagement was a whist drive in the airmens' mess on 13 November, while on 17 November he attended the outgoing CO's farewell party, a 'shindig' at which such notable fighter 'types' as Grp Capt Kingcome, Wg Cdr Duncan-Smith, Sqn Ldr Lance Wade* and Sqn Ldr P. Stan Turner* were present.

While November proved to be a relatively quiet month for Mackie, others were steadily pushing up the score of the squadron which, on 22 November, had moved 25 miles north-east to Canne, near the Adriatic coast. Flt Lt J.H. Nicholls* claimed an FW 190 and Wt Off K. Warren a Bf 109 on 28 November, whilst on 30th, Lt A. Sachs* (SAAF) and Flg Off 'Curly' Henderson each bagged an FW 190.

Mackie broke his duck with 92 Squadron on 3 December, when he led 'Yellow' Section to 19,000 feet over the Sangro and saw 12 Bf 109 fighters and fighter-bombers flying east about 1,000 feet below him. He fired at two, and found that the enemy was, for once, inclined to 'mix it'. Getting on the tail of another, he got in a successful burst and saw it crash on the side of a hill west of Casoli. II/JG 77 lost Uffz Heinz Grundmann in combat with a Spitfire in the Casoli area that day, while another Bf 109 was lost to Spitfires over the Sangro by I/JG 53. However Sgt N.P. Hanson also claimed one of the Messerschmitts met by 92, while claims for two by 417 Squadron and for one by 601 Squadron were also submitted. That evening Mackie, Hanson and Flt Lt Nicholls were invited to 601 Squadron's mess to celebrate the day's successes.

Mackie's account of the action was:

Up: 1235. Down: 1350. December 3, 1943.
Aerodrome: Canne, Italy.

I was leading Yellow Section on Sangro River patrol when I heard Pyrex reporting bogies (12+) at 18,000 ft to Mustard A/C who

---

* (Wg Cdr L.C. Wade, DSO, DFC & 2 Bars; see *Aces High*, pages 610-11); (Grp Capt P.S. Turner, DSO, DFC & Bar; see *Aces High*, pages 597-8); (Wg Cdr J.H. Nicholls, DFC; see *Aces High*, pages 462-3); (Lt A. Sachs, DFC; see *Aces High*, page 658).

we were about to relieve. We climbed rapidly to 19,000 ft and barely one orbit to port to keep in the area, I sighted approx. 12 strange A/C just north of Casoli, flying SE at about 18,000 ft. They were leaving black smoke trails behind them. Suspecting that these were the bogies I dived to attack definitely identifying them as Me 109s. They immediately split up, some losing height while others gained cloud base at 20,000 ft. I fired several bursts of cannon and machine gun at two Me 109s from approx. 300/350 yds but there were too many others around for me to concentrate much on these. Seeing my tail was clear I picked on another 109 and fired several bursts from about 10 degrees astern at about 300/350 yds range. I saw several flashes on the fuselage near the cockpit. The machine then went into a screaming dive towards the mountain taking no avoiding action. I did not fire any more but followed the 109 down to about 4,000 ft when I turned to port to avoid the mountain and saw it crash in the foothills at approx. H.1989. About the same time I saw another machine crash in flames near H.2495.

Claim: 1 Me 109 destroyed.

An 80-minute patrol over the Sangro River at 20,000 feet on 4th was not challenged by the Luftwaffe, but Lt Sachs, one of many South African Air Force pilots with RAF units in Italy, and Mackie kept the pot boiling on 5th. Flg Off Cornish tells the story graphically in the squadron's ORB: "Lt Sachs destroyed two 190s and probably destroyed another. His story is an epic. He positioned himself behind the 12-plus fighter-bombers while two others attacked the fighter cover. After destroying an FW 190 with a one-second burst, Lt Sachs saw another on the tail of a Spitfire, so he turned into it, firing a 30-degree deflection shot, then fired again from point-blank range astern.

"The aircraft blew up, and portions hit Sachs' windscreen, smashing it, while another large piece struck his starboard wing.

"FW 190s were then diving on him from both sides and one shell exploded on his tailplane, blowing off his starboard elevator. He turned toward another FW 190 which was attacking him at point-blank range on his port side, and felt a jar as he collided with it. The enemy aircraft dived away out of control minus its fin and rudder.

"The attack continued and finally, after his elevator and aileron control were useless, Lt Sachs was forced to bail out. He landed safely in his own lines within 60 yards of the wreckage of his Spitfire.

"This success brought the number of enemy aircraft destroyed by this squadron since it left England to 100, while the total is now 293½ confirmed. 'On to the 300th' was the slogan of the eight pilots as they took off on the final patrol of the day and they were not disappointed because the CO, Mackie, who was leading, destroyed an Me 109 which went down in flames. Eleven aircraft destroyed in 11 days without losing a pilot!" Uffz Werner Jahnke of I/JG 53 was killed on this date when he crash-landed following combat with a Spitfire; FhjFw Arno Fischer of the same unit also crash-landed after similar action, but survived unhurt.

Mackie's combat report:

> Up: 1450. Down: 1600. December 5, 1943.
> Aerodrome: Canne, Italy.
>
> I was leading Yellow Section of 4 A/C on patrol in the Sangro River area when Pyrex reported 15+ bogies approaching from the west at 20,000 ft. I climbed rapidly to 22,000 ft, but the plots had failed and we were given no further information for a few minutes. Pyrex then reported 2+ bandits flying east near Casoli. I could not see the ground at all owing to dense cloud below, except for the snow covered top of Mt. Amaro. Just east of this mountain my No.3 reported four 109s at 3 o'clock above. I immediately spotted these as they tried to dive onto our tails. They dived away westwards with myself and Yellow 2 in hot pursuit. We were going too fast to fire and as they were diving for cloud I broke away and climbed to about 20,000 ft again straight into sun as we were in the midst of 10 or 12 109s which appeared to be orbiting at 12,000 ft.
>
> From 20,000 ft I spotted a 109 getting away westwards about 15,000 ft, so I dived down and opened fire with cannon and machine gun from about 300/350 yds closing to 100 yds. I fired 8 to 10 bursts with the 109 weaving and diving and then climbing in front. At about 100 yds it blew up in a sheet of flame. Sgt E. Budgen my No.2 witnessed this. I then climbed to 20,000 ft again and resumed patrol. I saw 10 109s flying westwards over the mountain at about 1,200 ft, but as I did not know how much ammunition I had left and I did not know where Yellow 3 and 4 were, I did not attack.
>
> Claim: 1 Me 109 destroyed.

That was the squadron's last patrol over the Sangro. For the next two weeks its task would be to maintain standing patrols along the bomb line, between Ortona and Casoli, at anything from 9,000 feet to 20,000 feet.

On 9 December Air Chief Marshals Sir Charles Portal, Chief of the Air Staff, and Sir Arthur Tedder, AOC Mediterranean, with Air Marshal Sir Arthur Coningham, AOC Mediterranean Tactical Air Force, visited 244 Wing.

For more than a week no advance was made on the squadron's score, and then came a frustrating 16 December: "Sgt Hanson made no claim after firing, but the forward controller reported that an Me 109 had crashed," recorded the ORB. "Again in the afternoon, we met over 20 FW 190s and Me 109 fighters and fighter-bombers. Flt Lt M.S. Hards*, DFC, DFM probably destroyed an Me 109 while Sqn Ldr Mackie and Sgt Hanson damaged a 109 each."

Mackie's report of the incident:

Up: 1340. Down: 1425. December 16, 1943.
Aerodrome: Canne, Italy.

I was leading Yellow Section of 8 A/C on patrol over bomb line at 16,000 ft when Pyrex reported 20+ bogies approaching from the west at 18,000 ft. I climbed to 19,000 ft and Red Leader who was at 7,000 ft reported smoke trails coming from the west, just north of the mountains. These were hidden behind cloud at 19,500 ft so I flew north west. Yellow 3 reported bandits below at 2 o'clock so I turned starboard and saw 7 or 8 109s breaking cloud at 3 o'clock. I gave chase as these turned away from me and closed in behind No. 2 of a section which turned to port and detached itself from the others. I gave three or four deflection shots (the A/C being hidden under my nose) at about 250 yds closing to about 150 yds. I gave two more bursts as the 109 started to dive, and I distinctly saw several large flashes immediately underneath the cockpit.

The A/C went into a vertical dive from about 18,000 ft between Orsogna and Poggiofiorite. I did not follow it down or watch what became of it, because a 109 was behind my No.2 and I had to break.

Claim: 1 Me 109 damaged.

18 December brought some new postings to 92 Squadron, with Flt Lt Hards being promoted to command 111 Squadron, and Flt Lt J.F. Edwards*, DFC, DFM, being posted from 417 (RCAF) Squadron to become OC 'A' Flight. 'Eddie' Edwards (later to become widely

---

* (Sqn Ldr M.S. Hards, DFC, DFM; see *Aces High*, pages 313-4); (Wg Cdr J.F. Edwards, DFC & Bar, DFM; see *Aces High*, pages 248-9).

known as 'Stocky') was a notable pilot in his own right. During the Libyan and Tunisian Campaigns he had flown Kittyhawks with 260 Squadron, and had been commissioned from Flight Sergeant direct to Acting Flight Lieutenant. By the time his first tour had ended in early summer 1943, his personal tally stood at 12 and two shared, plus nine destroyed on the ground.

Recalling Evan Mackie from his home in Comox, British Columbia, in 1996, this highly-successful Canadian recorded: "Even though I knew him only a short time on 92 Squadron, he impressed me as the top of the line RAF fighter pilot – keen, aggressive, solid – ready to take the fight to the Hun – good CO and popular. Ran a 'tight ship' as they say."

The ORB noted that the pilots hoped for some clear days to coax the enemy into the air, to give them a chance of claiming the squadron's 300th before Christmas. Meanwhile, patrols between Ortona and Casoli continued, weather permitting. Low cloud and rain were common as winter established itself, and always there was the bitter, freezing cold – particularly noticed by those airborne.

"For some reason, in Italy, I found that the temperature dropped considerably with altitude," said Mackie. "In other parts of the world, like England, it was possible to keep warm with silk gloves plus your fur-lined sheepskin gloves. You got by. Over there it did not matter what you put on, your hands still got cold. It was phenomenal. And the rain set in."

He had a lot of admiration for the ground crews, who had to service the Merlin engines and Spitfire airframes out in the open in every sort of weather: "The ground crew had special hot-air blowers to warm them up prior to starting. It must have been a Herculean task in those conditions. We never actually had snow, but we certainly had ice and cold. No hangars," he added.

On Christmas Eve, 1943, there was no chance of 92 Squadron's aircraft taking off for patrols owing to heavy rain and a low ceiling. "In the afternoon we kept four aircraft at readiness for local defence but they were not scrambled." According to the record book: "The pilots and officers had their Christmas dinners this evening and a very fine meal it was. Pilots invited their crews into the party after dinner and everyone had a merry time in 92 style!"

Mackie: "I can remember Christmas and the New Year, how cold it was, with ice and frost right down to the water's edge. Our airfield virtually ran down to the sea and our tents were not far away. I don't know how many blankets I used at night but there was a terrific weight of them – I know that! It was the only way I could keep warm."

On the afternoon of Christmas Day the pilots were released in time to assist the officers and senior NCOs in waiting on the airmen for their Christmas dinner in the traditional RAF fashion. "Each man had four bottles of beer to wash down the splendid meal of turkey, pork, plum pudding and mince pies, and Christmas cake – and there was a parcel of 70 cigarettes on each plate," the squadron record read. In the freezing and dismal weather prevailing, such a meal must have been physically warming as well as morally uplifting.

Lt Albert Sachs left the squadron next day, operationally time-expired. Since he joined at Castel Benito he had been credited with four enemy aircraft destroyed, two probably destroyed and three damaged.

Two of 92's Spitfires were scrambled on 28 December to escort a Dakota carrying General Montgomery to a landing strip near the River Sangro, and on the last day of the month the record book declared: "The Squadron is on the top line, ready to uphold the reputation of 92 throughout the year 1944. May our efforts bring victory next year!"

January ushered itself in with a vengeance on 5th. Gale force winds blew the airmen's mess tent down and a slight snow storm prevented the squadron's usual daily Casoli-Ortona patrol. A Bf 109 downed by Flt Lt Garner on 10 January brought the total to 295½, and confirmation on 13 January of Flg Off Henderson's 'damaged' Me 210 of 8 January as 'destroyed' advanced it to 296½.

Readying itself to provide cover for the coming invasion at Anzio and Nettuno by the US 5th Army, 92 Squadron moved 55 miles south-west to Marcianese landing ground, near Naples, on 17 January. There Mackie was only six miles from the Capodichino strip, where he had commanded 243 Squadron under the 25-pounder batteries.

When he led his squadron off Marcianese strip just before dawn on 22 January, it must have been with a sense of 'deja vu': "I was beginning to get quite used to this sort of thing, and regarded myself as a specialist, as I had been in the Dieppe invasion, then Reggio, then Sicily, Salerno, and now Anzio. Each time I was there just as daylight was breaking, so I guess that's an experience not too many pilots can claim."

One of 92 Squadron's pilots, Flg Off Dibden, certainly made no such claim. His aircraft ran off the runway on take-off and he was killed. Mackie recalled that the Marcianese strip had been carved out of the countryside and was not the best: "As usual, metal strips laid on earth, and to get to the patrol line before dawn we had to take off in complete darkness. Makeshift runway lighting was put up in some form of flares. It was one of those unaccountable things – you can't say – you couldn't see the flares – it was considered adequate – something went wrong – maybe he had a tyre burst – who knows?"

The remainder of 92 went on to an uneventful patrol, the ORB claiming that the unit "which provided the first cover of the Sicily/ Italy invasions, today provided first cover over British and American forces landing 30 miles south of Rome. No contact with enemy aircraft. Sorties over the Anzio battle area."

Roderick Owen, in his history *The Desert Air Force*, noted that there were 850 Allied aircraft "jammed cheek by jowl" on the airfields of Naples, and went on to set the scene of the invasion, with a tribute to Mackie's squadron.

"The invasion fleet was to be well screened. Coastal Air Force was responsible for providing air protection from Naples to the little island of Ponza. 12th Air Support Command (USAAF) took over from there onwards, employing aircraft stepped up in layers. Four Spitfire patrols at 20,000 to 25,000 feet over the beachhead and convoy; twelve Spitfires at 16,000 to 18,000 feet (eight over the beachhead and four over the convoy); 16 US Warhawks (half over the beachhead and half over the convoy). 64th Fighter Wing in Naples, a control ship off the assault beach, and finally a control post on the beachhead, directed the activities of the close-support fighter-bombers.

"Taking off in the palid glow of the waning moon, 92 Squadron were on patrol before first light on 22nd. Below, the troops were already disembarking; a British infantry division with supporting artillery and tanks on the left, five miles north-west of Anzio, and an American Corps consisting of infantry, Rangers, artillery, tanks and other units, on the right near Nettuno. By nightfall the ports of Anzio and Nettuno were in our hands, whilst inland, with little enemy opposition, the bridgehead was rapidly extending."

Mackie flew two sorties on that particular 'D' Day, and was next aloft on 14th, searching off Gaeta Point for Flg Off MacDermott, who was missing in the sea.

Patrols during the next two days were uneventful, but then on 27th, just as a 92 Squadron patrol had been relieved by another squadron, ten Bf 109s flew in from the north-west. Being officially 'off duty' did not worry Mackie, who went straight at the enemy. Unfortunately for him, the anti-aircraft gunners on the naval vessels below were also intent on success that day: "Our CO, Sqn Ldr Mackie, damaged one but interception was made difficult by accurate gunfire from ships off Anzio," recorded the squadron diary.

Mackie's account:

Up: 1235. Down: 1420. 27th January 1944.
Aerodrome: Marcianese, Italy.

I was leading Red and Blue Sections on patrol of the battle area when bandits were reported approaching Anzio from the NW, at

15,000 ft. I climbed to 16,000 ft and whilst orbiting the point saw several bomb bursts well clear of some large ships just NW of Anzio Point. I dived in that direction and I saw at least 5 Me 109s flying east about 2,000 ft below. I jettisoned my tank and attacked an Me 109 opening fire with cannon and machine gun at about 400 yds closing to 250 yds. Just as I saw cannon strikes on the starboard wing roots which caused flame and smoke, my engine started to run very rough, and thinking I had been hit by flack *(sic)* I broke away.

When I last saw this 109 it was in a very steep dive and if it crashed it should be within 10 miles of Anzio Point.

Claim: 1 Me 109 damaged.

The next day, while flying 'J', he shot down a meteorological balloon at 19,000 feet over the battle area – possibly just to practice his marksmanship.

The frustration felt by the squadron's pilots began to show. There they were, just four short of the magic 300, and the enemy was not "coming to the party". On 29 January Flg Off Cornish lamented: "Only 16 sorties were flown over the Anzio battle area today and no enemy 'kites' were airborne when our pilots were in the air. Do they know when 92 takes the air?" He recorded that during the month the squadron had flown 540 operational sorties, 38 non-operational sorties, totalling 775 hours 35 minutes of operational flying and 27 hours 15 minutes of non-operational flying during January – the most since July of 1943.

Rapidly, February promised to be a better month for 92 in terms of aerial success, and Mackie was right there to help his squadron make it so. On 2 February Cornish wrote: "25 sorties were flown over the Anzio area and during our last show six of our pilots encountered a gaggle of 15-20 FW 190s flying east to the battle area. The CO, Sqn Ldr Mackie, brought his personal score to 16 destroyed by chasing one of them until he saw it crash. Flg Off 'Curly' Henderson also destroyed one."

Mackie reported:

Up: 1230. Down: 1415. 2nd February 1944.
Aerodrome: Marcianese, Italy.

I was leading Red Section of 6 A/C on battle area patrol at 12,000 ft when bandits were reported NW of Anzio near the coast. When almost over Anzio itself a few minutes later, I spotted a gaggle of about 15 A/C half rolling and diving from about 13/14,000 ft, probably bombing some cruisers, through cloud just west of the Point. I intercepted one FW 190 as it levelled out over land and closing in to about 250 yds fired both cannon and machine guns. The 190 took evasive action by climbing, diving and weaving so I had no trouble in keeping in range. I fired many short bursts and saw strikes on the fuselage just in front of the cockpit and starboard wing roots. Streams of white smoke burst from the engine and there was a burst of flame. The 190 half rolled and diving through some cloud, crashed in a cloud of dust at approximately F.7846.

I was then at less than 4,000 ft and as much light flak was coming up I beat a hasty retreat and resumed patrol.

Claim: 1 FW 190 destroyed.

(II/SG 4, a fighter-bomber unit, lost at least one FW 190 to Spitfires on this date, Uffz Kurt Radebold being killed.)

It was undoubtedly a very proud Sqn Ldr Mackie who hosted four New Zealand nursing sisters in his squadron's pilots' mess three days later. With 16 enemy aircraft to his credit, a double DFC, and wearing the mantle of leadership of the RAF's 'crack' fighter squadron, things were certainly going his way. Even Mackie's natural modesty could understandably be relaxed to allow an equally natural pride to show through the chinks.

With 298½ enemy aircraft claimed, and only one and a half to go to the big 300, mechanical trouble which had been dogging 92 Squadron's Mark VIII Spitfires came to a head, causing even more frustration than the lack of opponents: "Since we have been in Naples at least nine pilots have had to make forced landings owing to their engines cutting, and after two episodes today our aircraft were grounded," Cornish recorded on 14 February.

At first the trouble was thought to be in the fuel. Samples analysed indicated the presence of corrosive sulphur. Special supplies of sealed petrol containers were obtained and all tanks and bowsers flushed out. This was not the main cause of the engine failure however. Lt J. Gasson* (SAAF) brought back a report from a squadron engineer at Nettuno that petrol was freezing in the petrol coolers on Spitfire VIIIs, causing the engines to cut.

"In the later marks of Spitfire like the VIII and the IX, the rate of climb was so great that in hot countries like Egypt they suffered from the petrol vapourising in the carburettor if they climbed quickly to a great altitude," explained Mackie. "The solution to that was to

---

* (Maj J.E. Gasson, DSO, DFC; see *Aces High*, page 657.)

put in a small wing radiator, about three inches in diameter, through which the petrol was cooled en route to the carburettor. In the cold conditions it was having the opposite effect; it was freezing the petrol before it got to the carburettor. This was quickly overcome by putting a sticky patch over the radiator aperture."

Technical problems solved, it required only the Luftwaffe to co-operate, but 32 sorties were flown by 92's pilots on 15 February without a sign of an FW 190 or a Bf 109. Then came what must have been remembered by squadron personnel as "the glorious 16th".

Flg Off Cornish takes up the tale of that day's events: "None of our pilots were able to get within range of 15 FW 190s sighted. In despair Sqn Ldr Mackie fired at four from 350 yards but he saw no results.

"After that show the squadron was at 30-minute readiness and the pilots were having lunch when a call came through from Wing operations asking if we could get a section airborne at once. In less than ten minutes, although several of our kites were under daily inspections, five of our pilots had taken off. They had been on patrol for 25 minutes when vapour trails were seen orbiting Rome, increasing in number and shortly afterwards a gaggle of aircraft was sighted flying down the coast.

"They were identified as 20 FW 190s in tight formation with a top cover of six Me 109s flying 5,000 feet above. Our pilots flew to intercept and met the enemy aircraft head-on as they dived to bomb the road north of Anzio. The Huns, continuing to dive, turned north-wards, but our pilots gave chase.

"Flt Lt J.F. Edwards, DFC, DFM, destroyed an FW 190 and Lt Gasson shot the tail off an Me 109. Thus was the squadron total of 300 enemy aircraft destroyed brought to the 300 mark." A young New Zealander who had recently joined the squadron, Flg Off Cedric Young, was awarded a Bf 109 damaged while flying No.2 to Gasson in the same encounter.

The celebration of the 300th victory was held that night (the record does not show whether it was Edwards or Gasson who bagged the 300th – or the sweepstake, although 'Stocky' Edwards confirms that the honour was his). Among the guests in the squadron mess were Grp Capt Kingcome, Wg Cdr Stan Turner (now 244 Wing's Wing Commander, Flying) and Wg Cdr C.P. 'Paddy' Green*, who had been a flight commander with 92 early in the war, and had contributed to the 300 victories; he was now a highly successful night fighter, commanding 600 (City of London) Squadron.

The evening of celebration was also the eve of Mackie's departure

---

* (Grp Capt C.P. Green, DSO, DFC. US DFC; see *Aces High*, pages 300-1.)

from 92 Squadron. On 18 February he flew his last Anzio patrol with the unit, while two days later Sqn Ldr G.J. Cox*, DFC, arrived to take over.

This time there was nothing untoward in Mackie's posting – it was, in fact, at his own instigation. "Air activity was very low and I realised I was getting near the stage where, in all fairness, I should go on rest. Whereas the normal tour is 200-odd hours of operations, mine had now extended to 492 hours, although I had had the various breaks of coming to the Mediterranean, and between actual campaigns. But the same thing applied to people in England. They weren't on operations every day.

"I'd done 349 sorties and 492 operational hours, so I put in for a posting. I would have liked to have gone back to England to a gunnery school to improve my air-to-air firing, because I could get on to aircraft very often, but I couldn't always hit them. I could have done better, had I been spot on the target."

Flg Off Cornish noted on 25 February: "Sqn Ldr Mackie said farewell to the squadron today. Since he took over command on 3 November,1943, we have destroyed 20 enemy aircraft, which is a tribute in itself to his leadership. We are sorry to see him go, but we realise at the end of a tour in which he has personally accounted for 16 destroyed, he deserves a rest."

Mackie had obviously made an impression on the squadron, and he also made an impression on Cedric Young, who cut his fighter pilot teeth in the Western Desert with 112 (Shark) Squadron, and was a member of the celebrated Late Arrivals Club (motto: It is never too late to come back), and who joined 92 in early February, 1944.

"I always considered it unfortunate that by the end of the month he was posted away and we got a new CO, as in the short time that I knew him I had come to regard him as a very fine pilot and a great leader," Young recalled at his Maketu home in 1993.

Young caught on quite quickly to Mackie's exacting standards. "On my second flight with 92, I was flying as his No.2 and shortly after take off I saw my oil pressure disappearing rapidly. So I called up and said I was returning to base, but forgot to give my call sign. And a very sharp voice came over the RT: 'What's your bloody call sign?'

"He did not say much, but he was the sort of person who asserted confidence. You felt that you could go anywhere with him and some-how or another you would be safe. He was just that type of fellow, and everybody had the greatest admiration for him. I was very disappointed when he left the squadron."

---

* (Sqn Ldr G.J. Cox, DFC & Bar; see *Aces High*, page 194).

Cedric Young added that Mackie seemed to think of everything in connection with his role as a fighter leader and gave an instance: "Whenever he flew he always wore a stout pair of boots, in case he came down in the hills or somewhere in enemy territory and had to make his way home on foot." And he confirmed that his fellow-Kiwi was not a great drinker of alcohol: "That was one of the reasons he gave for his success. While other chaps had a sore head, his head was always clear."

Mackie was certainly strict, said Young, but "usually in a nice way."

Without a doubt, Mackie had made his mark in the Mediterranean campaigns. He felt it was the right time to leave, but had he known what his next posting was to be in the United Kingdom, he might not have been quite so keen to go. He boarded the troopship *Almanzora* at Naples on 11 April (after a spot of local leave) for the 11-day voyage to Glasgow, and the British spring.

CHAPTER EIGHT

WESTERN EUROPE AGAIN – 122 WING

Mackie's departure from Italy proved to be anything but a pleasure cruise. "The roughest passage it was possible to have through the Mediterranean" was how he later described the pitching and rolling of the *Almanzora*. "You'd have to see it to believe it. We were just being tossed around like corks. I've never seen such rough water in my life."

The New Zealander was one of the few on board who was not seasick, and he watched with interest the futile efforts of the crew to launch an anti-aircraft balloon. Quite disillusioned with the Mediterranean, which he had previously associated with calm blue waters under sunny skies, he gained some comfort from the thought that the rough weather would make it difficult for enemy submarines to attack successfully. They did not, and *Almanzora* made a safe passage to Glasgow. Mackie, looking forward to polishing up his gunnery, took a train south. On reporting to a pool of RAF officers at Folkestone, he was again disillusioned. "Gunnery school? You don't want to go to gunnery school!" they said. "We want you to go to Headquarters at Stanmore."

In spite of all arguments, Headquarters it was. Bentley Priory, near Stanmore in Middlesex, the rambling mansion from where Fighter Command activities were directed, was to be his home for the next six months. Except that – it was no longer Fighter Command. The great force which Air Chief Marshal Sir Hugh Dowding had built up since 1936, which had expanded so vastly in the period from 1940-1943, had been reduced to one third of its size and given its old title, Air Defence of Great Britain (ADGB). The reason for the change, which had occurred in November 1943, was the creation of the Second Tactical Air Force (2nd TAF) to support the forthcoming opening of the Second Front in Normandy. Air Chief Marshal Sir Trafford Leigh-Mallory had left his post as Commander-in-Chief, Fighter Command, to head the new air force, and the pared-down home defence fighter force remaining was placed under the command of Air Marshal Sir Roderic Hill. It was to Sir Roderic that Mackie reported when he arrived at Bentley Priory in May 1944, to take up the post of Training II – effectively, the second most senior staff officer in the fighter training establishment.

His duties were to convey the Air Ministry's instructions on training to the training establishments, and to ensure that aircrew were being trained in accordance with them. He was not impressed. "I drove a desk for the next six months almost to the day. Most of the time was spent in the office dealing with what seemed to me useless paperwork. I could truthfully say that I didn't add much to the war effort – not through any fault of my own.

"If I had been doing something with my hands I would have been much happier. But just dealing with paperwork, handing it on, commenting, visiting stations which were run by very competent staff, didn't appear to me to be doing very much."

There were, however, two brighter aspects to his new post. One was access to Spitfires and communications aircraft at nearby Northolt airfield. The other was the presence at Bentley Priory of a certain Women's Auxiliary Air Force (WAAF) Sergeant, Marjorie Dear.

His logbook shows that Mackie seized every opportunity to escape from his desk and fly to training establishments. During the six months, he managed to visit 31 RAF stations in the United Kingdom, and three on the Continent (once the Normandy invasion had taken place in June 1944); some stations he visited several times. In all he flew seven versions of the Spitfire from Northolt – Marks IIA, IIB, VB, VC, VII, IX and IXB – as well as an Auster III and several Percival Proctors.

He went south to Selsey, Appledram and Bognor on the Channel coast; west to Montford Bridge on the Welsh border, near Shrewsbury; east to Southend in Essex, and as far north as Tealing, a training station north of the Scottish city of Dundee. He also re-visited his old OTU at Grangemouth.

Working not far away at 2nd TAF's 85 Group Headquarters at Uxbridge, was his old friend from Waihi, now Flg Off Owen Morgan. A radar technician, he was part of a team planning radar control for the Group's 12 fighter squadrons in readiness for when they would fly cover over the forthcoming D-Day invasion of Occupied France.

Mackie would much rather have been involved in such operations himself instead of being tied to the desk to which he was condemned. 6 June 1944 did at least find him aloft in a Spitfire IIB – even if it was flying in the opposite direction, to Annan, between Carlisle and Dumfries in Scotland. That same day he visited training units at

Acklington and Deenethorpe, before returning to Northolt after flights totalling three hours 35 minutes – a long day in a Spitfire cockpit.

Itching as he was to get more gunnery instruction and re-join the war effort more positively, he realised there was little point in seeking a re-posting immediately. Instead, he applied himself to his paperwork and furthered his acquaintance with Sgt Marjorie Dear. In less than two years they would marry. Her parents owned a public house in Garston, near Watford, and her brother was a pilot with Bomber Command. "He used to bring his crew home with him, seven of them, and my home was always filled with airmen," she recalled. Her affinity with the RAF led her to join the WAAF in 1941, and after basic training she was posted to Fighter Command Headquarters at Bentley Priory.

"We were 12 WAAFs posted to Stanmore amongst 1,000 airmen," Mrs Mackie remembered. "The airmen didn't want us, so they put us to work making cups of tea and running errands. Within 12 months there were 1,000 WAAFs and a dozen airmen – the rest had all been posted to the Middle East for the battles there."

While serving in the operations section she was promoted to Corporal, and in 1943 she was posted in charge of the accident records section with the rank of Sergeant. There she worked in what she described as a League of Nations of tour-expired aircrew, including a South African and a Canadian. "I had a navigation officer with a broken back," she said. "He was in plaster from his neck to his bottom and he sat very uncomfortably as his plaster would not bend. The rest of the officers played darts on his chest!" One of her team was a 22-year-old fighter pilot who was missing a leg and a hand; he had been shot down by British anti-aircraft gunners.

When she first met Evan Mackie, Marjorie Dear was still recovering from the loss of her fiancee in France, and was not much interested in men, but she found him to be "a great tease". When he declared that there were no pretty walks around the Priory she took umbrage, and challenged him to take a walk with her: "I thought, I'll take you for a walk – a long one. However, I ended up with a big blister on my foot, and he had to help me home. We became very friendly and he met my parents."

Mackie also found time to mix pleasure with business and on 17 July, 1944, he agreed to fly Owen Morgan in a Proctor from Northolt to Newcastle to see his brother. Tom Morgan was a ship's engineer who was ashore briefly to sit his extra Chief's ticket. Although the Battle of the Atlantic against the German U-Boats was beginning to be won, life at sea was still precarious, and Mackie knew how precious those rare wartime meetings were for the two Morgan brothers. He and Owen landed at Ouston, an RAF station just west of Newcastle, after a two and a quarter hour flight. Mackie then flew on to Eshott and Boulmer, nearby training establishments, and returned the next day to Ouston.

Owen had brought brother Tom to the airfield to meet Evan, who readily agreed to take Tom aboard for a short flight to Usworth, an airfield nearer to South Shields, where Tom was attending the Maritime College. A Royal Canadian Air Force ground staff member also managed to talk himself aboard the Proctor. "As it was a four-seater aircraft, I agreed," recalled Mackie. "But I hadn't counted on the fact that he had four suitcases! These were duly stowed aboard, and I can only say that we waffled into the air. Still, flying conditions were good and there was plenty of length of runway and I don't think we were in any great danger at any time."

While at Stanmore he also met up with Marty Hume, an old friend from 485 Squadron days. They flew in an Auster to Detling in Kent, and on to Selsey in Sussex where the squadron was then stationed. Hume had recently completed a stint as CO of 485, and that was quite a reunion – the Mediterranean ace and the former CO back with their old unit. On a later occasion Mackie took Hume with him when he visited Bognor airfield from Northolt.

Then came an invitation from Buckingham Palace. His Majesty wished to invest the Squadron Leader from New Zealand with both his Distinguished Flying Cross awards personally. "My future mother-in-law celebrated the occasion by hiring none other than a Rolls-Royce taxi to take us from Watford to the Palace and back," said Mackie. It was the second occasion on which he had met George VI. "He had little to say other than: 'You're a long way from home', that type of thing."

Being at the centre of things at Stanmore, Mackie had been well placed to keep in touch with movements, and with new developments in aircraft. In particular he had his eye on the Tempest fighter, which was just coming into prominence. A friend from 485 Squadron days, Grp Capt 'Jamie' Jameson, was commanding a Tempest Wing in Holland. Mackie obtained permission to fly over and see what his chances were of joining it.

He left Northolt in a Spitfire VB on 20 November, 1944, and flew to Volkel via Maldeghem and Eindhoven, arriving the following day. He was obviously persuasive during the four days he spent with Jameson at 122 Wing Headquarters, for he flew back direct to Northolt on 25 November with an invitation to join at any time. "There was no immediate post for me in the Wing, which was a five-squadron wing," said Mackie. "Therefore, I would join as a super-numerary Squadron Leader."

At about this time Marjorie Dear had volunteered for service abroad, and been posted to the staff of Supreme Headquarters, Allied Expeditionary Force (SHAEF). The Headquarters were at Hampton Court Palace, and V-1 flying bombs fell near on most nights. "We didn't know where we were going, but we knew it would be Germany or Japan, so I went to night school to learn German," she remembered. "Evan said that if I was on the Continent and he was flying somewhere abroad we wouldn't be able to see much of each other, so he gave me an ultimatum: either marry me, or we would not see each other again!

"So I put in my notice and was transferred to Ruislip Records Office until I was demobbed." By then her work at Bentley Priory had been recognised with a Mention in Despatches – which Marjorie Mackie was later to describe as "for good service pushing a pen!"

On the eve of his departure from Stanmore, Mackie was keener than ever to rejoin what he called the real war. By October 1944 the much-disliked title Air Defence of Great Britain had been banished for a second time. "Fighter Command was once again relabelled Fighter Command," wrote one historian, "and now sat back like a cat in its home garden, relaxed but watchful, not missing a movement and ready to pounce in a moment on any suspicious movement." Mackie wanted more than that.

His position at Bentley Priory was undoubtedly a much coveted one. Safely distanced from the front line, cushioned as it was in the comfort of Fighter Command Headquarters, with Spitfires and other aircraft on hand, many would have fought hard to retain the post. Mackie on the other hand, could not leave it fast enough.

On 29 November, 1944, he handed over to his successor and was flown from Northolt to Tangmere in an Airspeed Oxford. There he joined 83 Group Support Unit (GSU) and set out to master his new mount, the Hawker Tempest V.

The origins of the Tempest V can be traced back to April 1937, when the Napier company was testing its new 24-cylinder H-section Sabre engine, which promised an output in excess of 2,000 horse power. Sydney Camm, Chief Designer for Hawker, and his team had already produced the very successful Hurricane fighter. Now they began investigating the possibility of building a single-seat interceptor capable of being powered either by the Sabre, or by the 24-cylinder X-section Rolls-Royce Vulture of similar power. Two prototypes resulted, the Tornado with the Vulture and the Typhoon with the Sabre. The failure of the Vulture resulted in the demise of the Tornado, but the Typhoon was ordered into production, and rushed into service as a high-altitude interceptor well before all the 'bugs' had been ironed out of the design of aircraft or engine.

The wing design was in many ways similar to that of the Hurricane, featuring a thick aerofoil section which proved aerodynamically disadvantageous. A failure in its designed role, subject to considerable initial unreliability both of the engine and the airframe during its early service, the Typhoon was almost dispensed with by the RAF. Luftwaffe low-level fighter-bomber attacks on Southern England proved its salvation however, for a very high low-level maximum speed allowed it to catch and despatch these predators in a manner which the Spitfire could not match at the time.

Subsequently, following strengthening of elements of the airframe and improvements in the reliability of the Sabre IIA engine, the Typhoon found its true forte as an extremely successful ground-attack aircraft, carrying bombs or newly-developed rocket projectiles. In this role it was to achieve considerable fame in support of the Allied armies in Western Europe when the invasion commenced.

In a successful effort to overcome the high-speed compressibility which had adversely affected the Tornado and Typhoon, Camm, in an object lesson in aerodynamic refinement, designed a much thinner semi-elliptical wing with a slim aerofoil section. Indeed, the new wing was so thin that the Typhoon fuselage had to be lengthened by 21 inches to provide room for fuel tanks previously incorporated into the wing. Special narrow-section tyres had to be developed for the undercarriage, while for the armament new, slender, Hispano V 20mm cannon were also developed. But it was all worth it, for the new aircraft, dubbed Tempest I, was to achieve a top speed of 466 miles an hour at 24,500 feet from its 2,240 hp Sabre IV engine. In August 1942 the Tempest I was the fastest piston-engined fighter in the world, and would have given the Allies an enormous edge on the opposition. That however, was not to be.

Delays in the Sabre IV production programme resulted instead in orders being placed for the Tempest V, powered by the 2,180 hp Sabre IIB engine, and fitted with the same new, thin and highly-efficient wing. The Tempest V had a top speed of 427 mph at 18,500 feet, which was still faster than most Axis fighters when it came into service in February 1944 – notably the FW 190A-6 and Bf 109G-10. When the FW 190D-9 'long nose' version of the Focke Wulf fighter appeared in quantity later in 1944, this Junkers Jumo 213A-powered aircraft proved to have a very similar performance and a marginally better climb rate. However, the Tempest enjoyed the Spitfire's advantage in being able to turn inside the Focke Wulf, and could also dive faster.

Armed with four 20mm Hispano Mark V cannon, the Tempest V was a formidable machine, and from September 1944 onwards had become 2nd TAF's primary air superiority fighter at low and medium altitudes. Mackie was impressed with the Tempest from the outset. Having followed its development closely, perhaps he was prepared to be.

By the time he first took a Tempest V aloft on 1 December 1944, most of the bugs in the type had been eliminated. He was fortunate in that respect, because both the Typhoons and Tempests had been rushed into service, and many had been lost because of airframe failures (in the former) and engine failures (in both).

Even so, the Tempest V had its little peculiarities. Try and take off after ten minutes of taxiing and idling without clearing the engine with a sustained burst at 3,000 revs per minute, and the Sabre was likely to cut out completely on opening up. The aircraft would also develop a vicious swing on take-off unless the throttle was opened very smoothly, and appropriate rudder corrections applied immediately.

Landing could also be a dicey matter for the unwary. The aircraft weighed a little more than five tons fully laden and was designed to touch down at about 100 mph. A heavy landing could easily result in a burst tyre – and that meant a terrifying ground loop at best.

A wheels-up crash landing in a Tempest was treated with great respect. The massive radiator housing beneath the engine had a tendency to dig in and flip the aircraft upside down, which usually resulted in a fire from which escape was almost impossible. Many Tempest pilots abandoned their aircraft and parachuted to safety if they knew the undercarriage had been damaged. Some tried a crash-landing; a few survived. Mackie was to be one of the latter lucky ones.

For all its idiosyncracies, the Tempest was to become his favourite fighter, above even his beloved Spitfire. "Like all other Spitfire pilots at the time I would be the first to agree that they were the finest aircraft ever made. You wore them. You didn't just get in them and fly them. You became part of them and I can imagine nothing nicer than the later types.

"But for the class of work that was in progress on the Continent and from what I could see of the Tempest, it had more to offer; greater fire-power, greatly increased range and higher speed, particularly low down. They were particularly good in the dive and a very stable platform from which to fire."

By 5 December Mackie had made 12 flights in three different Tempest Vs, logging nine hours and 50 minutes, and decided that he liked the machine very much. "It seemed to have very few faults in my opinion. It was easier landing, having a wider under-carriage than the Spitfire, slightly improved vision, and easier taxiing. And it could be thrown around the sky like a piece of paper, it was so manoeuvrable."

He was sure that the Tempest had the edge on the latest types of Bf 109 and FW 190 in speed, flying straight and level. "I found that the harder and faster you flew them, the better they went," he said. It was a point of view he established early, for during his conversion to Tempests at Tangmere, most of his time airborne had been spent in aerobatics and dogfighting practice, with two sessions of air-to-ground firing on Studland range. It was appropriate that that was the nature of his gunnery practice, for on the Continent he was destined to bag rather more ground transport and locomotives than German aircraft.

It was a new type of warfare that the Mediterranean veteran was about to enter. The fighter squadrons in which he had served and led so far had flown almost entirely in the air superiority role (referred to more recently as 'counter-air'), their quarry being limited in the main to hostile fighters and bombers. Over Western Europe this was changing, due in the main to the very scarcity of aerial opposition from the overstretched and weakened Luftwaffe.

The German Army was on the defensive, as it had been in North Africa, Sicily and Italy – although it was to revert to its offensive mode briefly, but devastatingly, during December 1944. Then a final offensive was launched in the Ardennes in an effort to reach the Belgian port of Antwerp, and thereby split the British and Canadian armies in the northern part of the front from the US forces further south. This offensive, known colloquially as the 'Battle of the Bulge', was about to be launched at the moment when Evan Mackie joined 122 Wing.

Whilst the Wing's primary role remained that of air superiority patrols, increasingly all fighter units were encouraged to join the fighter-bombers in attacking targets of opportunity of all types on the ground. In this role the main enemy became the opponent's anti-aircraft defences – the Flak. But this was not the familiar black shell bursts of the 88mm heavy Flak at high altitude – it was the deadly streams of tracer from the automatic light Flak, which the Germans had developed to a considerable degree of efficiency and sophistication. One particular weapon had become the nemesis of the Allied ground-attack pilots – the gyroscopically sighted, quadruple-barrelled 20mm automatic Flak guns. These were plentiful, and were manned by well-trained and experienced crews. When used in battalion strength, as they were to protect the most worthwhile targets, there were six of them, supported by nine single 37mm guns – together they hurled 250 shells a second into the air.

Two aspects of this type of ground attack were hated by pilots. An effective attack took the aircraft necessarily very close to that most dangerous of elements for an aircraft – the ground itself. It also required the pilot to keep his machine on a steady course for the last few seconds of the attack if he was to aim his guns accurately. And theoretically, there is no target more easy to hit than one coming steadily and directly towards the gunner.

In consequence, losses to Flak were frequently to become more severe than to enemy aircraft. This resulted on occasion during the autumn and winter of 1944/45 in 122 Wing receiving orders to desist from attacking ground targets in order to husband available numbers of these relatively scarce and valuable aircraft for their primary purpose.

Flak therefore was to be probably the most dangerous enemy which Mackie was now to meet, and he was to find that it took a new kind of courage to hold a Tempest steady on a ground target, ignoring the bursting shells and the glowing tracer, concentrating on the gunsight and the target, until that wonderful moment when, with stick back, 2,180 hp of snarling Sabre could be used to haul one skyward to comparative safety. By its very nature, ground attack had the potential of greater danger than air-to-air combat. In front of every Tempest pilot lay the sheer inevitability of flying through a barrage of automatic anti-aircraft fire. There was no way he could avoid doing so, for it was likely to be the only way to the target.

Such activities lacked, perhaps, the 'glamour' of aerial combat, which appeared much 'cleaner' in its application. It was nevertheless, effective and necessary, and contributed greatly to the ultimate defeat of the German forces. However, after a notable absence by the Luftwaffe as it rebuilt and re-equipped its shattered units after the terrible losses which had been suffered in Normandy during the summer, the Ardennes offensive was to bring it out in force again. Once more formations of up to 50 fighters and fighter-bombers were to be encountered, together with growing numbers of the radical new Messerschmitt Me 262 jets, employed in the main as fighter-bombers. These aircraft were so fast that interception by the Allied piston-engined fighters became a matter of luck, either catching them unawares, or following an engine failure (which was not uncommon at the time), or during their landing or take-off approaches at their home airfields, when they were at their most vulnerable.

This then, was Mackie's new war. By the standards of the time, he was already an 'old stager'. And he was very good. By his own admission, he was also very lucky. Before his new war ended he would inflict considerable damage on the enemy. To his credit, he would also look after the newcomers whenever possible.

122 Wing, a part of Air Marshal Harry Broadhurst's 83 Group, supporting the 21st Army Group, had been on the Continent since 25 June, 1944 – less than three weeks after the D-Day landings. At

that time the Wing comprised three squadrons of North American Mustang IIIs. Since 25 July the Wing had been under the command of Grp Capt Jameson, whilst during September and October the Mustang units had returned to the United Kingdom for other duties, their place being taken by five squadrons of Tempest Vs – 3, 56, 80, 274 and 486 (New Zealand).

When Mackie boarded the duty Anson on the 'milk run' from England up to the front line in Europe on 13 December 1944, the Wing was still based at Volkel, a Dutch air station recently vacated by the Germans. Jameson assigned him as a supernumerary to 3 Squadron, to give him the opportunity of gaining some operational experience on the Tempest before taking command of one of the Wing's other squadrons.

Weather on the Continent had been less than suitable for airborne operations, according to the 122 Wing history: "It was during this period of the 'Volkel vapours' of constant poor visibility that 'Desmond', the call sign of 122 Wing's flying control, became particularly well-known in the Group for the efficiency and speed of its homings. It was during these autumn months, too, that the Group Support Unit Ansons, bringing replacement pilots from Thorney Island, became objects of awed respect by flying in conditions when all sane men stayed firmly on the deck.

"A typical example of the flying weather at this time was quoted by a section of Tempests which landed after 45 minutes patrolling and reported: 'Weather considered unsuitable. Ten tenths at 700 feet. Top unknown. Rainstorms. Vis. poor.' On that particular day 34 sorties were flown."

The Wing had taken a new direction shortly before Mackie's arrival: "At the end of November the Wing was taken off defensive work," according to the Wing history, "and really came into its own, in the last six months of the war producing results unsurpassed by any Wing in the 2nd TAF."

In command of 3 Squadron when Mackie joined it briefly on 15 December was a familiar figure – Sqn Ldr Harvey Sweetman, a fellow Kiwi who had last flown with Mackie as a Plt Off in 485 Squadron. By now experienced in Tempest flying and tactics, having been in command of the squadron since September, Sweetman taught Mackie quite a few 'wrinkles' in his four days with the unit.

He suggested an air cannon test over the Zuider Zee on the first day, and blooded Mackie in the sport of ground attack on 17 December. In the Osnabrück-Rheine area Mackie felt for the first time the dubious thrill of shooting up trains – and learned again the sickening thump that Flak made as it slammed into his aircraft.

Transferred to 274 Squadron, commanded by Sqn Ldr Alexander

H. Baird, Mackie made his mark on his first patrol. It was Christmas Eve, and the squadron was at 10,000 feet over Aachen, not far from Eindhoven. Bad weather had kept 122 Wing's aircraft grounded for several days, but Feldmarshall von Rundstedt's counter-offensive in the Ardennes had begun on 16 December. American forces particularly were hard-pressed in the Wing's area and the Tempests were airborne at the first opportunity.

"I was flying what they call arse-end Charlie – I was the last aircraft in the formation," Mackie recalled. "I noticed a squadron of Typhoons heading in the opposite direction, down toward the battle area. I also noticed a stray aircraft at the back which moved up behind the others – a few puffs of smoke and the aircraft dived away."

It quickly dawned on Mackie that the Typhoons were under attack – and that only he had seen this. Indeed, two of the Typhoons (which were from 440 Squadron, RCAF) had already been shot down by the attacker. "I called up the squadron leader. He was leading the thing and it wasn't my place to break off on my own. I called him twice, there was no reply, so I did the inevitable." The reason there was no response from Baird, as Mackie later realised, was because he (Mackie) had failed to change to the proper radio channel.

Meanwhile: "I dived down, I came up under this 190. He must have seen me, because he went vertically up. I don't know how much longer he would have gone. I couldn't have gone on much longer, but I thought: Well, I'll go on as long as you will, mate! And I was gaining on him, because of the speed I had attained during the dive.

"I gave a short burst right at the top, and I more or less flopped off into a semi-spin. I saw no results, and it was with great trepidation that I returned to dispersal, expecting a rap over the knuckles for breaking away as I did. But word came through that the thing had crashed just near Eindhoven. So all was well. That justified it." He lodged the following claim:

Up: 1105. Down: 1255. December 24, 1944.
Place of attack: Eindhoven.

I was flying No.2 to Talbot Leader in Red Section on a patrol Julich-Malmedy and while we were returning to base and approaching Eindhoven, I noticed approx. 8 Typhoons flying in the opposite direction at about 4,000 ft. They were in open formation. When almost abreast of these A/C at about 6,000 ft I noticed one of the Typhoons suddenly break formation and dive into the ground on fire and I did not see anybody bale out. I then noticed the machine which had been flying behind that one, had moved behind another Typhoon, which then began shedding

large pieces and losing height. Although we were not close enough
to these aircraft to identify one of them as an enemy, I realised
that this particular one must have been, so I immediately
jettisoned my long-range tanks and gave chase.

There was no R/T communication between myself and the other
members of the section, as I had not heard the order to change
to channel 'A'. The E/A lost some height then pulled vertically
upwards. I identified it as a short nosed FW 190 and opened fire
with four cannons at a range of about 250 yds closing to 50 yds.
I then broke off the attack as I was then rolling over on to my
back. I gave about a 2½ sec. burst and numerous strikes were
seen on the wings and centre section of the FW 190 by myself
and F/L Malloy who was flying Red 3.

After I broke away, S/L Baird stated that the FW 190 levelled
out, going very slowly, dropped a wing and then spun into the
ground approx. 4 miles SE of Eindhoven, where it blew up.

Claim: 1 FW 190 destroyed.

It seems that Mackie had shot down Hauptmann Wolfgang Kosse,
Staffelkapitän of 13 Staffel, IV Gruppe, Jagdgeschwader 3. Kosse was
reported lost in combat with Typhoons in the Luttich area at about
1245, having reportedly shot down two of these aircraft first; two of
his pilots each claimed a further Typhoon during this engagement,
although only two were actually lost by the Canadian unit. These
final victories had brought Kosse's personal total to 28 – so he was
a worthy opponent for the New Zealander. "His luck ran out that
day," Mackie later commented, when told of the likely identity of
his victim many years later.

Altogether 122 Wing aircraft flew a total 142 hours on Christmas
Eve – an effort which they repeated on Christmas Day. "Plenty of
activity. Eight missions flown, no successes," recorded 274 Squadron's
Operations Record Book. Mackie was one who flew that day.

"In spite of this sudden rush of hard work, the traditional Christmas
dinner was served by the officers to all ranks," according to the Wing
history. "The chief feature of the season, however, was a party given
to 300 Dutch children, who enjoyed an afternoon they are hardly
likely to forget."

274 Squadron at this time was composed mainly of Britons. Mackie
was one of three New Zealanders, the others being Flg Off A.I. Ross
and Flt Lt N.A. Crofts. There were also some Canadian pilots, and
an Australian – just the sort of mixture Mackie thought made up a
good team.

Mackie flew an uneventful patrol on Boxing Day (26 December), but found more action on 27 December during a patrol over the Aachen area. "Two Me 109s were sighted at 1100 hours flying at 11,000 feet over Aachen," according to the squadron record book. "Sqn Ldr Mackie attacked one enemy aircraft and observed strikes at the wing roots of the fuselage – flew off emitting black smoke and he claimed this as damaged. Wt Off E. Twigg attacked the second enemy aircraft, which crashed and exploded at approx. seven miles S/E of Duren."

Mackie's report of the action:

Up: 1040. Down: 1210. December 27, 1944.
Place of attack: Duren.

I was flying as No.1 in Blue Section which was top cover to Red Section, on a bomb-line patrol, Julich-Malmedy. Huns had been reported in the St. Vith area, and the squadron became split up so a rendezvous over Aachen was ordered by Red Leader.

My No.2 W/O Twigg, and W/O Weir, who had been flying as Red 3, were flying with me towards Aachen at about 11.000 ft when two Me 109Es flying line abreast passed within about 300 yds of me. Long-range tanks had previously been jettisoned, so informing Blue Section of my intention I turned hard to starboard and gave chase. After about 3 or 4 minutes I overtook the 109s which were flying almost due east. Definitely identifying them as 109Es I opened fire with four cannons on the one which was flying on the starboard side, at about 300 yds closing to 200 yds. I saw numerous brilliant flashes on the wing roots and centre section, and the 109 began emitting large volumes of black smoke and I thought it was on fire. Also large pieces were seen to fall off it.

Both the strikes and the pieces falling off were seen by both the pilots flying with me, even though one of them was about 1,500 yds behind, having had trouble with long-range tanks.

I broke off my attack on this 109 and turned to port to see what had become of the other 109 which I had last seen at about 300 yds on my port side, but a Tempest was engaging it.

When I turned my attention back to the first 109 again, it was not in sight and must have gone down for the visibility at that height was perfect. There was smoke and haze coming up from the Ruhr which could easily have obscured the latter part of its descent. As there was great danger of a bounce by other enemy fighters I could not investigate its fate any further, but I am sure it did not make base.

Claim: 1 Me 109 damaged.

Mackie's firm identification of these aircraft as Bf 109Es is strange, since this model of the aircraft had disappeared from front-line service in Western Europe during 1941, and elsewhere by early 1943, the remaining aircraft of this type being in use only for the operational training role.

His next encounter with the enemy was a dicey one indeed. At first light on New Year's Day, 1945, he was sitting in the cockpit of his Tempest at dispersal, about to leave on a patrol. Most of the Wing was already airborne and just as he was about to taxi out, the Luftwaffe struck – in strength: "These aircraft whizzed by at treetop level, guns ablaze. Naturally, they had little time to pick and choose their targets, and I consider myself to be one of the lucky ones," he commented on his escape from injury.

It was Operation 'Bodenplatte'*, a final fling by the Luftwaffe. From all over, Luftwaffe General Hugo Sperrle had gathered together more than 800 fighters and fighter-bombers, in conditions of absolute secrecy. At dawn on 1 January he flung them against the Allied airfields in Belgium and Holland in simultaneous co-ordinated low-level attacks. Surprise was total, and on the face of it, the operation was in some ways a success, for the Allies had not believed the Germans were capable of attacking in such numbers any more.

Some 200 RAF and USAAF aircraft were destroyed, while an equal number were damaged where they were parked; of these however, many were non-operational types, or bombers from the US 8th Air Force or Bomber Command, which had landed at local airfields after raids on Germany, rather than flying back to the United Kingdom. Total losses of locally-based tactical aircraft amounted to 50 Spitfires, 19 Typhoons, 23 US P-47 Thunderbolts, and 11 Wellingtons. The latter were elderly medium bombers, now in use for night reconnaissance duties. 11 more fighters were lost in combat with the attacking Luftwaffe formations.

By a miracle Volkel was one of three airfields almost untouched. Some 70 German fighters from Jagdgeschwader 6 were briefed to attack Volkel, but owing to faulty navigation, only about a dozen arrived. According to the Wing history: "These passed smartly over the airfield at 0900 hours and did practically no damage. Three of the Tempest squadrons were airborne at the time, and although two of them were short of ammunition after ground-strafing, they succeeded in shooting down eight Huns, probably destroying one, and damaging four in a matter of moments without loss."

Mackie's old squadron, 485, was caught on the ground at Maldeghem

---

* (For a detailed account of the events of 1 January, 1945, see *Battle of the Airfields* by Norman Franks, published by Grub Street, 1995.)

in Belgium, and lost 11 Spitfires, burnt to ashes. Bill Crawford-Compton – now Wing Commander (Flying) of 145 Wing – with whom Mackie had shared his first victory, was nearly caught by 'Bodenplatte' fighters as he drove around the perimeter of another Low Countries airfield. He abandoned his car at ten miles an hour and sprawled in a gutter as cannon shells churned up chunks of tarmac only 12 metres away. He too was lucky, for the Germans missed him, his car and some nearby petrol tanks!

Whilst losses of aircraft had been fairly heavy, they were much lower than they might have been had all bases targetted been attacked with full effectiveness. Further, relatively few Allied pilots had become casualties – 12 killed, two wounded and one POW – and aircraft losses could now be made good from the stocks held at Maintenance Units, with remarkable rapidity.

For the Germans however, the operation ended as an unmitigated disaster. Their own Flak opened up on several formations in error (due to the very secrecy that almost gave success), inflicting heavy losses, whilst Allied fighters and AA units did likewise. 255 pilots were lost – 170 killed or missing, 67 prisoners and 18 wounded. These totals including 19 irreplaceable unit and formation leaders, three of them Geschwader Kommodore, seven Gruppenkommandeuren, and nine Staffelkapitane. JG 6, targetted with Volkel, alone suffered the loss of 23 of its 70 pilots, including the Kommodore, Oberstleutnant Johann Kogler, two Gruppenkommandeuren and two Staffelkapitane.

By energetic action, Air Marshal Broadhurst had sufficient fighter squadrons on line to hold the front within 24 hours. The destroyed aircraft were quickly replaced – and during that time 122 Wing, as the only fully operational Wing in 83 Group, provided the necessary patrols.

'Bodenplatte' was effectively the swan song of the Luftwaffe – a gamble that did not pay off. Although formations of German fighters and fighter-bombers would still be met, the Luftwaffe was never again to wage war with anything like the force marshalled for this operation. As a tactical fighting force it was finished.

On 13 January, 1945, Mackie succeeded another New Zealander, Sqn Ldr R.L. 'Spud' Spurdle*, as commander of 80 Squadron. It was a traumatic time for Spurdle. He had completed 564 operational sorties and five tours of operations (including one with the RNZAF in the South Pacific), and he had just led 80 Squadron through six months of hectic fighting. He later told the author that he did not remember meeting Mackie, or handing the squadron over to him. "I was exhausted, tour expired," he explained in correspondence.

---

* (Sqn Ldr R.L. Spurdle, DFC & Bar; see *Aces High*, pages 561-2.)

"It was goodbye to 80 and my pilots. It was goodbye to the strongest bond a man can know; the brotherhood of arms," he wrote in his autobiography, *The Blue Arena*. "I hated to hand over the lives and well-being of my boys to a stranger. But the die was cast."

Mackie, on the other hand, found it easy to assume command of 80 Squadron. He was not unfamiliar with the pilots, having met them in the Wing mess. On his first day with the squadron he led it on a reconnaissance over the St. Vith area, and within a week, shown largely by example, the pilots of 80 Squadron knew what their new CO expected of them. Within two weeks Mackie had logged the following results from his personal sorties:

Shot up four locomotives, one MT (motor transport) and dummy FW 190s.
Shot up two locomotives and one MT.
Shot up four locomotives and training gliders – lots of German bods.
Shot up four locomotives, three MT and six hangars.
Shot up four locomotives – fired at Me 109.
One Me 109 destroyed, fired at two others, shot up four locomotives.
Shot up four trains.
Shot up four trains and one MT – lots of trucks.

With leadership like that, the pilots of 80 Squadron were scrambling to keep up. His combat report for the Bf 109, the 19th enemy aircraft he had been involved in shooting down, read:

Up: 1242. Down: 1420. 23 January, 1945.
Place of attack: 12 miles north of Osnabrück.

I was leading a formation of 8 aircraft on an armed recce in the Osnabrück-Minden area, when the leader of the top section reported an aircraft landing on the aerodrome about 8 miles north of Osnabrück. Both he and his No.2 went down to strafe this aircraft and while covering them I noticed a single-engined aircraft flying north between the two aerodromes almost on the deck. I dived down, closing range to 200 yards and identified as an Me 109, just as it was making the last turn of its approach to land at the 'drome about 12 miles north of Osnabrück, I fired a one-second burst at approx. 200 yards using almost full deflection so that the E/A was actually hidden from my view under the nose, at the moment of firing. I therefore could not see the direct results of my fire, but on lowering my nose I saw the nose of the E/A drop sharply and it dived vertically into the ground approx. 1 mile east of Hesepe A/Fd where it began to smoke. As it was going down in this dive I noticed that both the landing wheels were lowered. The actual crash was witnessed by several members of my section. The E/A was camouflaged dark grey.

My cine camera was exposed.

Claim: 1 Me 109 destroyed.

Sweetman, who had blooded Mackie on Tempests, and had watched with interest his performance as a supernumerary with 274 Squadron, was also in a position to assess his early leadership of 80 Squadron: "An above average pilot," he wrote to the author in 1986. "Had the ability to sum up a situation quickly, and as a fighter leader led from the front with clear, decisive leadership. Aggressive but tempered this with a sincere consideration for the welfare of all his pilots. He was essentially a team man, not interested in any self-aggrandisement. Extremely modest, with a quiet but friendly demeanour and a keen sense of humour. Mixed well and was a popular member of the squadron."

Not everyone agreed. Flt Lt Leslie Withers, 80 Squadron's adjutant during Mackie's command, was led to comment to Spurdle in a letter many years later: "I found Mackie a difficult man to work with – always interfering in admin. which he did not understand but wanted to boss; reluctant to grant the slightest privilege (and even quibbling about legitimate leave); and cool and over-efficient with the pilots, whatever his own flying prowess." And this in spite of Mackie having made it clear that he had no interest in fighting the paper war while the real war was going on.

It may be that Mackie proved to be a somewhat less indulgent and accommodating, and rather more demanding CO than had the tired 'Spud' Spurdle. When Christopher Shores was writing the history of 80 Squadron, one of the veterans of 1945 confided to him regarding Evan Mackie: "We didn't like him very much." But then comparisons are always odious.

As Mackie settled in with 80 Squadron, the weather gradually improved. Warmer spring temperatures cleared Volkel airfield of its snow, and more sorties were flown. "Most days we were flying," he said. "Often the cloud base would be at about 2,000 feet, which suited us very well. We would fly out to a designated area above the cloud, and if we could see the ground at 1,000 feet we started operating under the cloud. If not, we'd go up again and look for some other area.

"We knew the terrain pretty well. No high obstacles. Northern Germany is pretty flat, and the cloud gave us great cover for getting to and from our areas. Unfortunately, we encountered very few enemy aircraft. To start with there was quite good hunting close in, in the

way of trains and road transport, but gradually they became more
and more elusive, so we went further and further afield. In fact, before
the war ended, we were going in 150 to 200 miles, just a section of
four of us, in search of targets. If a good area was found it was quickly
passed on to other squadrons, and they made the most of it."

Mackie said that the heavier flak did not worry the Tempest pilots
much, because they operated at such low levels. "But if we continued
at a steady height, say 8,000 feet, we could expect to see heavy flak
come at exactly 8,000 feet. They were very good on height."

"Our biggest enemy in this type of work was the light Flak. Another
was flying debris from trains and the like, some of which really blew
up. I remember coming home one day, and I said to the ground staff
as I parked the aircraft: Seems something queer with the tailwheel.
It's not castering. Would you mind having a look at it? He did, and
he found that a .303 bullet had struck the pivot gear and jammed it.
Now, if that had been 30 feet further forward I probably wouldn't
have got home. Just one bullet . . ."

On 2 February, 1945, Mackie was not so lucky: "We were about
150 miles inside Germany," he recalled, "on our usual mission and
I'd just shot up an ordinary Army truck. I was pulling out from the
attack when I sensed, rather than felt, something had touched or
affected my aircraft. I just caught a flicker on the oil gauge. I thought,
this could be serious, so I headed for home."

At that stage he was at about 1,000 feet, so he gained another
1,000 feet, meanwhile advising his section of what he was doing, telling
them to carry on. No sooner had he settled on a course for Volkel
than the Sabre's oil pressure began to drop. Mackie worked out that
his best chance of getting home was by keeping his revolutions per
minute to a minimum, compatible with a reasonable speed. Having
worked out the most efficient equation, it was just a matter of sweating
it out.

"I was on my own. There was little danger from other aircraft really,
because we hadn't struck any in the area for ages. But I still had 150
miles to go, and the oil pressure went lower and lower. About 80
miles from home it was on zero.

"From there on the temperature started to go up and up and up,
and me – I was in a real dither. Shall I bale out? Shall I crash-land?
What will I do? It was a big decision to make, and for anyone to say
that they are not scared or frightened silly, because in those conditions
you naturally must be – and I was.

"My chances of a successful crash-landing would have been alright,
but I would have been sure of capture and becoming a prisoner of
war. Baling out would probably have enhanced my chances of
escaping capture, but it also had its dangers.

"Anyhow, I stuck with it, and the temperature went up and up until it was right off the clock. Smoke started to appear from under the bonnet just as I got within sight of the airfield, which was about three miles away. I decided it wasn't worth the risk of trying any further, when it would inevitably catch fire, so I crash-landed," said Mackie. "I remember tipping the tops of the trees on the boundary of a postage (stamp) sized ploughed field and landed, wheels up naturally. It pulled up mighty quick, but broke the back of the aircraft. But at least I was in home territory, no more than three miles from the aerodrome."

According to 80 Squadron's record book, he actually nursed the aircraft for 190 miles. The offical account concluded succinctly: "Excessive damage was caused on a/c (but) the pilot was okay." Tempest NV657 was written off as beyond repair.

That Mackie landed the high-speed Tempest with its scoop-shaped 'chin' radiator without injury was testimony to his airmanship skills. Tempests are reputed to have killed far more pilots than ever got out of them alive in wheels-up landings.

Thereafter he had a considerable respect for the Napier Sabre engine, which was of sleeve-valve design and even more dependent on oil lubrication than the more conventional poppet-valve engines. To keep going for about 80 miles with no oil pressure was a feat which appealed to Mackie's appreciation of well-designed machinery.

A later inspection of his aircraft revealed a crack in the supercharger casing through which 14 gallons of lubricant had leaked, for the oil tank was completely dry. Mackie thought it possible that the strain under which the aircraft was placed as he pulled it out of the attack had cracked the casing – more evidence of his 'ham-fisted' flying!

The record book noted the next day: "Eight a/c led by Sqn Ldr Mackie broke cloud to find an exceptional target – two trains loaded with MT. Forming two left-hand circuits a fine beating-up took place."

Mackie claimed two locomotives, three flamers, three smoking and 15 damaged from the sortie, and commented: "This is one aircraft, so you can imagine what our Wing of 48 aircraft was doing to the German war effort. Anything that moved on the landscape, we were on to. In fact, one morning there was a large trailer being drawn along by a tractor at a crossroads. Couldn't quite see what it was, anyhow, shot it up – no flames, no nothing. Worked around the area a bit and happened to pass back over the same spot later and the ground was all white around it. We realised it was a milk tank!"

On 8 February he logged: "Mixed with Me 109, shot up four locos, barges etc." and he then flew seven more sorties before going on leave to England on 15th. While he was away Wg Cdr R.P. (Peter)

Brooker*, who had been posted in as Wing Commander (Flying) of 122 Wing in early January, led the squadron at times. The record book noted: "Flt Lt A. Seager often leads sweeps and Flt Lt L.R.G. Smith sometimes leads them."

Louis Graham-Smith had been with Mackie on No 12 Course at 58 OTU, Grangemouth, in Scotland. Coincidentally, he had also served with 92 Squadron. Mackie promoted him as 'B' Flight commander soon after taking over as CO of 80 Squadron. "It's a pity I had only two and a half months with Evan, as he was a great fellow," Graham-Smith wrote to the author from his home in Port-of-Spain, Trinidad, in 1986. "He was considered by all to be an excellent pilot and leader."

Mackie arrived back on the Continent on 28 February, 1945, travelling by Dakota from Northolt to Eindhoven. He was airborne with 80 Squadron on 1 March, leading it on a sweep over Paderborn at 10,000 feet. The next day he led a section of four Tempests which became involved in a combat which he logged simply as: "Mixed with 16 FW 190s", and which the Tempest pilots were probably very happy to get out of with their skins intact! Weakened the Luftwaffe may have been, but 16 FW 190s against four Tempests was over the odds.

During the afternoon of 7 March, Mackie led a sweep by 80, 274 and 486 Squadrons over the Nienberg, Hanover and Hamm area. At Rheine nine long-nosed Focke Wulf 190Ds were seen. Mackie at once engaged one in what was to be the toughest and most memorable fight of his life. He later said that he could have almost wrung the sweat out of his battledress on return to base. His combat report graphically describes the engagement:

> Up: 1431. Down: 1620. March 7, 1945.
> Place of attack: North of Rheine.
>
> I was leading 80, 274 & 486 Squadrons on a sweep in the Rheine-Quackenbrück area, when bandits were reported high in the Rheine area. Climbing through cloud at about 8,000 ft, I saw 6 or 8 A/C making vapour trails at approx. 15,000 ft. I was flying with No.80 Squadron, so climbing up we eventually made contact at about 13,000 ft as the E/A were diving down on other Tempests. I picked out a long-nosed FW 190 which, after several manoeuvres, dived vertically down to 3,000 ft just below a 5/10 layer of cumulus cloud. I then found myself alone with this 190, over open country, so we proceeded to have a good uninterrupted dogfight.
> For over five minutes I tried to position myself for a reasonable

---

* (Wg Cdr R.E.P. Brooker, DSO, DFC & Bar; see *Aces High*, page 151.)

shot at him, but he proved to be a very clueful opponent. We were both leaving almost continuous wing-tip trails. I found that with full revs and boost, I could gain slowly on him in about 3 complete turns, but when almost ready to open fire at him, he would throttle back suddenly and turn sharply, causing me to over-shoot. These tactics were to some extent successful and he actually took one wild shot at me on one occasion, but the deflection was full and he must have been almost stalled at the time so I was not unduly worried. After each of these overshoots, I found myself back where I started, and so another vicious turning circle developed. Once or twice he attempted to dive away on the deck, climbing up again when I began gaining on him, and even went up into cloud which was not sufficient cover for him.

Eventually two Tempests of 274 Sqdn. arrived on the scene, which distracted the attention of the Hun sufficiently for me to get in a 1½ sec. burst with 30-degree deflection from approx. 200 yds. On lowering my nose I saw that a fire had started right in the cockpit. The fire grew, developed into a huge sheet of flame and the E/A crashed in a mushroom of smoke and flame N. of Rheine.

This was witnessed by two pilots of 274 Sqdn.

Cine camera used.

Claim: 1 FW 190 destroyed.

It was his last solo victory over an armed aircraft, and a combat which he would never forget. Years later he commented: "I could have outrun him if I had decided to go for home, but he was a real cracker." However, "go for home" was simply not a phrase in Mackie's book when the odds were even, and if anything the fight put up by the "real cracker" only increased the New Zealander's determination to come out on top.

There seems little doubt that the opposing Luftwaffe unit on this date was III Gruppe of Jagdgeschwader 26. Eight or nine of this unit's FW 190Ds had taken off from Plantlunne at around 1500, seeing Tempests below them near Enschede and becoming involved in a wide-ranging dogfight. Four of these aircraft failed to return, two pilots being killed and two surviving with wounds.Mackie's victim would appear to have been one of the latter – either Lt Heinz-Wilhelm Bartels or Unteroffizier Otto Salewski.

All the excitement of the chase occurred on 15 March when 56, 80 and 486 Squadrons, led by Mackie, came across a jet bomber during a sweep over the Rheine – Dummer Lake – Münster area. It was an Arado 234, a twin-engined aircraft capable of reaching speeds well in excess of 500 miles an hour. Mackie had a crack at it, but saw no results. Flg Off F.A. Lang, an Australian with 80 Squadron, closed to within 200 yards of the bomber in a dive and managed to damage it with his cannon – but not enough to stop it making off at a much higher speed than the Tempest could aspire to.

Those members of 80 Squadron with a sense of history were in for a treat on 20 March, when they assembled to meet the man known as 'The Father of the Royal Air Force' – Marshal of the RAF Viscount Lord Trenchard, known to all as 'Boom', who was on a tour of the front lines on the eve of the crossing of the Rhine.

Activity flared up again on 22 March, when 56 and 80 Squadrons claimed the destruction of six FW 190s and damaged three more – all aircraft of II/JG 26. At the end of this engagement, Mackie, who was leading, said on the R/T: "Okay chaps, that's all. Reform and go home." Immediately a small meek voice was heard saying: "Don't go yet – I'm still fighting five!"

Then came 23 March, 1945. For weeks tension had been mounting along the Rhine. From Bourg Leopold to Nijmegen the roads were packed; pontoons, Bailey bridge material and all the customary divisional convoys had been pouring through Uden village by day and night, while coloured smokescreens obscured Germany's last natural defence. The detailed preparation was second in magnitude only to that for D-Day. At last, in the evening, the pilots were briefed for the final great operation, the Rhine crossing, or, as 80 Squadron's ORB put it rather more melodramatically, "the final phase of the battle against the European scourge," noting that "the first wave of troops crossed the last bastion of Teutonic defiance at 2100 hours."

The entry for 24 March read: "For the first time in ten months the Met. men appear to have indented – and obtained – perfect weather from the equipment officer. So warm and clear and sunny is it that it would be insulting to say it is as good as an English summer. The Rhine operation has been highly successful, with the world's greatest airborne operation. Our first op was at 0645 – a standing patrol off Rees–Wesel, meeting no E/A and finding it difficult to see much for the Allied smokescreen and artillery dust. The same area patrol at 0940/1110 had some success, led by Wg Cdr R.E.P. Brooker, when some of our aircraft managed to find a gap in the aerial carpet of Lancs, Halifaxes, Dakotas and gliders and nipped down through and back again, leaving 'the leading people in Europe' three MET less in which to get away from the 21st Army Group."

The book noted that a New Zealander, Sqn Ldr J.A.A. Gibson*, who was flying with the squadron, had been hit by Flak but had force-

---

* (Sqn Ldr J.A.A. Gibson, DSO, DFC; see *Aces High*, pages 279-80.)

landed safely by Mook Bridge "and returned merrily to find he had a DSO awaiting him."

The Wing operations book recorded that its aircraft flew 193 hours that day, maintaining a standing patrol over the bridgehead between Wesel and Rees from 0515 to 1945: "There was no air opposition. The defensive work continued for two days, and then the Tempests reverted to their more profitable occupation of attacking communications, mainly road vehicles."

Mackie flew eight sorties between 26 March and the end of the month, destroying seven military transports and damaging 12, also damaging six locomotives and shooting up a searchlight post.

Although he was not having any success with enemy aircraft, other members of his squadron were mixing with them to some effect, according to the squadron history. "Locos and MT were the order of the day for some time after this, but three Me 109s which were popping about a bank of cloud like fleas, were damaged by Flt Lt Seager, Plt Off Ross and Plt Off Dopson on 28 March, and a Ju 188 was written off while flying at deck level on 31st." The Ju 188 was a development of the Ju 88 bomber, and the aircraft shot down was undoubtedly being used in a reconnaissance capacity. The conflict exacted a steady toll of 80 Squadron pilots, however. The history continued: "The day before the Squadron lost another favourite, Plt Off 'Bluey' Rankin, who said goodbye on his R/T after being hit by Flak."

There were some lighter moments, which the squadron history also preserved for posterity: "On 1 April, on some excuse or other, an excellent party was held at dispersal, complete with such delicacies as chicken, hares, eggs and the members of Ralph Reader's 2nd WAAF Gang Show, who enlivened proceedings with song and dance."

On 6 April, 1945, Mackie was advised that he had been appointed a Companion of the Distinguished Service Order – an award Gazetted on 24 May, 1945. The citation read: "Acting Squadron Leader Mackie has led the Squadron on numerous sorties within recent months. During these operations more than 70 locomotives have been put out of action. A good number of barges, trucks and mechanical vehicles have also been effectively attacked. Ten enemy aircraft have been destroyed. The successes obtained are a fine testimony to Acting Squadron Leader Mackie's exceptional leadership, great skill and courage. Among his achievements are the destruction of 18 enemy aircraft."

It would be 13 June before Mr T.A. Barrow, the New Zealand Government's Air Secretary, conveyed a copy of the citation to Mackie's family in Waihi, together with his personal congratulations, but its late arrival would by no means diminish the pride with which it was received.

"We continued to hound the enemy with great gusto," said Mackie. "Every possible moment was spent in the air, hounding him and any-thing that moved in his territory." He scarcely had time to get his new ribbon up before flying on 7 April to the assistance of Allied ground forces pinned down by mortar fire at the River Weser bridgehead.

"Naturally, there were pockets of resistance to the Rhine crossing, and Leese village was one of these," Mackie remembered. "We were called upon to strafe certain houses. We had forward control. In fact, my predecessor, Sqn Ldr Spurdle, was up near the site directing the aircraft in the operation."

According to the Wing history: "The Army reported later that they had asked for this attack because 54 sappers had been killed by mortar fire while trying to build a bridge. As a result of the Tempests' assaults the bridge was built and 'several hundred' Huns were killed as they lay in slit trenches. In the course of the attacks one of the squadrons also knocked out a nearby train, and this proved to be laden with V-2s."

On 9 April, 80 Squadron caught a number of Arado Ar 96 trainers in the circuit at Fassberg aerodrome, although these were mistakenly identified as Messerschmitt Bf 108s. Three were claimed shot down, two by Mackie and the other by Flg Off W.R. Sheaf. Mackie reported:

Up: 1815. Down: 2030. April 9, 1945.
Place of attack: Fassberg.

I was Black Leader and engaged on an Armed Recce of the Weser bridgehead. Whilst flying on an easterly course in the area of Fassberg aerodrome I sighted an aircraft flying low in approx. the same direction. I dived down to attack, recognising the A/C as an Me 108, and experienced difficulty in avoiding an overshoot. I positioned myself behind him and gave a 2-3 sec. burst from 300 yards closing to 80 yards allowing 10 degrees deflection, obtaining strikes near the cockpit. I overshot towards the end of my attack and as I broke away, I saw the enemy aircraft dive down and level out at deck level. After Black 2 had also attacked this A/C, Black 3 and 4 saw it crash in flames in some woods.

After I had broken round to starboard, I saw a further two Me 108s approx. 50 feet above the ground. With my number 2 firing at the starboard aircraft, which crashed in a field in flames I attacked the port aircraft, giving a 3 sec. burst at 200 yards closing

to 50 yards allowing 30 degrees deflection. I obtained strikes on
the fuselage and cockpit and the aircraft burst into flames and
crashed from about 20 feet in a field about a 100 yards from the
A/C shot down by my No.2.

Claim: 2 Me 108s destroyed.

Uncharacteristically, the usually meticulous Mackie logged the combat
under 10 April in his logbook. He noted: "Two Me 108s destroyed
(Ar 96s)". The correction in brackets is believed to have been written
in much later, after Christopher Shores had advised him of the correct
identity of the aircraft, having seen a print from his combat film during
1969.

In the wake of the 21st Army Group, 122 Wing Headquarters
moved in to Germany on 10 April, 1945; next day the Tempest
squadrons flew to an airfield they had fired many cannon shells at in
recent weeks, B-122/Hopsten, and landed there. The Wing history
recorded the ground move: "As the long convoy moved over the
pontoon bridge across the Rhine at Xanten it was impossible not to
feel a thrill of pride. The Channel, the Seine, the Rhine . . . surely
the end of a long journey could not be far away?"

On 12 April patrols were being flown as usual from the new base,
the squadrons making the most of fine spring weather as the war
moved rapidly towards its climax: "The MET claims far exceeded
those made during the Falaise Gap battle," according to the Wing
history. "This time the disintegrating German Army was fleeing north
and north-east across the Elbe, providing magnificent targets for the
Tempests' four cannons. On 13th April, 122 road vehicles were
claimed as 'flamers' and 260 as damaged. This day's work drew
another signal from the Air Officer Commanding congratulating the
Wing on its 'stupendous performance'."

During an armed reconnaisssance north-east of Hamburg on 15
April, Mackie became involved in his last air-to-air combat. His
opponent was an FW 190D pilot, and even though the German was
flying one of the best fighter aircraft of the time, he stood little chance
against the New Zealand ace and his No 2, Sgt W.F. Turner.

Mackie's claim, which included a half share on behalf of Sgt Turner,
who went missing on the following day, read:

Up: 0735. Down: 0954. April 15, 1945.
Place of attack: 10 miles S/W of Uelzen.

I was flying Black 1 and engaged on an armed recce in the Wismar
– Butzow area, when I heard 486 Squadron reporting FW 190s

to the south of me. I turned the formation south and when in the area of Uelzen, I sighted a number of FW 190s being engaged by 486 Squadron.

I selected one of these A/C for attack & followed him through a series of manoeuvres; during the course of which I got in three bursts of approx. 1 second each & allowing a wide deflection. On the third of these attacks the E/A was making a tight turn to starboard & allowing 60-70 degrees deflection I got in a 1 second burst from 150 yards. My height at this time was 5,500 ft. I saw strikes in the area of the cockpit, the cockpit hood flying off. I also saw what appeared to be holes in the fuselage just behind the cockpit. He turned on his back & went vertically downwards, pieces flying off on the way down. I did not see the pilot get out & the A/C crashed in a sheet of flames in some woods. Black 2 (Sgt. Turner) made an attack on this A/C as it was diving vertically, obtaining strikes on the tail & seeing pieces fly off.

Claim: ½ FW 190 destroyed, shared with Sgt. Turner.

In view of the fact that Sgt. Turner became missing on the day following this combat, it is impossible to submit a report of his attack. The details contained in S/Ldr Mackie's report are confirmed & a half share in a FW 190 destroyed is claimed on his behalf.

Without detracting in any way from Sgt Turner's attack on the FW 190, it does seem that Mackie was generous indeed in ensuring that his No 2 was credited with a half share. At the stage of Turner's attack the German fighter was diving vertically, shedding bits and pieces, its pilot apparently badly wounded or dead. However, Mackie was never known to claim anything which he did not believe was rightfully his; this combat brought his total of confirmed air-to-air victories to 20 and three shared – or if added arithmetically, to 21½.

During the war a small minority of fighter pilots undoubtedly lodged claims for aircraft which they well knew they had not destroyed. Many undoubtedly claimed aircraft in the genuinely mistaken belief that they had shot them down. Even Mackie's first champion and editor of this book, Christopher Shores, was constrained to write to the author: "Don't expect Mackie to have definitely got something for every claim – very few pilots ever do – but he was good – substantially more accurate than most." So the absolute accuracy of his total claims of 20 and three shared will probably never be known. What is known is that every aircraft in that total was confirmed as destroyed by the Royal Air Force at the time.

Meanwhile, all the excitement of that last combat was not yet over. Possibly by the violent manoeuvres Mackie had been putting his Tempest through, the propeller mechanism malfunctioned and an over-speed developed. "A very embarrassing situation," said Mackie. "Its similar to a clutch going on a motorcar. Plenty of power, but no drive."

At the time he was at about 4,000 feet and not far from Celle, a front-line airfield not yet recommissioned since being abandoned by the Germans. It was for Celle that he headed, but on arrival the prospects did not look good.

"Naturally, it had been well pock-marked with bomb craters and these were in the process of being filled in. Bulldozers and scrapers were still working on parts of this field. I slowly circled down, and when I came in to land I found the hydraulics had gone on the blink too and only one wheel would come down. So I was committed to a landing which was on one wheel followed by one wingtip and the tailwheel and, unfortunately, the propeller tips.

"It was very noisy, with this wingtip scraping around on the tarseal (macadam). I can to this day see the repair gangs taking to their scrapers as I veered around in almost a complete circle." He thanked his lucky stars that, although he had suffered two propeller failures, he had been within range of an airfield on each occasion.

It was a sad day for 122 Wing when Peter Brooker, the Wing Command (Flying), failed to return from an armed reconnaissance. He had led a section of four Tempests off from Hopsten runway just as dawn was breaking on 16 April, and his Tempest had been seen to catch fire after attacking a train in the Osnabrück region. Brooker was unable to release the cockpit hood and his No2 was flying desperately and uselessly alongside him when two FW 190s moved in unnoticed and shot them both down.

This loss would soon affect Mackie, but the New Zealander did not know that when he led 80 Squadron on a two-hour flight from Hopsten to Warmwell in Dorset on 18 April, 1945. There, at 17 Armament Practice Camp, they were to be taught the finer points of using their Tempests as fighter-bombers for the first time.

"We were taught to dive at an angle of roughly 45 degrees and, using the ordinary reflector sight on the target, to release the bomb at a certain time and a certain height," recalled Mackie. "We started from between 5,000 feet and 4,000 feet. We did not get very good results as far as accuracy went."

The Wing history was scathing of this exercise, the author lamenting the unit's reduction to three squadrons at such a time: "Of all ironic fates, when real-life targets were ten-a-penny!"

The squadron was only on its third day at Warmwell when Mackie was advised that he had been promoted to Wing Commander. At the same time he was offered an interesting choice. He could choose to command 616 Squadron, the first RAF squadron to fly jet fighters operationally, which had just joined 122 Wing, or he could replace Brooker as Wing Commander (Flying) within the Wing.

He at once realised the honour accorded him. Many of his contemporaries would have given their right arms to lead the unit flying the Gloster Meteor III jets, which were capable of flying at 458 miles an hour at sea level, and 493 mph in level flight at 30,000 feet. 616 was the only RAF squadron flying single-seat aircraft which rated a Wg Cdr as its commanding officer. Wg Cdr A. McDowell*, who had led the unit since it was first equipped with Meteor Is in July 1944, was now due for posting.

Mackie weighed the pros and cons. The development of jet propulsion interested him enormously, yet he chose to stay with his tried and trusted Tempest. After all, he reasoned, as Wing Leader he would have operational control of 616 Squadron anyway.

He signalled Jameson his decision, and although he handed command of 80 Squadron over to Major R.A. 'Dutchy' Henwick (SAAF) on 20 April, he stayed on at Warmwell until 28 April, practising low-level bombing, high dive-bombing and air firing – he could never get enough of the latter! Henwick, recently promoted from Captain, was one of 80 Squadron's longest serving pilots, having been with the unit right through the Western Desert and Italian campaigns.

Meanwhile, Mackie's refusal of 616 Squadron had been good news for a fellow New Zealander, Sqn Ldr W.E. Schrader, CO of 486 Squadron. He was also promoted to Wg Cdr and was posted to lead the Meteor squadron. 122 became known as the 'Colonial Wing', with Jameson, Mackie, Schrader and Henwick all holding senior positions.

After a few days leave in London, Mackie flew from Warmwell to Fassberg, where 122 Wing had meanwhile located itself, in a two hours 20 minutes flight. It was 2 May, 1945, and the European conflict had only a few days to run. Mackie might have known something, for he made the most of the remaining time. That same day he was out on an armed reconnaissance of the Eutin area, and damaged a military transport.

His second sortie as Wing Leader might well have dampened his enthusiasm for a last crack at the enemy. It was 3 May and he was over the Fehrmarn/Echernforde area, shooting up a locomotive in time-honoured Tempest fashion, when the thing exploded under him. The logbook entry: "Hit by debris, jammed aileron, shaky do!"

---

* (Wg Cdr A. McDowell, DFM, AFC; see *Aces High*, page 432.)

scarcely does the incident justice. "On this particular attack I came as near to flying into the deck as I ever wished to," he remembered. "Just as I passed over this locomotive which I'd been firing at and went to break to the left, the ailerons froze – completely froze in the position they were. And I exerted all the strength I could muster with two hands on the control column; I was actually afraid that I might bend it or break it!"

At the time he was in a slight turn to the left which would have taken him into the ground had it continued, but he managed to get out of the gradual dive and begin a climb. Then he found that he could not maintain a course. "It would gradually veer round to port. So all I could do was let it do a complete circle now and then, straightening it up as much as possible before I got onto course. Using all my force again, I would try and keep it flying straight and level, which I could not, and then let it drift around in another circle until I came to the course I was trying to make good."

Looking out to starboard Mackie could see something sticking up through the aileron, a foreign body which had clearly jammed it immovably. He eventually reached the end of the Fassberg runway and prepared for the landing with great trepidation, but luckily, as the Tempest slowed to landing speed, so were the forces on the ailerons reduced: "I made quite a normal landing. But it shows you what a small thing can happen and how pilots come to grief."

The object proved to be a piece of steel about eight inches long, an inch wide, three-eighths of an inch thick, with a half inch hole at each end. Mackie kept it on his desk as a souvenir of what he called "a very close go".

The incident put something of a damper on what had been his first flight in his 'own' Tempest V, bearing his initials EDM. The right to have personal initials painted on the Wing Leader's aircraft instead of the usual squadron codes was a jealously defended privilege dating back to the appointment of the first wing commanders (flying) in 1941, and was almost unique in operational units to the pilots of single-seat fighter aircraft.

Mackie's Tempest V, SN228, was painted in the standard camou-flage scheme of the time; dark green alternating with sea grey (medium) on the upper surfaces, and sea grey (light) on the under-surfaces. Distinctive to 2nd TAF, the upper wing roundels were similar to those on the fuselage – red, white, blue and yellow from the centre outwards. The initials EDM were in light grey. It carried the standard fin flash of broad blue and red bands separated by a thin white stripe, and a wing commander's pennant below the wind-screen, together with (eventually) 25 black crosses.

Altogether Mackie was to have confirmed 3½ aircraft destroyed on the ground (three and one shared), as well as 21½ in the air (20 and three shared) . The arithmetic addition of these figures appears to make up the total of 25, although they are a disparate grouping. However, he was yet to destroy any aircraft on the ground – and he was not going to be able to do that in his pristine EDM, now damaged by the locomotive explosion.

He was up again that same day in a Tempest coded 'F', leading 3 Squadron in a sweep over the Schwerin area, where many German aircraft had been caught in the air on the previous day. Success was again with the Tempests, and 14 aircraft were claimed in the air and on the ground. Mackie claimed an He 111, a Dornier type and a Fieseler Fi 156 Storch, all destroyed on the ground:

> Up: 1900. Down: 2058. May 3, 1945.
> Place of attack: Landing ground 12 (miles) N/E of Kiel.
>
> I was leading Filmstar Squadron on A/R and saw A/C burning on the ground on a landing ground to the NE of Kiel, with a T/E E/A taxying at the end of the strip. I attacked this which I believe was a Do type and set it on fire. On my next attack I set a He 111, which was covered by a camouflage net, on fire, and followed this on my third attack by setting a Fi 156 on fire. I saw the Ju 87 burning after this attack by W/O Saunders.
>
> Claim: 1 Do type, 1 He 111 and 1 Fi 156,
> all destroyed on the ground.

"The Germans were sort of evacuating areas not far beyond, and there was no opposition," Mackie explained.

The next day, flying at the head of 486 Squadron, he made his last claim when he shared with fellow Kiwi Wt Off J.R. Duncan in the destruction of one of two Fi 156s on the ground.

> Up: 1128. Down: 1315. May 4, 1945.
> Place of attack: Oldenburg area.
>
> I was leading the Squadron on an armed recce and anti-shipping strike when, in the Oldenburg Area, 2 Fi 156s were reported on the ground.
>   W/O Duncan attacked first gaining strikes and I followed firing a short burst. I saw strikes on the centre section and E/A immediately went up in flames.
>
> Claim: 1 Fi 156 destroyed shared with W/O Duncan.

This was the last time Mackie fired his cannons in anger. It was an inconsequential end to a brilliant career in air fighting – a tiny, unarmed fabric-covered observation aircraft left blazing on the ground, smashed by the fire of two Tempests. The fortunes of war, as Mackie often said.

It must have been reasonably apparent to the 122 Wing personnel that evening that the end was not far away, for just on dusk several FW 190s, Bf 109s and Me 262s skimmed across the lowlands and landed back at their old base – Fassberg! Luckily for them, Grp Capt Jameson had ordered the airfield anti-aircraft gunners to shoot only if enemy aircraft were committed on an offensive act – in anticipation of something like this happening.

"They came in at deck level, right at dusk, landed, taxied in and gave themselves up and said: Right, now what are we going to do about these Russians?" Mackie recalled. "In other words, they were all ready to throw in forces and take the Russians on. They had already emptied their guns and dropped what bombs they had on Russian lines. The following morning peace was declared, so naturally they were just put in the cooler." Mackie said he did not meet the German pilots personally, but he did examine and photograph their aircraft. He observed that the Me 262 was a very "rough-built" machine.

The official ceasefire in Western Europe came into effect at 0800 hours on Saturday, 5 May, 1945, and for Mackie and his Tempests the war was over. He had flown 634 hours and ten minutes on operations during 433 individual sorties.

"The Wing sat back rather dazed and uncomprehending," according to its history, "for everyone had been much too busy to follow with much understanding the comings and goings of Count Bernadotte."

Inaction did not last long, however. Soon after midday two squadrons took off to escort five Dakotas loaded with British troops to Copenhagen. During the flight "the pilots flew low and were impressed by the vast numbers of people crowding the roads, waving and cheering."

For some, however, the end of the war had come too late for cheering. Belsen concentration camp was only 20 miles from the Fassberg airfield, and members of the Wing were able to see for themselves that the official reports had not been exaggerated.

"I've never seen or smelt anything like it," said Mackie. "The smell was indescribable. No pigsty could compete. The inmates had been in tiers of four or six bunks in these long sheds and some of them were still living, were still there, just walking skeletons, club feet, in tatters, just on bare boards or netting, whatever the bunks happened to be made of, no mattresses.

"I was told that when the Army arrived there, there were 5,000 dead laying around in the yards. They got the guards to collect them up and put them in pits, and they said the guards could put two under each arm and carry them to the pits. And they said that they pushed the guards in after them and buried the lot. It was quite an experience."

The Wing would remain at Fassberg until June. Although offensive operations had ceased there were still plenty of ceremonial flypasts and 'showing the roundel' flights, so Wing and squadron formation practices had to be taken seriously. Almost certainly Mackie, forever striving for perfection, took them more seriously than most. It was probably just as well for the pilots that he led from the front, and did not fly at the rear where sections slipping out of alignment, and individual pilots flying a little too low or too high would have drawn comments very much to the point.

For the sheer joy of it, because he remained a Spitfire man at heart, Mackie took a Spitfire XIV aloft on 11 May and threw it around the sky for 55 minutes.

It was also time to take stock. The summary for 122 Wing between D-Day and 8 May, 1945 was extremely impressive. First with its squadrons of Mustangs, and latterly with the Tempest units, the Wing had claimed the destruction or damage of the following:

	Destroyed	Damaged
Aircraft	391½	302
Road Vehicles	1,615	4,252
Locomotives	78	1,077
Railway Wagons	170	2,248
Tugs and Barges	100	436

In addition there had been attacks made on gasworks, oil refineries, radar stations, midget submarines and motor launches, whilst the Mustang units had bombed headquarters, bridges, gun positions, marshalling yards, food and ammunition dumps, V-1 and V-2 sites – and that was just by one wing in one group! However, the cost had not been inconsiderable, for during that period the Wing had also lost 141 pilots to all causes.

CHAPTER NINE

PEACE

With the conclusion of hostilities Mackie was reaping the benefits of his rank and of the peace. As well as having his personalised Tempest, he also had his own light communications aircraft – an Auster IV, also coded EDM.

The show, however, had to go on. A Wing formation over Hamburg and Kiel on 14 May was followed by a similar flypast over Kiel and Lübeck on 19th. And just to reinforce the fact that Germany had indeed been conquered, there was another flight over Kiel and Hamburg on 26th – and over Luneburg on 31st. It was on Luneburg Heath on 4 May, in front of Field Marshal Montgomery, that Admiral Friedeburg had signed the surrender of all German forces in north-west Germany, Holland, the North Sea Islands, Schleswig-Holstein and Denmark.

After leading another Wing formation over Luneburg on 1 June, Mackie flew his Auster over Hamburg, taking LACs Young and Keight along for the ride. The next day he was airborne in front of the Wing again, in formation over Kiel.

On 3 June Mackie made a circuit of Fassberg airfield in a captured Focke Wulf FW 44 Stieglitz (Goldfinch). A radial-engined biplane which had seen service throughout the war with the Luftwaffe in a training role, the Stieglitz had two open cockpits in tandem. He took a member of the ground staff identified only as 'Ginger' with him for the 15-minute flight.

The chance of spending some time in the sun at Cannes on the French Mediterranean coast came his way on 6 June, and he seized the opportunity. He flew a Colonel Lockwood to Luneburg in the Auster and there boarded an Anson piloted by Grp Capt McGregor. With two other officers aboard, the twin-engined communications aircraft cruised steadily southwards over Belgium and France, landing in Brussels and Lyons, before reaching its destination in the evening.

There they had a week's holiday in a rest home right in the city of Cannes, enjoying the fine weather and the swimming. "Even in wartime it was a beautiful place." Mackie recalled. "We visited Monte Carlo in the evening. Didn't make any money, by the way. Nor did I lose any!"

While Mackie was basking in the sun his Wing was still doing its stuff for public relations. "Wing, led by Sqn Ldr R.B. Cole*, DFC & Bar, made flypast over Frankfurt on the meeting of Marshal Zukov, General Eisenhower and Field Marshal Montgomery" according to the 10 June entry in 3 Squadron's operations book. (Cole was the CO of 3 Squadron, having succeeded the New Zealander, Sqn Ldr K.F. Thiele, DSO, DFC & two Bars in February 1945 when the latter baled out to become a prisoner after his Tempest had been hit by flak.)

With McGregor again at the controls, Mackie and his fellow-officers flew back from Cannes on 14 June, via Marseilles, Paris and Brussels, arriving at Fassberg the same day.

The opportunity of trying another captured aircraft came Mackie's way on 17 June. He spent 25 minutes in the Fassberg circuit in a Focke Wulf FW 56 Stosser (Falcon), a high-wing single-seat advanced trainer capable of 173 miles an hour.

While at Fassberg, 122 Wing personnel collected spare clothing and other articles to help relieve the plight of the inmates at Belsen. According to the Wing operations book, 22,905 articles were collected, including 13,830 pieces of crockery, 900 boots, 170 matresses, 1,230 blankets, 430 bed linen articles, 45 bedsteads and 30,000 cigarettes.

Mackie flew his Tempest 'EDM' from Fassberg to Manston in Kent on 20 June, and on 22nd flew direct from Manston to Kastrup airfield near Copenhagen, Denmark, to which 122 Wing had relocated. He made the 570-mile flight in a single hop, taking two hours and 45 minutes – his longest flight in a Tempest V. Of 183 flights Mackie made in Tempests, 33 were of two hours or longer duration – indicative of the considerable range of the aircraft, consistent with its high performance.

On the day he arrived at Kastrup the Headquarters of the United States Strategic Air Forces in Europe published General Order No.80, in which Mackie was awarded the US Distinguished Flying Cross. The citation read: "Squadron Leader (*sic*) Mackie has an outstanding record of operational flying. He has proved himself to be a courageous and relentless pilot and has obtained many successes over various battle areas. He has contributed greatly to the Allied war effort by destroying at least 19 enemy aircraft as well as making successful

---

* (Sqn Ldr R.B. Cole, DFC & Bar; see *Aces High*, page 185.)

attacks on numerous ground targets. The keenness and great fighting ability of this officer have been an inspiration to his fellow airmen."

Mackie noted that the only time he had worked with American forces was during the Ardennes 'push', the 'Battle of the Bulge', when he had shot down the FW 190D. He presumed the award was recognition for that.

At Kastrup 3, 56 and 80 Squadrons rejoined 486 Squadron which had gone there in May on attachment to 125 Wing. Mackie had the Wing airborne on 26 and 30 June, practising formation flying, rehearsal for an air pageant over Copenhagen on 1 July which was watched by an estimated 250,000 spectators.

In Copenhagen Mackie renewed his acquaintance with Sqn Ldr C.J. Sheddan* DFC, the New Zealander who had been appointed CO of 486 Squadron in May, and who was to command the unit until it was disbanded at Dunsfold in October 1945.

Sheddan and Mackie had known each other for most of their operational service, although, as Sheddan told the author in 1987, "it was a stop-go sort of arrangement." They had served together in 485 Squadron, and then both been in 122 Wing at Volkel at the same time. "He was one pilot whose name was a household word through-out Fighter Command," wrote Sheddan. "Wherever fighter pilots gathered, be it crewroom or bar, it would not be long before his name would crop up."

During the latter stages of the war, when Sheddan was leading his Tempests a long way over the front line into Germany, and control reported German aircraft massing, "it was very comforting to hear Rosie talking quietly to his flight. It made you feel a lot better just to know that he was around. He was one of those rare people who had the ability to inspire confidence by just being around."

On 26 July, Mackie flew Tempest EDM from Kastrup to Bückeberg in Germany to be presented personally with his US DFC by General Otto Weyland, Commander of the US XIX Tactical Air Command. He returned the same day.

It was during 122 Wing's ten weeks at Kastrup that a policy of switching the squadrons around was adopted "to give as much of the Group as possible a change from the unpleasant atmosphere of stricken Germany," according to the Wing history. "In turn 175, 181, 182, 184 and 400 Squadrons came in and 3, 56 and 486 moved away. Inevitably, the Wing deteriorated into a not-very-efficient boarding house, although practice flying was still energetically carried on."

Mackie and Grp Capt Jameson had meanwhile found a new interest:

---

* (Sqn Ldr C.J. Sheddan, DFC; see *Aces High*, page 543. See also autobiography *Tempest Pilot*, written with Norman Franks and published by Grub Street 1993.)

"Jamie had somehow discovered that there was a flash yacht, a German-owned yacht, in the harbour with some German crew still aboard – two crew. It had evidently belonged to the commander of the area prior to our arrival. These two crew were a fairly meek and mild sort of pair . . . and they seemed quite happy to stay where they were. We made full use of the yacht at weekends and whatever opportunities we had with them as crew – just sailing in the waters around Copenhagen and really enjoying ourselves." The yacht was named *Ryhr*, and Mackie still had a blanket from it, with the name embroidered on, more than 40 years later.

Generally, RAF activity on the Continent was scaling down quickly during August, and 122 Wing was no exception. The only growth area was the establishment of the British Air Forces of Occupation – a service in which Mackie would play a brief role before his return to New Zealand. Otherwise, the emphasis was on the reduction of the wartime buildup.

The Wing flew its last ceremonial formation over Aarhus on 15 August. Mackie further extended his experience of flying German aircraft with two flights as a passenger in a Fieseler Storch. Sailing with Jameson was his main relaxation. In early September, 122 Wing moved south, over the border to Flensburg in Germany, and there, on 17 September, it was formally disbanded. For Mackie, the days of real command were over, as was his flying life.

He was given an interim posting to 121 Wing in nearby Schleswig, spent two weeks on leave in England, and returned on 1 October to be posted to 83 Group Control Centre, also in Schleswig. "There I think I was even more like a fish out of water," he said. "I was called Wing Commander in charge of radar, and I had several GCCs (Ground Control Centres) under my wing. I didn't know how one worked, let alone the others! And I can't remember doing one bit of useful work while I was there."

On 12 October he made his last flight in a fighter aircraft, and appropriately it was in EDM, the Tempest V in which he had led 122 Wing. Airborne from Schleswig for 80 minutes, he practised homings and ground-controlled approaches with his new equipment. When he ran up the great Napier Sabre engine to clear the plugs before switching off, it was the end of an era for Evan Mackie. Only twice more in his lifetime would he again take the controls of an aircraft.

He had flown a total of 230 hours and 25 minutes in Tempest Vs, and had claimed the destruction of five enemy aircraft in the air while flying the type – one of them shared.

Now he was back to flying a desk – and he did not like it. "I had given some thought to my future when the war finished – whether I would like to continue in the forces or return to civvy life. I couldn't make up my mind, but I had applied to join the RAF Staff College at Bracknell."

On 9 and 10 November, 1945, he made his last flights as pilot-in-command when he flew a Percival Proctor from Schleswig to Buckeburg and back. He simply had no inclination to fly again after jumping from the cabin of the low-wing monoplane that autumn day in Germany.

Mackie returned to England in February 1946, and on 18th of that month (her birthday) married Marjorie Dear in the village church at Garston, just outside Watford, and about 20 miles north-west of London. They honeymooned in Aberdeen.

While on honeymoon, Mackie was posted as 'Operations II' with the British Air Forces of Occupation (BAFO). Meanwhile, back in the Air Department in Wellington, the administrative wheels were grinding away steadily regarding his application to join a Staff College course. On 19 March, the Air Member for Personnel recommended to the Minister of Defence: "On the basis of his early success as a student and of his later achievements as an officer of the RNZAF, it is considered that (Wing Commander Mackie) is eminently suitable to represent the RNZAF at the Staff College . . ." In the same letter the Air Member noted that Mackie had "distinguished himself both as a fighter pilot and as leader of men. By the end of the war he had achieved the outstanding result as a fighter pilot that he had shot down 21 enemy aircraft, which meant that he was the fourth highest scoring fighter pilot of the RNZAF." Just how the Air Member arrived at that total and analysis is difficult to tell. Mackie's 20 and three shared was by that time well documented in official records, and perhaps he was including Gray, Deere and Crawford-Compton, New Zealanders with the RAF, and all of whom were believed at the time to have higher totals, as members of the RNZAF.

In any event, the Minister approved the Air Member's recommendation the same day. Mackie had flown to the Continent on 7 March, but he held his BAFO posting for less than a month, arriving back in England on 3 April.

No. 34 Staff Course (No.17 War Course) at Bracknell ran from 1 April to 28 October, 1946. The Commandant was Air Vice-Marshal Sir Arthur Sanders, and there was one New Zealander, Grp Capt R.L. Kippenberger, a career RAF officer, on the directing staff. Mackie, who reverted to his substantive rank of Sqn Ldr for the course, was out-ranked by the majority of the 94 course members, and appeared in the course list with his name mis-spelled 'MacKie'. He was also the only New Zealander on the course.

"My records of the Wing Commander are confidential," wrote Grp

Capt W.G. Abel, the then Staff College Secretary, in 1986. "but I can tell you that he passed successfully through his course and was awarded the (wartime) Staff College qualification. His reply to his joining instructions shows that he did not bring a motor car to Bracknell (few had the money or the influence to possess one in 1946), but he did rejoice in a three-valve mains-operated Echo radio. Such details were obviously considered important by the College authorities forty years ago!"

Abel observed that "there were very many distinguished individuals at Bracknell with Evan Mackie, and just as many seem to have gone on to greater distinction thereafter."

Mackie would later regard the course as one of the high points in his life, although he did not find it easy. "It was very high class, very sophisticated. My education had not extended beyond the age of 14, two years at high school. I did not have a very good command of the English language, and I found it rather hard going." But he appreciated the "wonderful collection" of lecturers, amongst them General Jan Smuts, and Sir Robert Watson-Watt of radar fame.

While he was attending the course he was again invited to attend an investiture at Buckingham Palace, this time for his Distinguished Service Order. Again his mother-in-law insisted on a Rolls-Royce taxi. Mackie said it was the third occasion on which he had met King George, "but he didn't look as if he recognised me! Or even as if he had ever seen me before!"

It was with some regret, as the course neared its end, that he decided that the forces were not for him. "I felt ill at ease most of the time, especially socially. I had a narrow background. I could see that I was not fitted out well for a future in an office – not that I was sure that I would have been employed in an office. But during peacetime office work flourishes. I had spent almost five years destroying things and I reckoned it was time that I did something constructive."

There was another reason. "I had every admiration for the bulk of Air Force personnel, but in the higher ranks there were quite a few who were a bit in the background when there was action and they started to come out of the woodwork when the war finished. I didn't like the prospects, in many cases, of working with a lot of them.

"The idea of playing war games, which is what we did mostly at staff college, didn't appeal to me at all. The purpose of it had gone. I just wanted to show what an electrical apprentice could do if he set his mind to it."

Having shown them, Mackie applied for a transfer back to New Zealand and demobilisation. He and Mrs Mackie joined the RMS *Rangitiki* at Tilbury docks on the Thames, and sailed for Wellington

on his birthday, 31 October. They went via Curacao, Colon and
Pitcairn Island, and he kept his adminstrative hand in on the voyage
when he was appointed returning officer, in charge of the votes cast
by the hundreds of troops on board, for the general election then
being held in New Zealand. In Colon he was responsible for making
'going ashore money' available to the troops.

Rangitiki berthed at Wellington on 12 December, 1946, and Mackie
was formally granted furlough on 15 January, 1947 – effectively the
date of his discharge from active service with the Royal New Zealand
Air Force. He had served six years and 75 days, of which five years
and 222 days were spent overseas. He had a total of 1,230 flying
hours, 634 of them operational, accumulated during 433 operational
sorties. He had flown ten different types of aircraft, and landed at
102 different aerodromes. The 29-year-old had seen enough death
and destruction to last him a lifetime. Now he wanted nothing more
than to go back to his electrical trade and to reconstruction, doing
things to help people, and which gave him personal satisfaction.

On the same day that he was discharged, Mackie was formally
promoted to Wing Commander (temporary) and transferred to the
RNZAF reserve of officers, class 'A'. His personal file was annotated
"unlikely to be recalled for further service". He had been offered a
permanent commission in the RNZAF on his return, and in spite of
his feelings on completing the staff course, had given it serious
consideration – but turned it down. "I could not imagine myself
playing war games in New Zealand any more than in England."

CHAPTER TEN

HOME

Evan's brother Allan was working with an electric power board in the central North Island, and Mackie heard there was a job there as a faultman if he wanted it. He did, and he entered service with Waitomo Electric Power Board in February 1947, living at Otorohanga.

A tour of New Zealand came first, however, catching up with friends and relatives, introducing his new bride, and showing her her new country.

In Waihi he was guest of honour at a civic reception, at which Sqn Ldr J.R. Cullen was also welcomed home. Mr M.W. Wallnutt, the Mayor, referred to Mackie as "the Dominion's second ace" and said he "symbolises the fighting spirit of all the sons of New Zealand". He listed his successes, attributing him with the destruction of 25 enemy aircraft, and recalled his biggest 'jam' which took place on the Italian front: "He was attacked by six enemy aircraft, but successfully fought them off single-handed after a lively combat in which his Spitfire reached the thrilling speed of 600 miles an hour in a dive for the sea." It was all good, if slightly exaggerated stuff, and just what the Waihi folk wanted to hear of their home-town boy.

The Mackies went as far south as Invercargill. A newspaper account has them staying with his relatives, Mr and Mrs A. Beattie, when they visited Dunedin – and also credits him with 25 enemy aircraft destroyed. Clearly, the reporters were not distinguishing between aircraft destroyed in the air and on the ground.

Yet another newspaper article of the time referred to him as "New Zealand's second fighter ace", whatever that meant, and attributed him with 25 aircraft destroyed. It also had him making "more than 600 sorties over enemy territory" and quoted his reason for leaving the service as being that fighter pilots were not wanted at the end of the war, the demand being for transport and bomber pilots.

Mackie stayed with the Waitomo Power Board until 1950, when it became obvious to him that he was not going to be able to save enough money to buy a house of his own. He went into business on his own account as a cartage contractor to Worth's Limeworks at Otorohanga. "I kept this up for three years and achieved my objective," he said. Then he went back to the power board, as an inspector faultman, working out of Te Kuiti and Otorohanga.

By the late 1950s the two sons who had been born to the Mackies, Keith and Brian, were entering their teens and showing an interest in boating and fishing. "Otorohanga was about as far from the sea as you could get, so we decided it would be a good idea to move to the sea," said Mackie.

In 1960 he secured a position as inspector-faultman with the Tauranga Electric Power Board at Mount Maunganui, and in 1963 he was promoted area superintendant in nearby Te Puke. A further promotion to chief inspector in 1969 took him to the board's head office in Tauranga, and it was from that position that he retired in 1978.

During his last years with the board he worked closely with the chief engineer, Mr N.R. White, who soon discovered that his chief inspector had wide-ranging skills quite outside his profession. White was leader of a team which established a Wurlitzer organ in the Tauranga town hall, and Mackie helped on the project. "Evan . . . could do anything," he said. "He could lay bricks, he could chop holes through concrete, he could do timber work. He really was a very accomplished person apart from his electrical skills. He used to take quite a delight in solving problems – nothing to do with electricity, and he made no secret of the fact that he enjoyed doing that."

White, himself a keen harbour fisherman, had seen first-hand evidence of Mackie's ability with rod and line on many occasions. As organiser of fishing contests among the power board's staff, he had to introduce a new trophy because of Mackie. "I thought someone else other than Evan ought to be able to get a cup, and the only way they were going to do that was to have a lucky guess at the weight of the biggest fish caught. So I gave a Cup for Excellence in Piscatorial Judgement!"

Evan Dall Mackie, fighter pilot, leader, electrical engineer, practical man and family man, died in the Tauranga Hospital on 28 April, 1986, aged 68.

Just as his coffin was being carried from the funeral chapel on the afternoon of 1 May, an RNZAF Douglas Skyhawk of 75 Squadron thundered low overhead in final salute – the service paying tribute to one of its own. Mackie would have appreciated the precise timing of Flight Lieutenant Glen Todd's arrival.

He always did like a tidy ending.

APPENDIX I

CLAIMS OF WG CDR E.D. MACKIE

Date	Place	Rank at Date	Sqdn	Aircraft Flown	Type Claimed	Result
26.3.42	5m W Le Havre	Plt Off	485	Spitfire VB	Bf 109E	Destroyed; shared with Flt Lt W.Crawford-Compton
26.4.42	Mardyk-St Omer	Plt Off	485	Spitfire VB	FW 190	Probably Destroyed
7.4.43	near Medjez	Flg Off	243	Spitfire VC	Ju 87s	2 Destroyed
9.4.43	near Medjez	Flg Off	243	Spitfire VC	Bf 109	Damaged; shared with Sqn Ldr J.E.Walker
10.4.43	Medjez	Flg Off	243	Spitfire VC	Bf 109	Destroyed
13.4.43	Euston/Tabarka	Flt Lt	243	Spitfire VC	Bf 109	Destroyed; shared with Flt Sgt Hill
16.4.43	W Medjez el Bab	Flt Lt	243	Spitfire VC	Bf 109	Destroyed
18.4.43	SE Teboursouk	Flt Lt	243	Spitfire VC	FW 190	Damaged
27.4.43	E Medjez	Flt Lt	243	Spitfire VC	Bf 109	Destroyed
28.4.43	Medjez-Pont du Fahs	Flt Lt	243	Spitfire VC	Bf 109	Destroyed
8.5.43	Cap Bon	Flt Lt	243	Spitfire VC	Bf 109	Destroyed
4.7.43	Catania	Sqn Ldr	243	Spitfire VC	Bf 109	Destroyed
5.7.43	Gerbini	Sqn Ldr	243	Spitfire VC	Bf 109	Destroyed
11.7.43	S Gerbini	Sqn Ldr	243	Spitfire VC	MC 202	Damaged
12.7.43	N Augusta	Sqn Ldr	243	Spitfire VC	MC 202	Probably Destroyed
13.7.43	3m SW Gerbini	Sqn Ldr	243	Spitfire VC	Ju 87s	2 Destroyed, 1 Damaged
„	10/15m N Augusta	Sqn Ldr	243	Spitfire VC	MC 200	Re 2002 Destroyed
11.9.43	Salerno/Agropoli	Sqn Ldr	243	Spitfire VC	Do 217	Destroyed
15.10.43	Volturno River	Sqn Ldr	243	Spitfire VC	Bf 109	Damaged
3.12.43	Sangro River	Sqn Ldr	92	Spitfire VIII	Bf 109	Destroyed
5.12.43	Sangro River	Sqn Ldr	92	Spitfire VIII	Bf 109	Destroyed
16.12.43	Ortona-Orsogna	Sqn Ldr	92	Spitfire VIII	Bf 109	Damaged
27.1.44	Anzio area	Sqn Ldr	92	Spitfire VIII	Bf 109	Damaged
2.2.44	Anzio area	Sqn Ldr	92	Spitfire VIII	FW 190	Destroyed
24.12.44	Eindhoven	Sqn Ldr	274	Tempest V	FW 190	Destroyed
27.12.44	Duren	Sqn Ldr	274	Tempest V	Bf 109	Damaged
22.1.45	8m W Dulmen	Sqn Ldr	80	Tempest V	glider	Damaged on ground
23.1.45	12m N Osnabruck	Sqn Ldr	80	Tempest V	Bf 109	Destroyed
7.3.45	N Rheine	Sqn Ldr	80	Tempest V	FW 190D	Destroyed
9.4.45	Fassberg	Sqn Ldr	80	Tempest V	Bf 108s	2 Ar 96s Destroyed
15.4.45	10m SW Uelzen	Sqn Ldr	80	Tempest V	FW 190	Destroyed: shared with Flt Sgt Turner
3.5.45	landing ground 12m NE Kiel	Wg Cdr	122 Wg	Tempest V	Do type	Destroyed on ground
					He 111	Destroyed on ground
					Fi 156	Destroyed on ground
4.5.45	Oldenburg area	Wg Cdr	122 Wg	Tempest V	Fi 156	Destroyed on ground; shared with Wt Off Duncan

TOTAL: 20 and 3 shared Destroyed; 2 Probably Destroyed; 8 and 1 shared Damaged; 3 and 1 shared Destroyed on the ground, 1 Damaged on the ground.

APPENDIX II

THE TACTICAL USE OF TEMPEST V AIRCRAFT

(Paper believed to have been prepared by Wg Cdr E.D. Mackie during 1945.)

The primary role of Tempest aircraft with 83 Group was that of "armed recce", for which they were admirably suited by virtue of their great speed, fire-power, long range, excellent vision etc. Nevertheless a goodly toll was taken of enemy aircraft on fighter sweeps, patrols, and recces themselves.

Briefing
Before each sortie, a thorough briefing was carried out by the formation leader, usually in the Wing briefing room when up to the minute information was available such as enemy positions, movements, position of our own forces etc. A careful study was made of the flak map, and routes, and heights planned accordingly.

For armed recccs, the area to be searched was of great importance and its possibilities were usually discussed in detail. If a specific target was to be attacked, detailed instructions were given regarding recognition, direction, and method of attack, break away etc.

For fighter sweeps, emphasis was laid on the disposition and call signs of other aircraft, routes to be covered, positions to fly relative to other sections and sun, heights etc.

For patrols it was usually a question of positions, heights, control, speeds etc.

In all cases, accurate courses were worked out for predetermined heights and speeds, and information given on R/T channels, diversionary landing grounds, safe areas to head for in the event of being forced down in enemy territory etc. Deputy leaders and section leaders were chosen and safe courses for base given. The importance of accurate timing by all pilots was always emphasised.

Take-off
The Tempest proved to be a temperamental starter at the best of times so that for a sortie of 8 aircraft, a spare was always briefed. It is difficult to taxi on account of the necessity to maintain sufficient revolutions to prevent or reduce rough running and at the same time swing the nose for forward vision. Adequate time had to be allowed between "press buttons" and actual take-off, as frequent runs up to 3,000 rpm were necessary if a safe take-off was desired.

When taxi tracks were long and narrow, it was the practice to carry an airman on the starboard wing to give directions and so obviate the necessity to swing. Great care however, had to be taken whilst braking, turning, or on rough ground, for it was only too easy to throw him off as he had very little to hold on to.

It was essential to run engines up to 3,000 rpm immediately prior to take-off, until all signs of oil smoke had vanished from the exhausts. Failure to do this after 5 or 10 minutes ground running often ended up by engines cutting completely on opening up.

Once 8 aircraft were lined up on the runway, it was only a matter of about 3 minutes before they were airborne, taking off in pairs echelon starboard and with a minimum time interval between sections. This was the secret of a quick form up. Great care had to be taken by section leaders as a swing can easily develop unless the throttle is opened steadily and corrections made immediately.

Form up

Armed recces were usually carried out with 8 aircraft and for fighter sweeps, 8 per squadron. Once on course from base, sections flew in "finger 4's" or as near line abreast as possible, but in the aerodrome circuit it was the practice to remain in close line astern unless of course there were enemy aircraft reported.

Sections of 4 or 8 aircraft usually formed up and left the circuit in close formation after one-half to one-whole circuit. This was made possible by an orderly take-off, and by the leader climbing straight ahead to almost 1,000 ft before turning slowly through 180 degrees to come back close to and parallel to the runway. Each succeeding pair flying for a progressively shorter time straight ahead was thus able to "cut corners" and come quickly into formation. No.2 in each pair of course fell into close line astern immediately after take-off. Care had to be taken by sub-section leaders to take relative speeds into consideration to prevent being left behind even though a good "interception" was initially gained. This was greatly assisted by the leader throttling back when 1,000 ft was reached.

For armed recces, the sections of 4 changed to line abreast (finger) formation as soon as course was set, remaining close until cloud, if any, was climbed through.

For sweeps, squadrons flew in close line astern with four's leaders line abreast, orbiting base thus until the "set course" order was given. It was always a debatable point as to whether the leading squadron should take off first or last.

Flying out

In clear weather, sections opened out into battle formation immediately course was set, climbing up thus to 7-8,000 ft before crossing the bomb-line at a suitable spot. It was found that 4,000 ft was the maximum height at which targets such as Motor Transport could readily be spotted, but as flying at this height necessitated greater vigil for flak positions, 7-8,000 ft was maintained as long as possible. When the desired area was reached, the leading section would go down to 4,000 ft or lower and concentrate entirely on searching for targets while the other section would fly 1,000 ft or so above and down sun, giving cover and protection against surprise attacks from enemy aircraft.

After several targets had been attacked, the two sections would change roles, and so on until either ammunition was running short or it was time to return to base. 7-8,000 ft was gained once more and the sections returned to base in battle formation.

In cloudy weather a high standard of airmanship was demanded of all pilots, especially when long-range tanks were used and targets up to 250 miles away were attacked by the more venturesome leaders. Ascent through cloud was made on course in close finger formation, opening out into battle formation when once in the clear, which was usually 8-9,000 ft. It was usually possible to search for ground targets through up to 6/10 cloud or in large breaks, but for greater amounts it was abandoned until the desired area was reached by "dead reckoning".

Sections closed into close finger formation, for the descent through cloud, each four going its own way from then on. A steady course was maintained with throttles closed slightly to keep the speed below 350-360 mph and if cloud base was not reached at 1,000 ft the sections climbed straight ahead to return to base or try elsewhere. Providing there was 500 to 1,000 ft clearance even in mist or light rain, attacks were carried out and good scores obtained.

In such conditions it was of vital importance that each and every member of the section should stick together as once he lost contact he was entirely dependent upon his R/T for a safe return journey. This called for steady flying in cloud and well disciplined attacks.

When the "cease fire" order was given, the sections once again closed in and climbed through cloud on course for base. Whenever flak was encountered unexpectedly and cloud cover had to be taken, it was usual for the leader to order the section to climb through cloud on a given course and then form up again.

On fighter sweeps squadrons usually made rendezvous above cloud and then made the necessary height for crossing the bomb-line when on course. Normal cruising revolutions and boost were 3,000 and zero or +1, which were sufficient to prevent "leading up" of plug points. Up to 15,000 ft was sometimes gained without using the high speed supercharger which was uneconomical and troublesome.

Long-range tanks

Two 45-gallon jettison tanks were frequently carried especially as profitable hunting grounds were discovered up to 250 miles away. These were turned on as soon as possible after take-off (1,000 ft) and used equally on the journey out. To start with, it was the practice to jettison tanks before attacking ground targets as there was a supposed danger of them exploding if hit by flak.

However, due to absence of known cases of disaster and the fact that they often failed to release in any case, they were usually retained when enemy aircraft were encountered. They were however, always turned off during actual attacks. Retaining tanks greatly speeded up time taken to turn around between sorties and were scarcely noticeable in flight, reducing speed by only 5 to 10 mph.

Attacking ground targets

(1) The basic section was a No.1 and his No.2, both the section and sub-section leader taking the initiative whenever "beating up" commenced. It was decided that a locomotive could not be "destroyed" by 20mm cannon fire and that it was better to badly damage as many as possible instead of wasting ammunition on a few. To this end a locomotive was considered to be "out of action" providing at least two aircraft had each scored a good burst from close range, and it had emitted clouds of steam.

(2) Motor Transport often burst into flames after only a short burst but others, presumably those using gas producers, refused to ignite and often caused further waste of ammunition. Here again, two good bursts were considered sufficient.

It was further decided that except in isolated cases, the element of surprise was difficult if not impossible to attain, and it was not always an advantage in any case. Rushing-in in an unpremeditated attack so often meant a poor approach and an abortive attack. Attacks were carried out with the No.2 about 300 to 350 yards behind his leader so that he could get in a good burst after the latter had broken away.

Using about 3,000-3,200 rpm and increasing boost to maybe +1, the approach was made from far enough away to allow time for accurate trimming at a steady speed of about 350-360 mph, concentrating almost entirely on sighting from about 600 yards.

A 1½ to 2 second burst was usually given from 350-200 yards or 300-150 yards approximately, breaking away up and to whichever side it was decided to orbit. Frequent cases occurred of pilots prolonging fire too long and damaging their aircraft by debris thrown up.

The approach was considered to be the secret of a successful attack. Attacks were usually made at right angles to roads and railways and usually out of the sun, although this was dependent upon the terrain, relative position of towns, flak positions etc.

If a locomotive was emitting clouds of steam and smoke from a first attack it was often necessary to attack downwind in order to be able to see it at all.

Attacking downwind gave a greater ground speed with less danger from flak, but a shorter attack. Allowance for wind was made by aiming low. Attacking into wind gave reduced ground speed but a longer attack, allowance being made by aiming high. Varying amounts of deflection were necessary during cross-wind attacks, or for the speed of moving targets. One common mistake was to open fire out of range and lift the point of aim to compensate for this resultant bullet drop, with the result that shots appeared to be "drawn through" the target. The rule was "reduce range to reduce bullet drop".

Unless flak was coming from the vicinity of the target itself, height up to 2 or 3,000 ft was immediately gained in readiness for further attacks. After attacks, the sub-section came into line abreast of the leader who carried on in search of more targets.

At one particular period the Hun had a nasty habit of including up to 3 flak-cars in trains – one at each end and one in the middle. These were left severely alone whenever possible as targets were plentiful, but sometimes attacks had been started before these were spotted. To combat this menace, a system was employed whereby the section of 4 would make their approaches simultaneously, coming down in line abreast about 100 to 150 yards apart. Should guns suddenly appear on the train the scheme was for an attack to be made directly at them, either disabling them or keeping the gunners under cover, while the leader attacked the locomotive.

This method was however, very cumbersome, and much delay was caused by inexperienced pilots not keeping stations, but with a good team it had promise. On one particular occasion when a No.2 came down in line abreast with his leader, he was able to deal effectively with a flak post placed beside a viaduct, on which the leader had very foolishly chosen a target.

As a general rule, aerodromes, towns, bridges, viaducts, and marshalling yards, were given a wide berth. Stationary trains were always regarded with suspicion as so many turned out to be "flak traps". A varied assortment of targets, both pre-arranged and ones of opportunity, were attacked, including an oil refinery near Celle where containers up to 110 feet in diameter were set ablaze.

When attacking aircraft on aerodromes it is essential for all aircraft to fly line abreast and, if possible, for complete surprise to be achieved. When attacking such targets, it was the practice to remain as low as possible afterwards until a safe area in which to climb up, was reached. Sometimes carriages and goods wagons were strafed along their length in an endeavour to find something explosive or inflammable, but usually ammunition was conserved for prime movers.

Gun buttons
Cannon selector buttons were tried for a time so that either inboard or outboard cannons could be used independently. This, however, did not prove to be any decided advantage, as a short well-aimed burst with 4 cannons was preferred. As a rule each aircraft carrying 130 rounds per gun was able to make 6 to 8 attacks.

Ammunition
Ammunition carried was 2 HEI and 2 SAPI alternately spaced throughout

the belt with 5 rounds of tracer placed 50 rounds from the end. This loading proved very effective against practically all targets, strikes being readily observed.

Harmonization
The type of harmonization which was generally accepted was that which gave the most uniform concentration at all ranges up to about 800 yards, spot harmonization being so only at one particular range.

Cine guns
Cine camera guns were usually fitted and excellent films obtained.

Enemy aircraft were often encountered on armed recces, but the Tempest proved to be superior except in climb, to all the German orthodox fighter aircraft, especially below about 5,000 ft where most combats took place. The Hun pilots usually flew at deck level in clear weather making spotting difficult, and at cloud-base in cloudy weather.

Fighter sweeps
These were usually carried out at 12-15,000 feet, using the low speed supercharger, unless of course, enemy aircraft were encountered or a rapid climb was necessary. The "finger 4" formation was invariably used, with squadrons and sections stepped up away from the sun. The importance of pilots keeping well up in line abreast so as to make full use of mutual cover, could never be over emphasised. A straggler was a menace to himself and his section.

The Tempest could not compete with the Hun in a climb, but could outdive them with ease and compare favourably in a turn. One particular combat with a long-nosed FW 190, took place at 3,000 feet on a clear day, uninterrupted by either flak or other aircraft. Using + 11 lb boost and 3,750 rpm, the Tempest would almost get into a position to fire after about 3 complete turns, when the Hun would throttle back completely and disobey the golden rule of not changing bank, by stall turning the opposite way, thus almost meeting the Tempest head-on or at least at a big angle. Thus the Hun made a very elusive and formidable target, for after executing this manoeuvre for the fourth time, he managed to take a big deflection shot at the Tempest as it went steaming past.

The Tempest makes a bigger orbit than the FW 190 but at about 220 mph it completes the actual turn quicker. After each of these stall turns, the chase would start afresh, the Hun making several unsuccessful attempts to dive away. After about 10 minutes of this, a pair of Tempests appeared on the scene and distracted the Hun's attention sufficiently for a short burst to be given which finished him off.

The loading previously described, in the Tempest, was particularly effective against aircraft. The Tempest scored many victories against jet aircraft, but this was usually only made possible by the Hun not keeping a good look-out or having a distinct disadvantage in heights. The straight-and-level and diving speeds were far superior to the Tempest.

Landing procedure

After crossing the bomb-line on the return to base, height was rapidly lost and the circuit approached in close finger formation, changing to close line astern when actually in the circuit. If descent through cloud had to be made, this was done in close finger formation as usual.

With 9 or more squadrons operating from the same airfield, circuit discipline had to be of the best and to this end any orbiting of base, waiting for permission to land, was done in close line astern. Sections of 4 opened out into long line astern at the last possible moment, it being the responsibility of each 4's leader to get his section in as soon as possible after the No.4 of the preceding one, without leaving unnecessary gaps or having to go round again.

The 4th aircraft was usually touching down as the leader turned off at the end of a 1,600 yard runway, but sometimes up to 6 have been rolling along simultaneously. Every pilot had strict instructions to land on the opposite side of the runway to the machine ahead, and to keep rolling right up to the end of the runway.

Landing in pairs was definitely not permitted as there was always danger of burst tyres and in any case leaders leave too big a gap between sections and nothing is gained. Engines were always revved up to 3,000 rpm before switching off.

R/T control

Practically all armed recces were carried out well beyond radar coverage and even R/T control, important messages often having to be relayed by sections suitably situated. A good reliable homer was essential, but once pilots had confidence in it they were encouraged to navigate their own way home as it would stand them in good stead for the occasion when their R/T failed, and they were above 10/10 cloud. The most popular procedure for reporting either ground targets or aircraft was as follows:

1. "Bulldog leader reporting aircraft 2 o'clock below travelling opposite direction."
2. "Bulldog Red 2 reporting MT 1 o'clock."

Pilots were always encouraged to make their initial reports to include all the necessary details so that futher interrogation by the leader was unnecessary.

BIBLIOGRAPHY

General Reference
The Anzacs Patsy Adams-Smith, Thomas Nelson, Australia, 1985; *The Second World War* Winston Churchill, Halstead Press, Sydney, 1951; *Straight and Level* Air Chief Marshal Sir Kenneth Cross, KCB, CBE, DSO, DFC, Grub Street, 1993; *Years of Command* Air Chief Marshal Sir Sholto Douglas, Collins, 1966; *Battle of the Airfields* Norman Franks, Grub Street 1995; *Out of the Blue* P.B. 'Laddie' Lucas, Hutchinson, 1985; *So Few; The Immortal Record of the RAF* David Masters, Eyre & Spottiswoode, 1941; *New Zealanders in the Air War* Alan W. Mitchell, George Harrap & Co, 1945; *Desert Air Force* Roderick Owen, Hutchinson & Co, 1948; *The Channel Dash* Terence Robertson, Evans Bros Ltd, 1958; *Aces High* Christopher Shores & Clive Williams, Grub Street, 1994; *Above the Trenches* Christopher Shores, Norman Franks & Russell Guest, Grub Street, 1990; *Fighters over Tunisia* Christopher Shores, Hans Ring & William N. Hess, Neville Spearman, 1975; *2nd Tactical Air Force* Christopher Shores, Osprey, 1970; *The Typhoon & Tempest Story* Chris Thomas & Christopher Shores, Arms & Armour Press, 1988; *New Zealanders with the RAF* Wing Commander H.L. Thompson, NZ Government Printers, 1953

Unit Histories
Strike True; The Story of No 80 Squadron, RAF Christopher Shores, Air-Britain, 1986; *An Illustrated History of the New Zealand Spitfire Squadron* Kevin Wells, Hutchinson NZ, 1989; *Pik-AS Geschichte des Jagdgeschwaders 53* Jochen Prien, Struve-Druck; *Geschichte des Jagdgeschwaders 77* Jochen Prien, Struve-Druck IV./Jagdgeshwader 3; Chronik einer Jochen Prien, Struve-Druck Jagdgruppe, 1943-1945; *101 Gruppo* Tuffatori Giuseppe Pesce, Stato Maggiore, 1975; *Il 5 Stormo, 1934-1984* Giuseppe Pesce & Nicola Malizia, Mucchi Editore, 1984

Fighter Pilot Autobiographies
Nine Lives Grp Capt Alan C. Deere, DSO, OBE, DFC, Hodder & Stoughton, 1959; *Test Pilot* Neville Duke, DSO, OBE, DFC, AFC, Czech MC, Grub Street, 1992; *The War Diaries of Neville Duke* Neville Duke & Norman Franks, Grub Street, 1995; *Flying Start; A Fighter Pilot's War Years* Hugh Dundas, Stanley Paul, 1988; *Spitfire Patrol* Grp Capt Colin Gray, DSO, DFC, Hutchinson, NZ, 1990; *Spitfire Strikes* Johnnie Houlton, DFC, John Murray, 1985; *Tempest Pilot* Sqn Ldr C.J. Sheddan, DFC with Norman Franks, Grub Street, 1993; *The Blue Arena* Sqn Ldr Bob Spurdle, DFC & Bar, William Kimber, 1986

INDEX

This index is arranged as follows: – i) Personnel; ii) Places; iii) Military Units and Terminology – a) British Commonwealth; b) US; c) Allied Commands; d) German; e) Italian. (Ranks generally those appertaining at the end of the war; units listed are those in which individuals were serving when referred to in the text.)

i) Personnel

ii) Places

iii) Military Units and Terminology
a) British Commonwealth – Royal Air Force

b) US

c) Allied Commands   SHAEF 138

d) German – Luftwaffe

e) Italian – Regia Aeronautica